# Presenting the Holy Spirit

## Volume 1:
### Who Is He?

## Volume 2:
### Walking in the Spirit

D0908090

## Dr. Fuchsia Pickett

CREATION HOUSE

PRESENTING THE HOLY SPIRIT
by Dr. Fuchsia T. Pickett
Published by Creation House
A part of Strang Communications Company
600 Rinehart Road
Lake Mary, Florida 32746
www.creationhouse.com

Unless otherwise noted, all Scripture quotations
are from the King James Version of the Bible.

Library of Congress
Catalog Card Number: 97-69350
International Standard Book Number:
0-88419-518-X

0 1 2 3 4 5 6 BBG 10 9 8 7 6 5 4
*Printed in the United States of America*

## *Volume 1 is dedicated to:*

Mrs. Mary Wyman Stone Fraser
and her two daughters,
Mrs. Mary Wyman Stone Fraser Davis
Miss Laura Lawton Stone Fraser

These three precious friends made the publication of this book financially possible. Mary Fraser declared, "I moved into a new world when Jesus baptized me with the Holy Spirit. The consuming desire of my heart is to introduce the Holy Spirit to everyone I can and help them have a personal, intimate relationship with Him. That is why I want this book shared with the body of Christ."

## *Volume 2 is dedicated to:*

Carol Noe responded to the burden the Lord laid on her heart to help ensure that the teachings of this ministry were preserved in writing for the generations that follow. Her countless hours of transcribing and editing these teaching have helped me present "my Teacher." We both pray that those who read these volumes will come to know the blessed Third Person of the Godhead—the Holy Spirit—more personally and intimately, and enjoy a deeper communion with Him as He reveals Jesus to them.

# Acknowledgments

I would like to acknowledge:

The faithfulness of "my Teacher," the Holy Spirit, who not only filled me with Himself, but also created within my spirit a desire to know Him personally and intimately, which thereby allowed Him to fulfill the mandate and mission in and through my life.

Carol Gwen Noe, of Blountville, Tennessee, a competent, Christ-like young teacher and minister of the Word and music, on whom the Holy Spirit laid the burden and commission to help me prepare for publication what she calls the "legacy of my life and ministry." Because of her faithfulness to Him, and her unity of desire with me, this book *Presenting the Holy Spirit* has become a reality. Without her ministry in helping to prepare this book, it might never have been printed.

Rev. Sue Curran, pastor of Shekinah Ministries, Blountville, Tennessee, for constantly insisting that I not bury with me the revelation I have received and taught concerning the Third Person of the Godhead, but that I write it as part of my legacy to the body of Christ. It is her persuasion that this "unique understanding of the person of the Holy Spirit" belongs to the body of Christ, and she has gently persisted in reminding me of my responsibility to leave it in good form for those who follow. I am grateful for her encouragement in this endeavor.

My beloved husband, Leroy, for his support, love, and companionship that enables me to fulfill the purpose of God for my life. He is a constant encouragement as I preach, teach, dictate, and write, traveling with me throughout the nation and other countries.

Dr. Judson Cornwall, my real spiritual brother and colleague, for editing the manuscript and for his words of encouragement and commendation to me.

The members of Shekinah Church Ministries for their continued prayers for the anointing of the Holy Spirit to be upon this ministry of the Word, and for their many expressions of physical help during these days of special physical needs.

# Contents
# Volume 1: Who Is He?

# Foreword

The world today seems to be caught in a tide of confusion, conflict, and aimless activity. Politicians, educators, economists, medical scientists, and governments appear baffled by the magnitude of the problems and challenges facing our world. New laws, policies, legislative programs, and schemes all seem to be temporary feeble attempts to place a man-made band-aid on a fatal wound.

Why can't man solve these problems? What is the real problem? What is the cause? What is the answer?

The answer is that man has lost his internal regulator, the Holy Spirit. The fall of man left him without the Spirit of God, like a child without a guide. Paul said in Galatians 5:18, "But if you are led by the Spirit, you are not under the Law" (NAS). In essence, without the Holy Spirit, man needs to be controlled and regulated by external law. Therefore the Holy Spirit is the missing ingredient in our world. For this cause Jesus came into the world, that we all might receive the "promise of the Father." The Spirit is God's major and key agent in the earth today. So much has been focused on Jesus (the Word), that we forget the Spirit "gives life" to the Word.

Dr. Fuchsia Pickett has given most of her life in intimate relationship with the Holy Spirit. It is out of that relationship and communion that she wrote this book. Her wealth of knowledge and revelation will not only bless you, but also transform the lives of generations to come. I am so happy she has written her heart that she might continue to speak to generations beyond the grave. Her deposit in my life will always be a permanent part of my development and I encourage you to receive the wealth of deposit in these pages. Read and feel yourself change as your mind is renewed.

Dr. Myles E. Munroe
President/BFMI
Nassau, Bahamas

# Introduction

Some readers might think it rather abstract and impractical to write a book that answers the question, "Who is the Holy Spirit?" Others may deem it presumptuous of me to say, "I would like to present to you the Holy Spirit." To many people the Holy Spirit is nothing more than a name in a religious creed recited in liturgical services. To others He is merely a vague influence mentioned in the Scriptures. Even those Christians who think they know who the Holy Spirit is many times do not recognize Him as a divine Person. I do not blame anyone for thinking about the Holy Spirit in these ways, for I remember the time in my life when I too would have thought it strange to address the Holy Spirit as a personal friend and teacher. Even though I referred to Him as the Third Person of the Godhead, when speaking theologically, He was not a real Person to me.

The doctrine of the Holy Spirit as a divine Personality is not only extremely practical, but also fundamental to our knowledge of God and our relationship to Him. Anyone who knows God the Father and God the Son without having a true understanding of God the Holy Spirit has not attained the Christian conception of God, nor has he come to the fullness of Christian experience.

I must mention the doctrine of the Trinity here to give us a proper foundation for the study of the Holy Spirit. In Genesis 1:26 reference is made to the plurality that exists in the Godhead: "And God said, Let Us make man in Our image, after Our likeness...." God referred to "Our" image and "Our" likeness, using plural pronouns to refer to Himself. Many such references confirm the reality of the Triune Godhead. Even the passage in Deuteronomy that some use to discount the validity of the Trinity, actually confirms the fact of the Trinity. We read there, "Jehovah our God is one Jehovah" (see Deut. 6:4). The Hebrew word for God that is used here is a plural form. That indicates, in spite of the intense monotheism of the Hebrews, the plurality of persons in the one Godhead. So we refer to the Godhead in its original state, in the eons of eternity, as the Triune Godhead. Our study here focuses on the Person of the Holy Spirit, but we cannot ignore His integral relationship to the Triune Godhead.

The importance of understanding the Person of the Holy Spirit is seen first of all in His effect on our perspective of *worship*. If we think of the Holy Spirit as merely an impersonal influence or divine power, we will inevitably rob Him of the honor and the worship He is due. We will not relate to Him properly, or give Him the love and trust, and surrender and obedience, that we should. We need to acknowledge this Third Person of the Godhead as He does His work on the earth, and yield to Him in complete obedience to His will.

Secondly, it is important that we not relate to the Holy Spirit only as an influence or power so we don't try to "use" Him, or "it," for our own purposes. This mistaken concept of the Holy Spirit inevitably leads to self-exaltation. It causes us to strut in pride, thinking that we have received the Holy Spirit and therefore belong to a superior order of Christians. Instead we need to think of Him correctly in the biblical way: as a divine Person of defined majesty and glory. Then we will relate to Him properly by asking such questions as, "How can I surrender more completely to the Holy Spirit?" and "How can the Holy Spirit possess me and use me in a greater way?" Relating to the Holy Spirit as a divine Person is one of the most fundamental truths of the Bible—one that we must understand if we are to enjoy right relationship with God. Many earnest Christians are going astray on this point. They are trying to get hold of some divine power that they can use according to *their* will or giftings instead of surrendering their lives to the Person of the Holy Spirit. True maturity in Christ only comes through cultivating a right relationship with the Holy Spirit.

We need to acknowledge the Holy Spirit as a divine Person of infinite majesty who has come to dwell in our hearts, take possession of us, and work out God's eternal plan and predestined will in us, for us, and through us, until we are a praise to the glory of the Father. Then we will experience true holiness in the reality of self-renunciation, self-abnegation, and self-humiliation. I know of no other truth that can humble us and put us on our faces before God more quickly than this: The blessed Holy Spirit is the Third Person of the Godhead who has come to dwell in our hearts and to restore us to the image of our God as He, in His infinite wisdom, unfolds His predestined plan for our lives. Such love and infinite desire of the Godhead to dwell with mankind is incomprehensible to our finite minds.

Many Christians testify to the entire transformation of their lives and service to God when they become acquainted with the Holy Spirit as a Person. That is my personal testimony as well. After serving God as a Methodist professor and pastor for many years, I came into a fuller relationship with the Holy Spirit. I realized then that Someone had come to live in my life, Someone whom I was not personally or intimately acquainted with. When I surrendered my life completely to Him, He began to reveal to me that He had come to be my Teacher. He had come to unveil the Christ who had been living in me for 17 years. It was then that I began to become intimately acquainted with the Holy Spirit as a Person.

People often misunderstand what we are saying when we refer to the Holy Spirit as a Person. They think we are saying that He has hands, eyes, and ears and operates in a physical body as we know it. But those physical characteristics are attributes of corporeality, not personality. The generally accepted attributes of personality are intellect, volition, and emotions; i.e., knowledge, will, and feelings. One who thinks, feels, and exercises his will is a person. We finite human beings will one day lose our corporeality. Our earthly life in this world will end and we will depart from these bodies. That does not mean we will cease to be persons, however. The Bible says that when we are absent from the body, we are present with the Lord (2 Cor. 5:8). So we will be alive in the presence of the Lord without mortal bodies. The Scriptures ascribe to the Holy Spirit all the attributes of personality, which we have defined here, that make Him a divine Person. For example, knowledge is attributed to the Holy Spirit in the passage that says, "Even so the thoughts of God no one knows except the Spirit of God" (1 Cor. 2:11b NAS). The Holy Spirit is not just illumination or inspiration that comes to our minds so we can see truth. He is a Person who Himself knows the things of God and reveals them to us. We know also that the Holy Spirit came to instruct us, to become our Teacher. Jesus said, "But the Counselor, the Holy Spirit, whom the Father will send in My name, will teach you all things and will remind you of everything I have said to you" (Jn. 14:26 NIV). It is our privilege today to have the Holy Spirit, a living Person, dwelling within us, opening the classroom of our spirits 24 hours a day and letting us ask about anything we want to know. He never closes the classroom and He never scolds us for asking. It is wonderful to know that, as we study the Bible, we have the divine Author of the Book to interpret it and to teach us its real and innermost meaning according to His divine knowledge.

Volition or will is attributed to the Holy Spirit in the Scriptures that teach us concerning the gifts of the Spirit: "But all these worketh that one and the selfsame Spirit, dividing to each man severally as He will" (1 Cor. 12:11). The Holy Spirit came to earth to fulfill the will of God in the earth. Emotion is also attributed to Him in Paul's appeal to the Romans for prayer: "Now I beseech you, brethren, for the Lord Jesus Christ's sake, and for the love of the Spirit, that ye strive together with me in your prayers to God for me" (Rom. 15:30). Notice particularly the phrase, *"the love of the Spirit."* Isn't that a wonderful thought? It demonstrates that the Holy Spirit is not a blind influence or an "it." He is not tongues or gifts or just divine power. He is a divine Person, the Third Person of the Godhead, living in us and loving us with the most tender love.

Have you ever thanked the Holy Spirit for His love? We think of God the Father who "so loved the world, that He gave His only begotten Son…" (Jn. 3:16). We speak of Jesus' love for the Church being so great that He suffered outside the city wall in order to sanctify unto Himself a glorious Church. But have we considered "the love of the Spirit"? Often we thank our heavenly Father for His great love to us. We thank Jesus for loving us enough to die for us. Have we ever knelt in reverence to the Holy Spirit and thanked Him for His great love for us?

Yet we owe our salvation as truly to the love of the Spirit as we do to the love of the Father and the Son. If the Holy Spirit had not become the willing Servant to come to the world and seek out our lost condition and bring conviction to us, we could not have come to the Savior. I think we have missed a lot by not realizing who this blessed Third Person of the Godhead is. We have not fully understood the love He has for us, and the hurt-love He still experiences as a servant bringing us back to the Father's house.

I think if I tried to briefly summarize the message of this book, I would shout to the Church today: "This blessed Holy Spirit, the Third Person of the Godhead, is not an 'it!' He is not a fleshly manifestation of 'religious' people jerking their bodies. He is not just tongues or gifts. He is much more than an 'influence.' He is the infinite, omnipotent, omniscient, omnipresent, eternal Third Person of the Triune Godhead! He is a divine Person!"

I'm sure this is not a new concept to many. But I wonder how it affects our lives in a practical way. Do we treat the Holy Spirit as a Person? Do we honor Him, love Him, and acknowledge Him? Have we learned to communicate with Him? Do we know communion with the Holy Spirit that the Bible teaches we can have? Do we think of Him as One who is alongside us, in us, helping us, comforting us? Have we experienced His divine comradeship? His companionship?

My whole purpose in writing this book is to present my Friend and Teacher as He has revealed Himself through the Scriptures to me personally. As we study the personality of this Third Person of the Godhead as the Bible describes Him, it is my prayer that we come to know the blessed Holy Spirit in a more intimate and personal way and to learn to yield to Him and cooperate with Him more fully. It is with this desire that this book is presented to the Body of Christ.

# Chapter 1

# *The Holy Spirit Is a Person*

## *Part I: Relationship With a Divine Personality*

Modern theologians have declared this age to be the age of the Holy Spirit. The Holy Spirit came to earth on the Day of Pentecost (Acts 2) and has remained here to do the work the Father sent Him to do. He will not leave until God's eternal plan is accomplished. He came to fulfill the purpose God had for the Church, to fulfill what God had promised and prophesied in the Scriptures for hundreds of years. He was the Father's gift to the Church, sent under divine mandate to be the chief administrator of God's Kingdom on earth.

Today's Church must come to a right relationship with the Holy Spirit in order for the Kingdom of God to develop on earth as God has ordained. It is not enough for Christians to recite a liturgical creed that only mentions the Holy Spirit; neither is it enough to simply understand the doctrine of the Holy Spirit. The Holy Spirit is a divine Person sent to do a supernatural work in the lives of men and women who choose to know God. We need to become acquainted with the Holy Spirit as a Person to fulfill the purposes of God in our personal lives and in our churches. Only as we develop an intimate relationship with this Third Person of the Godhead can we hope to realize the abundant life that Jesus promised to all who followed Him.

It is unfortunate that even the evangelical church world often calls the Holy Spirit an "it" or describes Him as "tongues," or defines Him as an "emblem" like the dove or the wind. Some declare Him to be a mere "influence" or "power." He is none of those things! He is the Third Person of the Godhead who came to bring us into right relationship with God. The Holy Spirit wants us to commune and fellowship with Him in an intimacy that is greater than any we would share with another person. Many of us do not enjoy this kind of relationship with the Holy Spirit because we do not think of Him as a Person. We could even have received the baptism of the Holy Spirit and still not recognize Him as a *divine Personality*. Before we can relate to the Holy Spirit properly, we must accept the truth that He is, in fact, a Person.

## WHAT CONSTITUTES PERSONALITY?

When using the word, *personality*, we simply refer to the quality or state of being a person. Being a person involves the power of intellect or the mind; the power of volition, or the will; and the power of emotional response. In the populace of the world, these three aspects of personality combine to form such infinite variations of persons that we can truly say no two people on the face of the earth are alike.

There are many scientific approaches to understanding personality. Some have resulted in major branches of scientific study, such as psychology. For those who have researched it, the psyche has proved to be quite enigmatic in its complexities. The behavioral sciences have drawn their conclusions about man's "typical" behavior, only to find that they must constantly adjust those conclusions as man's behavior changes. Unfortunately, too many of these scientists have never come into a relationship with God, who created the human psyche. Therefore they have unwittingly abandoned the only valid premise for true knowledge and understanding of man. Without a relationship with God, it is impossible for man to understand either God or himself. True comprehension of

God and man results only from a relationship with God; after all, He defined the purpose of man in creation.

The three definitive elements of personality, then, include the *mind, will* and *emotional response*. Only as we learn to recognize and properly relate to these three aspects of the personality of the Holy Spirit can we intimately fellowship with Him as a divine Person. As the Third Person of the Godhead, the Holy Spirit reveals the *mind* of God as He fulfills the *will* of God for mankind. He also expresses the *emotions* of God in His loving and holy relationship to mankind.

The Holy Spirit simply has come to reveal Jesus, the lovely Savior, to all who will respond to His invitation to receive eternal life. The Spirit offers eternal life to all who will accept the sacrifice of Jesus' blood for their sins. Only the Holy Spirit has the power to save our souls and change us into the image of Christ. But it is when we accept that sacrifice for our sins that we can begin to know what the Father intended for man when He created Him.

## THE PERSONALITY OF MAN

When God created man as a tripartite person, with a body, a soul, and a spirit, He intended man to live in fellowship with Himself. God created man's body, perfectly adapted to Earth's environment, to be a home for man's soul and spirit. Man's soul, his personality, allowed him to respond to all of life in God's beautiful earth. Man's spirit allowed him to commune with God, who is Spirit.

God had warned Adam that in the day he ate of the fruit of the tree of the knowledge of good and evil, he would die (Gen. 2:16-17). But when the serpent deceived Adam's wife, he told her that they would not die if they ate of that tree. He declared that, instead, they themselves would become as gods (Gen. 3:4-5). Yet God's Word was true, and when Adam and his wife ate of the forbidden fruit, their spirits died to God. It severed their relationship with Him. Thus all mankind was doomed to live eternally in that state of being ruled by their souls, with no possibility of communion with God.

In a terrible sense, mankind has fulfilled the serpent's word to the first couple that they would be "as gods." Since the beginning of time nations have ravaged each other in an attempt to satisfy man's ungodly lust for power, for sovereignty, for dominion over other men. Without the life of God influencing man through his spirit, man's soul became warped and twisted. His mind turned hostile to God, his will became self-centered, and his emotions were filled with anger, envy, hatred, the desire to rule, and other negative forces. Man's personality was doomed to ultimate destruction.

Still, God had a plan to reverse that verdict and He has been unfolding that plan since the beginning of time. God's eternal plan was to have a family He could fellowship with throughout all eternity. Man's sin could not ultimately deter him from the fulfillment of God's dream.[1] Jesus came to earth to be our Savior so God's dream for a family could still be realized. When we receive salvation for our souls by accepting the sacrifice of Jesus, our spirits are born again and Christ comes to dwell in us with His divine life. Then the Holy Spirit can begin to transform our souls, or personalities, until we become Christ-like in our thinking, in our decisions, and in our emotional responses. *The better acquainted we become with the Holy Spirit, the more we can expect to be changed into the sons of God with knowledge.*

## THE PERSONALITY OF THE HOLY SPIRIT

The Scriptures reveal the personality of the Holy Spirit in many ways. In the Old Testament the Holy Spirit is present wherever God becomes involved with man. We may not always see the Holy Spirit clearly in these cases because He is concealed in 14 emblems that represent different aspects of His Person (Chapter 3 discusses this topic). He is typified in many ways in the Old Testament. One of the most beautiful types involves the ingredients of the holy anointing oil that was given to Moses (that is the topic of Chapter 4). Understanding the significance of each ingredient reveals a wonderful portrait of the Holy Spirit. A careful study of the emblems and types that God ordained to represent the Holy Spirit will unfold many aspects of the richness of His divine character and Person.

The New Testament reveals the Holy Spirit clearly to us, for it records His coming in Person to glorify Christ in every believer as He works to create God's family in the earth—that is, the Church. Jesus prepared His disciples for the coming of the Holy Spirit; He taught them many things about His personality. He called the Holy Spirit the *Spirit of Truth*, and the *Counselor* (Jn. 6 NIV). The Holy Spirit can take the truth of the words of Christ, breathe on them, life them, and reveal their depth of meaning to us. He writes the Word of God on the tablets of our hearts until the living Word becomes the Christ-life lived in and through us (Jer. 31:33; 2 Cor. 3:3). He is the Comforter who not only comforts us in our earthly sorrows, but also brings a peace into our hearts that the world cannot give.

Although the world defines peace as an absence of hostilities, the peace that the Holy Spirit brings does not depend on circumstances. Real peace is not based on happenings, but on a relationship with the Prince of Peace. When we do not walk in the peace of God, we do not walk in the Spirit. If we find ourselves venting anger, strife, and criticism that is evidence that we are not walking in harmony with the Person of the Holy Spirit. As we discover life in the Spirit, we learn to walk in truth, peace, grace, and holiness. Each of these virtues is a part of the divine life the Holy Spirit gives. So Jesus taught that truth, comfort, and peace characterize the personality of the Holy Spirit. He also taught that gentleness and patience are divine attributes of the Holy Spirit. It is especially interesting that at Jesus' baptism, the Holy Spirit was present in the form of a *dove*. The predestined plan and purpose of God for symbolizing the Holy Spirit as a dove was to reveal to us the gentle nature of the Holy Spirit. The gentleness of a dove characterizes the personality of the Holy Spirit. He is never harsh, rude, critical, or judgmental. He will convict, correct, instruct, teach, and lead, always in the patient gentleness of His divine personality.

The few characteristics of the personality of the Holy Spirit we have described here should help to establish in our minds that He is a Person. Our goal is to become intimately related to this wonderful Third Person of the Godhead. As we study the *offices* of the Holy Spirit, the roles He plays in building the Body of Christ in the earth, we will discover vital principles that govern our relationship to Him (Chapters 5 and 6 cover this topic). Understanding His divine *power* will build faith in our hearts to declare that there is no human situation too difficult for Him (see Chapter 7). God manifests the eternal, omnipotent power of the Holy Spirit through seven different *moods* of the Spirit (the topic of Chapters 8 and 9). His purpose is for us to become the expression of God in the earth as we yield our minds, wills, and emotions to the Holy Spirit. As we allow the Holy Spirit to fill us with His divine love, we become God-centered instead of self-centered. Then we begin to know the meaning of life and to fulfill the purposes of God in the living of our lives.

## HOW CAN WE RELATE TO THE HOLY SPIRIT?

God's ultimate desire is for all His children to know Him through true fellowship and communion in the Holy Spirit. The beauty of His Person as we have briefly described Him should create in us a desire to know Him for the Person He is. My intent is simply to recount the wonders of God as seen in the Person of the Holy Spirit so we might be inspired to make ourselves acquainted with Him personally. Paul declared, "...I count all things to be loss in view of the surpassing value of knowing Christ Jesus my Lord..." (Phil. 3:8 NAS). The Holy Spirit has been given to us so we might know Christ. Jesus said He would send a Comforter, the Holy Spirit, who "shall take of Mine, and shall shew it unto you" (Jn. 16:15). It is clear from what Jesus said that we need to know the Holy Spirit intimately in order to enjoy the kind of relationship with God that He intends for His children to enjoy.

### The Difficulty

Many Christians seem to have some difficulty in coming into the fullness of relationship with the Holy Spirit that the Scriptures teach we can have. Therefore it will be helpful to briefly examine the causes of this difficulty. Then we can overcome it. As I explained more fully in my book *God's Dream*,[2] there are three main reasons behind our lack of relationship with the Holy Spirit as a Person.

First, we have misinterpreted the scripture that says, "Howbeit when He, the Spirit of truth, is come, He will guide you into all truth: for He shall not speak of Himself..." (Jn. 16:13). We have interpreted this verse to mean that the Holy Spirit did not speak *about* Himself, that He drew no attention to Himself. Therefore, we have mistakenly concluded that we should not focus our attention on Him either. Although it is true that He came to exalt Jesus, the Holy Spirit, as the Author of the Scriptures, still refers to Himself more than 200 times in them. So we must have misunderstood the meaning of "He shall not speak of Himself." The more accurate understanding of that phrase is the Holy Spirit does not speak *out of His resources*, but speaks what He hears the Father speak. Because we misinterpreted that verse, we have often de-emphasized the importance of relating to the Holy Spirit as the Third Person of the Godhead.

A further difficulty to our coming into relationship with the Holy Spirit is our lack of a reference point for relating to a spiritual being. We can relate in our thinking to God the Father because we have earthly fathers who give us a concept of fatherhood. We identify quite easily with Jesus, since He became a man like us and lived among us. On the other hand, we have no human counterpart for the Holy Spirit, so we have difficulty with His lack of corporeality. We cannot see Him as an entity, nor relate to Him in a human framework. We can begin to overcome this difficulty though, when we learn to see the Holy Spirit in the Church, which is His Body on earth. Each believer becomes a temple of the Holy Spirit, reflecting His character and nature. Paul instructs us on how the Body of Christ functions:

> *But speaking the truth in love,* [you] *may grow up into Him in all things, which is the head, even Christ: from whom the whole body fitly joined together and compacted by that which every joint supplieth, according to the effectual work- ing in the measure of every part, maketh in- crease of the body unto the edifying of itself in love.* (Ephesians 4:15-16)

Since we are temples of the Holy Spirit, when we learn to be filled with the Holy Spirit individually, we will manifest His life on earth corporately as the Body of Christ.

Third, because we have difficulty with His lack of corporeality, we have tried to understand the Holy Spirit solely through emblems that represent Him or through gifts that He bestows. The Holy Spirit is not wind or oil or rain. The Scriptures use these metaphors merely to describe aspects of His Person for us. He is not an "it" or a "tongue" or an influence. He is the Third Person of the Godhead. When we accept the reality of the Holy Spirit being a divine Person, we can learn to respond to Him as the Person He is.

## The Way to Intimacy: Personal Communion

Once we have accepted the Holy Spirit as a divine Person, we can begin to acquaint ourselves with Him. We can learn to enjoy intimate communion with the Holy Spirit as we give ourselves to *prayer* and *fellowship* with Him (Chapter 9 discusses this further). We cannot develop a relationship with Him that enables us to walk in the Spirit without cultivating a life of prayer and communion with the Holy Spirit. Although we may sense the blessing of the Holy Spirit as we read the Word and receive His direction in witnessing for Christ, we still may not be truly walking in the Spirit because we lack communion with Him. He can even anoint us as we preach the Word, and give us understanding and discernment of spiritual things, without our walking in the *fellowship* with Him He had intended. As we discuss more thoroughly the scriptural meaning of "life in the Spirit" (see the second book of this series), we will discover the depth of relationship with the Holy Spirit that is available to believers.

Many of us who have been born again and filled with the Holy Spirit still think of His coming into our lives merely as an experience of power that brought spiritual gifts. In reality, the Holy Spirit comes into our lives as a Person, not as an experience. Getting to know the Holy Spirit requires spending time with Him, allowing Him to talk to us. As we do, we learn to become sensitive to His moods, which reveal His desires in a particular situation or for a person. Then He will pray the will of the Father through us for His Church, individually and corporately. And we will learn what pleases Him in even the small issues of our everyday life.

## Results of Communion With the Holy Spirit

**Victory.** Fellowship with the Holy Spirit makes it possible for us to live our daily lives in a way that pleases God. If in the morning we sense His freshness in our hearts, we can gain the strength we need to go through the challenges of that day, knowing that in every situation we will be completely victorious. Perhaps many have discovered, as I have, that we are not smart enough to solve the countless problems we continually face. As we develop a personal communion with the Holy Spirit, we can pray, "Holy Spirit, please lead me and teach me about this problem I am having. Give me Your answer from the mind of God." Then, with assurance, we can await the answer of the Holy Spirit who is faithful to answer and show us the way to victory.

**Revelation.** Much of the time we spend in prayer with God each day should be devoted to quietly meditating on the Word and allowing the Holy Spirit to speak to our hearts. Revelation comes from the Holy Spirit, who dwells within us. Each time God gives us fresh insight into the Word, He makes the *logos* (the written Word) become a *rhema* (a living Word) to our spirits. Just as the Holy Spirit caused Mary to conceive in her physical body, so the Holy Spirit can impregnate our spirits with the living Word. Reading the Scriptures in communion with the Holy Spirit, who is their Author, causes them to live in our spirits. Spiritual, mental, and physical renewal come to us because we wait in prayer on the Holy Spirit. The Holy Spirit transforms our minds to think God's thoughts, and we come into harmony with the will of God. It is the Holy Spirit who then anoints us to minister, with power and authority, that revealed Word of God to others.

**Protection.** Through our fellowship with the Holy Spirit, we receive His protection from the enemy. Many times the persecutions that come from the world do not wound us as deeply as the attacks that come from God's people. Our daily communion with the Holy Spirit can shield us, perhaps not from the actual attacks, but from the negative effects of those attacks. He enables us to come through our fiery trials, not as *bitter* people, but as *better* people.

**Anointing.** The anointing of the Holy Spirit for ministry comes to us through prayer and communion with Him as well. By yielding to Him in obedience and faith, He enables us to exercise the gifts of the Spirit

(1 Tim. 4:14-15). Even many who know about the gifts and manifestations of the Spirit do not know how to best operate in them. Paul wrote, "Now concerning spiritual gifts, brethren, I would not have you ignorant" (1 Cor. 12:1). We gain the understanding of spiritual gifts that we need as we fellowship with the Holy Spirit.

**Motivation.** Even the right heart motivation for exercising the gifts is a result of communion with the Holy Spirit. The apostle Paul taught that the proper motivation for exercising the gifts of the Spirit is love—love for God and for each other (1 Cor. 13). Some teach that love is the greatest *gift*. That is not what Paul taught. He said to "covet earnestly the best gifts: and yet shew I unto you a more excellent way" (1 Cor. 12:31). Love is not a *gift*, but a *way*. Fellowship with the Holy Spirit develops in us the way of love, which keeps all spiritual gifts and manifestations in proper order. Prayer causes individuals' gifts of ministry to work together in harmony, motivated by love and without unhealthy competition.

**Ministry.** Similarly, the five-fold ministry, given "for the equipping of the saints for the work of service..." (Eph. 4:12 NAS), must be released through the anointing of the Holy Spirit that comes through much meditation and prayer. Growth and development in ministry come through waiting on that ministry in prayer and fellowship with the Holy Spirit. Of course, the Holy Spirit administers the five-fold ministry gifts according to the Father's choice. Yet every Spirit-filled person can minister the life of the Holy Spirit. Whether or not you are an apostle, prophet, pastor, teacher, church administrator, elder, or deacon, your spiritual gift will grow and develop to properly edify the Body only through prayer and meditation in the Word.

**Boldness.** The Holy Spirit is God's provision to increase our boldness, inspire our obedience, and strengthen our faith. Obedience to the way He guides us often requires a courage that only prayerful communion and fellowship with the Holy Spirit can produce. Out of communion comes the necessary boldness and faith to obey God's Word, for the Holy Spirit believes everything our Lord says. The key to abundant victorious living is obedience to the Spirit of God. We cannot enjoy the quality of life Jesus came to give to us in abundance without obeying the Holy Spirit. Fellowship with Him strengthens our desire to obey Him. The Christian life can become dull, routine, and even negative if we don't enjoy consistent communion with the Holy Spirit.

Fellowship with the Holy Spirit becomes a way of life for the believer who learns to cultivate a personal relationship with Him. If you are not yet accustomed to this divine relationship with the Holy Spirit, but would like to be, you can simply ask Him to come and make the presence of Christ real to you. Ask Him to give you a new understanding of His Word, and to bring you into a new walk of fellowship with Himself. God delights to answer these requests, for they fulfill His will for us. We can learn to walk in a fellowship with the Holy Spirit that will continue to develop all our lives. It will bring us to the maturity that God intended for us to know and experience, thus making us sons of God with knowledge.

God has revealed all we need to know about the Holy Spirit in His Word. As we give ourselves to prayerful study of the Scriptures, we can expect to come into a more satisfying relationship with Him. When we invite Him to come into our lives, He comes to be our Counselor to guide us into all truth. In learning to walk with Him, we can know Him and love Him for the wonderful Person that He is. God intended us to commune with the precious Third Person of the Godhead in order to experience the full redemption of our souls. By becoming more sensitive to the Holy Spirit, we can obey Him more fully and so realize the fulfillment of God's promises in our lives. Then we will come to know His mind, the way He thinks about life. We will discover His will and become a part of it, surrendering our wills in the process. We will recognize His emotional responses, and begin to give correct emotional responses to Him as we learn what pleases and displeases Him.

Even now this beautiful Third Person of the Godhead is waiting for us to seek Him with all of our hearts. Only as we seek Him will we discover the true meaning and purpose of life in God.

### Notes

1. God's eternal plan is fully explained in the author's book, *God's Dream*, (Shippensburg, Pennsylvania: Destiny Image, 1991).

2. Ibid., pp. 27-33.

# Chapter 2

# *The Holy Spirit Is a Person*

## *Part II: Emotional Responses of the Holy Spirit*

I would hate to live life without expressing emotion. To some people expressing emotion is a sign of psychological imbalance, a display of weakness. They especially condemn emotion related to a religious experience. Although they declare it unhealthy to express emotion in religious experiences, these same people think nothing of getting angry with someone, or of expressing delight when they receive a gift. They often will make themselves hoarse from yelling excitedly at a ball game. Yet they feel justified in condemning emotional responses in religion. Weeping in prayer or rejoicing in songs of praise would be unacceptable behavior to them.

Some of these people also think it is unmanly to cry. However, psychologists and medical doctors disagree with that idea. They say that it is not healthy to bottle up our tears inside us. Pent-up emotion becomes poisonous to the health of men and women alike, both mentally and physically. Of course, we cannot ascribe to the philosophy that is prevalent today to "let them have it." Scripture does not advocate our venting anger and other negative emotions irresponsibly. It teaches us, instead, to develop self-control in our lives by yielding to the power of the Holy Spirit. Then we can overcome negative emotional responses. By "pent-up emotion" we refer to the repression of legitimate expressions of emotion as taught in the Word. Emotional health results from freely and correctly responding in each situation with our emotions as they are energized by the Holy Spirit.

In reality, it is not a sign of strength to repress emotion, but of stubbornness and selfishness. A hardhearted, self-centered person will not express emotions of gratitude or tenderness to God or to others. A man who is happy, complimentary, loving, and tender reflects godly character, not weakness. We need to learn to express emotions honestly and properly, as God intended. When we realize that our emotions constitute one third of our soul (the other two parts being intellect and volition), we begin to better understand their importance to our health and happiness.

The Holy Spirit is a Person who has definite emotional responses, as clearly described in the Scriptures[1]. He is God, and God is *love* (1 John 4:8). There is no stronger emotion than love. The strength of God's love is most clearly revealed in His willingness to undergo extreme suffering to rescue the object of His love: mankind. The Bible teaches, "For God so loved the world, that He gave His only begotten Son, that whosoever believeth in Him should not perish, but have everlasting life" (Jn. 3:16). It was because of His love for mankind that Jesus came to suffer and die on the cross and satisfy the justice of God toward sin. Although hate and anger have wrecked havoc through man's history, the whole universe will one day testify to the supremacy of love. The end of time will culminate in a reign of divine Love. The strength of godly love will always be expressed, as it was through Jesus, in sacrificial acts of giving. The love of the Godhead endured the pain of the crucified Savior, who gave His life for mankind. Today God still suffers the rejection of men and women who refuse to accept His love. As the Third Person of the Godhead, the Holy Spirit reveals the loving emotions of God. This intense love keeps Him seeking to save those who are lost, and rejoicing with the angels when one sinner repents (Lk. 19:10; 15:10).

It is incredible to think that human beings have the ability to refuse such divine love. As this divine Personality, the Holy Spirit, seeks to redeem our fallen human personality, we can choose to respond positively or negatively to Him. In human relationships, a positive action toward a person usually evokes a positive response. It is also true that our negative responses to people predictably bring unpleasant consequences. Similarly, the way we respond to the Holy Spirit either builds a loving relationship with Him or hinders the development of that relationship. Of course, the Holy Spirit will always be true to His nature of love. He does not abandon us as people whom we have offended might. He will continue to work in our lives to draw us into a relationship so we can be transformed into the image of Christ. On the other hand, He will never coerce us against our wills, for that would violate the meaning of relationship. He desires a love response that we choose to give to Him who first loved us. Our choices affect our fellowship with God just as they do with people. Satisfactory relationships with people depend largely on our responses to them. Our relationship to the Third Person of the Godhead is no exception to that principle.

## NEGATIVE RESPONSES

Scripture is full of examples and instruction regarding the emotional responses of the Holy Spirit. He responds to sin as God, who cannot tolerate it. He responds to mankind in the long-suffering, entreating way that the love of God uses to seek and to save sinners. He responds to the believer's worship and praise in one way, and to his disobedience in another. The Holy Spirit not only desires to respond *to* the believer, but also to express Himself *through* him. Paul taught that "the love of God has been poured out within our hearts through the Holy Spirit who was given to us" (Rom. 5:5 NAS). As we give Him our hearts, He will express the love of God through our lives. Thus, examining the emotional responses of the Holy Spirit that the Scriptures reveal to us will help us better understand this beautiful Third Person of the Godhead.

**Grieved.** First of all, the Scriptures teach that the Holy Spirit can be *grieved*. Paul exhorted the Ephesians, "And grieve not the holy Spirit of God, whereby ye are sealed unto the day of redemption" (Eph. 4:30). In this passage, Paul lists such sins as corrupt communications, stealing, lying, bitterness, wrath, and evil speaking, and instructs us to avoid these sins. We can safely conclude that if we do not follow these instructions and repent of these sins, we will grieve the Holy Spirit. We need to understand that because He is Love, whatever we do to sin against that love causes Him grief.

Rejection, rebellion, hardness of heart, disobedience, and lack of faith are sinful attitudes of the heart and mind that grieve the Holy Spirit. Sin is conceived in the mind before it becomes a deed. The Scriptures teach that "the heart is deceitful above all things, and desperately wicked: who can know it?" (Jer. 17:9) Jesus said that out of the heart proceeds "evil thoughts, murders, adulteries, fornications, thefts, false witness, blasphemies" (Mt. 15:19). The Holy Spirit alone can change our sinful hearts as we yield to Him. By continually surrendering to Him in obedience, we will live in right relationship with Him so that we do not grieve His heart of love through our thoughts, words, or attitudes and actions.

**Vexed.** The Scriptures also teach that the Holy Spirit can be *vexed.* The prophet Isaiah declared, "But they rebelled, and vexed His Holy Spirit: therefore He was turned to be their enemy, and He fought against them" (Is. 63:10). To vex someone means *to trouble and bring distress or agitation.* The people of Israel vexed the Holy Spirit when they rebelled against His ways. Rebellion against God will always produce negative consequences.

Failing to heed the conviction of the Holy Spirit will finally result in the judgment of God coming into our lives. Yet even in judgment God reveals the strength of His great love, for His intent is always redemptive, never destructive. He uses His judgments to bring us back to Himself with new desires to live in His will and to please Him. The psalmist understood this truth when he wrote, "Before I was afflicted I went astray, but now I keep Thy word.... It is good for me that I was afflicted, that I may learn Thy statutes" (Ps. 119:67,71 NAS). Although affliction is not always a result of disobedience, when affliction comes, we would still be wise to consider our ways. If the Holy Spirit convicts us of sin, and we turn from our rebellion, we can be assured that He will be there to receive our repentance and cleanse us of our sin. If we persist in our sin, we will be sure to vex the precious Holy Spirit and forfeit the peace of God that He brings to those who walk in obedience to Him.

**Offended.** As we have mentioned, at Jesus' baptism the nature of the Holy Spirit was represented in type by a dove that descended upon Him (Lk. 3:22). That gentle dove-like nature can be offended. The Holy Spirit is God and God is love. Therefore, though the Holy Spirit will never react in an unloving way Himself, He can be offended by our unloving responses to Him.

In human relationships we are sometimes offended because we are self-centered and "wear our feelings on our sleeves." That is a carnal reaction, and we need to repent of that. The closer we walk to God, however, the more sensitive we become to His presence, His love, and His nature. A closer walk also sensitizes us to anything that is incompatible to His nature. Our awareness of harshness, unkindess, and rudeness in people will be greater compared to our awareness of the loving presence of God. Though our responses to such negative attitudes may be more godly, we will feel more deeply the "unlove" of people when we have been communing with the love of God. If that is true in our limited human experience, what must the Holy Spirit, who is pure love, feel when He encounters our unloving attitudes?

Offending one of our brothers or sisters in Christ, our spouse, or our children, hurts the heart of the Holy Spirit, for He dwells in each of them. Paul exhorted the Ephesian Christians to "be kind to one another, tenderhearted, forgiving each other, just as God in Christ also has forgiven you" (Eph. 4:32 NAS). His instructions are very clear about how we are to treat one another as Christians. We are expected to respond to each other "with all humility and gentleness, with patience, showing forbearance to one another in love, being diligent to preserve the unity of the Spirit in the bond of peace" (Eph. 4:2-3 NAS). These attitudes are not natural to our human nature. Only the Holy Spirit can work them into our hearts as He fills us with His love for the brethren. When we offend the Holy Spirit by sinning against a person, even unintentionally, we need to repent for our sin against God's love.

**Quenched.** As a gentle Person, the Holy Spirit does not insist, against our will, that we obey Him. He waits to be invited and welcomed into our lives. Then He patiently persuades us of truth and righteousness. The Scriptures teach us to "*quench not* the Spirit" (1 Thess. 5:19). If we do not choose to obey the Holy Spirit, we will quench His work in our lives. The word picture in the Greek for quenching the Spirit is literally "choking the throat of the Holy Spirit." One way we can do that is by refusing to heed His convicting word to our hearts about our sin. As individual believers, we can expect the Holy Spirit to speak truth to us about our lives. It is imperative that we yield to His gentle but clear leading as He desires to counsel us and lead us into all truth. If we do not, we may be guilty of quenching His presence in our lives. In that case, we are left with our sin-nature in control until we choose to repent and allow the Holy Spirit to govern us again.

We must understand that it is possible to quench the moving of the Holy Spirit as church bodies also. We need to become sensitive to the Holy Spirit's desires for our worship services. For example, some churches have become embarrassed by the moving of the Holy Spirit through the gifts of tongues and interpretation. They relegate such "interruptions" to the prayer room on Wednesday nights. Other church programs leave no room for the Holy Spirit to change the agendas that their leaders judiciously control. Yielding to the Holy Spirit in faith, without knowing exactly how He will move, creates an uncertainty in their minds that they are unwilling to allow. They would rather quench the life-flow of the Holy Spirit than to lose "control" of the meeting. Such attitudes hinder our corporate relationship to the Holy Spirit in the Body of Christ by quenching His moving. To follow the Holy Spirit's guidance as He teaches us to worship requires our cultivating a sensitive relationship to Him. As we do, we can avoid quenching His moving and enjoy His presence.

**Lied To.** It is also possible to *lie* to the Holy Spirit as we would to any other person, but not without consequences. Ananias and Sapphira, people in the early church, lied to the Holy Ghost (Acts 5). Peter knew by the Holy Spirit that they were lying. He rebuked them, asking them why satan had filled their hearts to lie to the Holy Ghost. They had not lied to men but to God, and they died immediately because of God's judgment upon them. We must be careful when we make vows to God concerning our lives. Our loving heavenly Father is not waiting to pounce on us if we stumble in our commitment or even fail miserably. But if we promise Him one thing while fully intending to do another, we are not lying to men but to God.

**Defrauded.** We can *defraud* the Holy Spirit of His honor by taking to ourselves the honor due Him. The Bible records the fate of two prominent leaders who refused to give God the glory due Him. The Old Testament example is King Nebuchadnezzar of Babylon who gloried in the mighty kingdom he had built by the might of his power and for the honor of his majesty. Because he took credit for his own greatness, he lost his mind and went into the fields to live with the beasts for seven years. When he finally lifted up his eyes to heaven and praised God, his reason returned to him, and he was again established in his kingdom. Then he declared, "Now I Nebuchadnezzar praise and extol and honour the King of heaven, all whose works are truth, and His ways judgment: and those that walk in pride He is able to abase" (Dan. 4:37).

The New Testament records a worse fate for King Herod when he arrayed himself in his royal apparel and gave a grandiose speech to the people. They promptly acclaimed him to be a god. "And immediately the angel of the Lord smote him, because he gave not God the glory: and he was eaten of worms, and gave up the ghost" (Acts 12:23). It is dangerous for anyone to sin against God by breaking the first commandment, "Thou shalt have no other gods before Me" (Ex. 20:3). Although we would not blatantly bow down to another god, we need to examine our hearts when we take credit for personal accomplishments instead of giving glory to God, who enables us to succeed. When God gives us revelation in the Word and we share it with others, we dare not take credit for the blessing it brings to peoples' lives. It is the Holy Spirit who gives us the ability to understand the Word. We must be careful to acknowledge Him and give Him the glory for opening the truth to us. Similarly, when we have grace to give financially into the Kingdom, we need to guard against becoming conceited, as though we were doing a great thing. It is a work of the Holy Spirit in our selfish human nature that enables us to be generous, cheerful givers. We are not basically good, as the secular humanist insists. We are dependent on the Holy Spirit to enable us to live in a way that pleases God in every area of our lives. We must be careful not to defraud the Holy Spirit by taking glory to ourselves as though we are responsible for what He is doing in us to redeem us.

**Resisted.** Peter preached to the Jews on the Day of Pentecost, rebuking them as "stiffnecked and uncircumcised in heart and ears" who "always *resist* the Holy Ghost" (Acts 7:51). It is incredible to think that we finite human beings have the dubious power of resisting the plans and purposes the Third Person of the Godhead has for us. Yet when the gentle Holy Spirit comes to bring conviction to our hearts and we do not repent of our sin, we are guilty of resisting Him and we remain in our sin. His divine purpose is to continually cleanse us and change us into the image of Christ. As Christians we can expect the Holy Spirit to teach us the truth from the Word and to lead and guide us into all the will of God for our lives if we do not resist Him.

**Blasphemed.** Finally we must not omit the awful fact that it is possible for us to *blaspheme* the Holy Spirit. A simple definition of blasphemy against the

Holy Spirit is *to deliberately and willfully attribute the work of the Holy Spirit to the devil.*

The context of Jesus' teaching about this subject was the critical, defiant attitude of the Pharisees regarding His work of exorcising evil spirits. They kept accusing Christ of casting out demons by the power and authority of Beelzebub...Specifically, therefore, the Pharisees were blaspheming or slandering the Holy Spirit by giving the devil credit for Jesus' miracles of exorcism, when in reality these were wrought by the Spirit of God. But this false accusation was merely symptomatic of the underlying sin for which there is no forgiveness (Mt. 12:33-37). Their words would condemn them, for these evidenced a fixed, unrepentant attitude of mind that persistently rejected the wooing and conviction of the Spirit.[2]

Satan tries to frighten and condemn people with the threat that they have committed the unpardonable sin. No one is in danger of committing the sin of blasphemy against the Holy Spirit unless he has known God and then willfully turned from God in disobedience and rejection of Him. A hardened heart and a stiff neck of disobedience lead to a state of apostasy that can result in blasphemy (Jer. 10:26-31). If a person desires to be forgiven for sin, that is evidence that he does not have a heart that has committed the unpardonable sin of blasphemy against the Holy Spirit. God always forgives a repentant sinner if he turns from his sin and desires to be forgiven. It is comforting to know that if we are concerned about our sin, we are not in that unrepentant state of hardheartedness that results in apostasy and blasphemy. We need only rebuke satan's lie and repent of our sin to come into peace and relationship with the Holy Spirit.

If we are aware that we can displease the Holy Spirit in these ways, then we can guard against them and learn to please Him in all our responses to life. In cultivating a relationship with the Holy Spirit, unlike some of our relationships with people, we can be assured of His loving response to us. He will even enable us to respond lovingly to unloving people as we allow Him to live the life of Christ through us.

## POSITIVE RESPONSES

**Obeyed.** If our disobedience grieves the Holy Spirit, then we can be assured that our *obedience* delights His heart. As we yield to His convicting power and obey His truth as He reveals it to us, we will begin to know the righteousness, peace, and joy of the Holy Ghost in our lives and churches. The psalmist declared, "Thy word is a lamp to my feet, and a light to my path (Ps. 119:105 NAS). Walking in obedience to the Word of God helps us become properly related to the Holy Spirit. Not only will our individual lives bring glory to

God, but we also will enjoy His presence corporately in our churches as we walk in His precepts, obeying His commands with joy.

**Believed.** The Holy Spirit is the Spirit of Truth. We must respond positively to the truth He reveals by choosing to *believe* Him if we are to experience His divine power in setting us free from sin. Paul wrote to the church at Thessalonica that they were chosen "to salvation through sanctification of the Spirit and belief of the truth" (2 Thess. 2:13). Our salvation is not possible without our first believing the Spirit of Truth.

It is a true maxim that we live what we believe. If we believe that money is the most important thing in this life, we will spend all our energies in pursuing it. If we believe that obedience to God is the one great priority that will bring true success, then we will yield to the Holy Spirit and obey the Word of God. Actually, yielding to the Holy Spirit is not an option for the Christian; it is a command. Paul instructs believers to "yield yourselves unto God, as those that are alive from the dead, and your members as instruments of righteousness unto God. For sin shall not have dominion over you..." (Rom. 6:13-14). Obedience is a result of our yielding our wills to the will of the Holy Spirit.

All the promises of God belong to those who cheerfully obey the will of God revealed through the Word of God by the Holy Spirit. The Holy Spirit not only teaches us how to obey, but also gives us the desire and the power to do so as we walk in relationship with Him. Paul encouraged the Philippians, "Wherefore, my beloved, as ye have always obeyed, not as in my presence only, but now much more in my absence, work out your own salvation with fear and trembling. For it is God which worketh in you both to will and to do of His good pleasure" (Phil. 2:12-13). Only the power of the Holy Spirit can change a human heart from its natural bent toward sin and fill it with a delight in doing the will of God. That is why our relationship with the Holy Spirit is so imperative; we cannot obey God otherwise.

**Honored.** Giving honor is a prerequisite for having healthy relationships. We hear much teaching today about how to give honor in all our relationships, with both family and friends. Honor is defined as, simply, the esteem and respect bestowed on a person. The Holy Spirit teaches us how to honor God first and then how to bring that attitude to all our other relationships. We honor the Holy Spirit by acknowledging Him in all our ways, looking to Him as our Counselor, Comforter, and divine Guide into all truth. He is honored when we esteem the Word of God and obey it. Paul instructed Christians "...in lowliness of mind let each esteem other better than themselves" (Phil. 2:3). As the humility of Christ is worked into our relationships with one another, we honor one another as well as God.

This wonderful Third Person of the Godhead can make our lives victorious as we learn to hear and obey Him in all things. It is our responsibility to respond properly to Him by *yielding* to Him in obedience, by *believing* Him, and *honoring* Him in the living of our lives. We need to realize that we are responding to a Person, not to an influence or an "it." His loving response to us will encourage us to strengthen our relationship with Him. As we mature in our walk with God, we can know the true heart satisfaction in relating to the Holy Spirit as a Person and by enjoying His response to us as beloved children of God.

The beauties of this Third Person of the Godhead have been typified throughout the Scriptures to illustrate for us His infinite majesty. As we continue to study His Person-hood, we will discover His beauty in many of the Old Testament pictures or emblems of the Holy Spirit. We will learn to recognize many divine aspects of His personality in each of these eternal portraits.

### Notes

1. Scripture references to God's emotions include: Genesis 6:3, 6; Genesis 18:32; Leviticus 26:28; Joshua 7:26; Psalm 78:65; Isaiah 1:24; Jeremiah 7:13; Hebrews 10:12.

2. John Rea, *The Holy Spirit in the Bible*, (Lake Mary, Florida: Creation House, 1990), p. 128.

# Chapter 3

# *Emblems of the Holy Spirit*

## *Revelation of His Character*

Many of God's dear teachers, ministers and students seem to have the mistaken idea that the study of emblems and types found in the Scriptures is fanciful and farfetched, or at best, of very little importance. The fact is, types and shadows that tell of future realities run through the entire Book and contain untold wealth for the reverent student who is willing to become a miner of the hidden treasures of God's Holy Word.

In the Book of Moses and the historical books there are many typical characters, events, and institutions.

In the poetical books, we have typical utterances by typical characters. In the prophecies, we again have typical characters and events where the fulfillment of types is foretold, while throughout the New Testament they are constantly referred to and explained and the great anti-type is presented.[1]

It is important for us to clearly understand what we mean by a "type". As I have explained in my earlier books, a type prefigures, or symbolizes, something or someone. It is a person, place, thing, event, or incident that is recorded in the Bible to teach us spiritual lessons and to open to us some truths about God or His people. These persons and places were not mythical; they were actual historical facts. The typical events recorded in the Scriptures really happened; they are not mere allegories. But they each convey a truth in type that is larger than the natural realities they represent.

We should always be careful not to set forth anything as a type that the Scriptures themselves do not so designate. But if we dig deeply enough, we shall find that almost every incident in the Old Testament history that is referred to in the New Testament has been "typical" in its teaching. This becomes especially clear when we remember that the apostle Paul, after summing up the main events of Israel's history, wrote: "Now all these things happened unto them for ensamples [types]: and they are written for our admonition, upon whom the ends of the world are come" (1 Cor. 10:11). Let us bear this great statement in mind as we proceed to study the types and emblems of the Holy Spirit.

Old Testament types may be compared to pictures in a beautifully illustrated book. The New Testament can be compared to the "captions" in that book that explain the pictures of the Old Testament. If we were to read the captions without ever looking at the pictures they refer to, we would miss much of the book's inspiration as well as find it much more difficult to understand. In the same way we Christians lose great blessings and inspiration if we study only the New Testament and try to comprehend its deep truths without referring to the Old Testament, where those very truths are set forth in types and emblems that make them easier to understand.

An emblem represents, metaphorically, an abstract idea or an invisible element and helps to define its general ethical or spiritual meaning.[2] There are at least 14 emblems used in the Scripture to represent various aspects of the Holy Spirit. Each emblem reveals a beautiful facet of the Holy Spirit's nature and of His work on earth. Of course, this divine Personality can be truly understood only by the revelation of Himself to our hearts. But just as similes and metaphors give our minds a picture to grasp, so types and emblems help to open our understanding to the revelation of His Person.

Why are there so many types and emblems in the Scriptures? It is because the beauty of our glorious Savior is so transcendent, so wonderful, that no single picture could ever express the depth of truth contained in Him. Neither can the infinite beauty of the Holy Spirit be fully revealed through one or two pictures or emblems. That is why we find so many pictures of the Holy Spirit in the Old Testament. When there is repetition in some illustrations of the Holy Spirit, it is because our heavenly Father knows our weakness of comprehension and the shortness of our memory. Even so, we shall discover that each picture or emblem illustrates a distinct revelation peculiar to itself.

Often the same object is used, on different occasions, as one type in order to express different spiritual concepts. For example, the serpent is used as a type of the devil (Rev. 12:9). Jesus changes the picture when He uses the serpent as a type of Himself being lifted up on the cross (Jn. 3:14). Then He tells His disciples to be wise as serpents and harmless as doves (Mt. 10:16). In each case the serpent represents a different spiritual reality. The context of the Scripture will make clear to us the use of the type or emblem. As we study in a humble, yielded spirit, looking to the Holy Spirit for guidance at every step, He will not fail to open to us these wonderful treasures of His own Word.

## *THE DOVE*

The Spirit of God descended on Jesus at His baptism as a dove (Mt. 3:16). It must have been a moving experience for those standing on the river bank that day to see a dove light on Jesus and hear the voice of God from Heaven saying, "This is My beloved Son, in whom I am well pleased" (Mt. 3:17). Although they were not accustomed to witnessing supernatural events, surely they must have thrilled to the presence of God manifested in that hour.

As we mentioned earlier, the gentleness of the dove characterizes the personality of the Holy Spirit. The dove that Noah sent out of the ark became his servant to bring him news of the earth's condition after the flood. In that same way the Holy Spirit is God serving mankind, bringing us to a knowledge of eternal life and filling us with that life at our request. The gentleness and servant spirit of the dove show us the kind of God that is without a hint of harshness or violence. He gently persuades us of the truth of God's love, then waits for us to invite Him into our lives. He will never coerce us to repent or to obey Him. The Holy Spirit will always deal with mankind in a way that is in character with His gentle nature.

Even in our most painful situations, we dare not think that God allowed our difficulties because of any unkindness in Him. He cannot treat us unkindly, for His divine nature is kind and gentle. Jesus said, "Come to Me, all who are weary and heavy-laden, and I will give you rest. Take My yoke upon you, and learn from Me, for I am gentle and humble in heart; and you shall find rest for your souls" (Mt. 11:28-29 NAS). The Spirit of God, who came to reveal Jesus to us, reflects that gentleness in all He does.

## THE SEAL OF PROMISE

*Now He who establishes us with you in Christ and anointed us is God, who also sealed us and gave us the Spirit in our hearts as a pledge.* (2 Corinthians 1:21-22 NAS)

The purpose of a seal is to ratify and confirm, to give guarantee and assurance of certain claims. Paul taught the Ephesian believers that they were sealed in Christ "with the Holy Spirit of promise, who is given as a pledge of our inheritance" (Eph. 1:13-14 NAS). In this same passage, Paul referred to the believer as "God's own possession" (v. 14). The seal, in this sense, represents the proprietorship of God's love. God has stamped us as His possession, His very own property. This scriptural seal of promise represents the security of the believer and the guarantee that God's promise of eternal life is real. When the devil tries to convince us that we have sinned too terribly to be called Christians, we need to remind him that the Holy Spirit of promise has sealed us. Simply repenting of present sin will bring a cleansing of the blood of Christ and we can resume fellowship as though we had never sinned. The Word declares that "if we walk in the light, as He is in the light, we have fellowship one with another, and the blood of Jesus Christ His Son cleanseth us from all sin" (1 John 1:7). The seal of promise is a present reality that guarantees our eternal future with God. It is the presence of the Holy Spirit in our lives that reminds us we belong to God and will live eternally with Him.

## ACT OF ANOINTING

God ordained the act of anointing when He instructed Moses to create the anointing oil (see Chapter 4). It symbolizes the Holy Spirit's consecrating grace and guidance for the believer. Paul declared that his anointing was from God, "who also sealed us and gave us the Spirit in our hearts as a pledge" (2 Cor. 1:22 NAS). He meant that God has made us like the anointed One, Christ Jesus, in the sense that the same Spirit has anointed both Christ and us.[3] The Scriptures teach us that "the anointing which you received from Him abides in you, and you have no need for anyone to teach you; but as His anointing teaches you about all things, and is true and is not a lie, and just as it has taught you, you abide in Him" (1 John 2:27 NAS). The abiding presence of the Holy Spirit is the anointing that gives believers the capacity to know the truth and to be set free from every form of deception.

It was written of Jesus, "Thou hast loved righteousness, and hated iniquity, therefore God, even Thy God, hath anointed Thee with the oil of gladness above Thy fellows" (Heb. 1:9). Jesus lived His life in complete separation from sin. He consecrated Himself to the Father to do only His will. For that reason, the Father gave Him the Spirit without measure (Jn. 3:34). He was fully consecrated and divinely qualified for ministry through the anointing of the Holy Spirit.

We see the Old Testament counterpart of this consecration experience in the lives of the priests. The holy anointing oil was poured over the heads of Aaron and his sons to consecrate them to the ministry of the priesthood (Ex. 29). As New Testament believers, we are called to be a holy priesthood, "to offer up spiritual sacrifices, acceptable to God by Jesus Christ" (1 Pet. 2:5). The Holy Spirit empowers us to fulfill our priestly calling. It is the anointing of the Holy Spirit that qualifies us for ministry in the same way the anointing oil did, in type, the Old Testament priests.

## OIL

A most useful characteristic of oil is the light it provides when it is burned in a lamp. People living in Bible days perhaps appreciated that fact more because oil was the chief source of illumination, apart from the sun. That light symbolizes the power of the Holy Spirit to illuminate truth to us. Jesus taught the parable of the wise virgins who took plenty of oil for their lamps and the foolish virgins who did not. The foolish virgins were away buying more oil when the bridegroom came (Mt. 25:1-13). Without the oil of the Spirit being plentiful in our lives, we will not be ready when the Bridegroom comes. We must "buy the truth, and sell it not"

(Prov. 23:23), and allow the Holy Spirit to teach us all things so we will be prepared for the coming of the Lord.

Jesus said, "I am the light of the world" (Jn. 8:12). The Holy Spirit filled Him and He walked as Light in the darkness of this world. Then He declared to His disciples, "Ye are the light of the world" (Mt. 5:14). Only as the Holy Spirit fills our lives can we have truth illumined to us. Then we can become light to the darkened minds of men who do not know God.

## FIRE

Many times the Scriptures refer to fire to typify the presence of God. When the children of Israel were in the wilderness, the presence of the Lord was with them in a cloud by day and a pillar of fire by night (Ex. 13:21). Later in history, God declared through His prophet Malachi that the coming of the Lord was like a refiner's fire (Mal. 3:2). John the Baptist preached this:

> ... *He that cometh after me is mightier than I, whose shoes I am not worthy to bear: He shall baptize you with the Holy Ghost, and with fire: whose fan is in His hand, and He will thoroughly purge His floor, and gather His wheat into the garner; but He will burn up the chaff with unquenchable fire.* (Matthew 3:11-12)

Why fire? We sometimes fear fire, having seen the devastation it can cause to a home and anything else it touches when it's out of control. Fire has the power to destroy. But that is not the reason God uses fire to represent the Holy Spirit. The work of the Holy Spirit is redemptive, not destructive. When under control, fire is an invaluable element that provides warmth and light and that cleanses and purifies whatever it touches. The Scriptures teach that "our God is a consuming fire" (Heb. 12:29). His holiness is the essence of that fire. The fire of God that appeared in the cutting of the covenant with Abraham showed God's approval of Abraham's worship (Gen. 15:17). When Elijah called fire down out of Heaven on Mount Carmel, it consumed the sacrifice and proved to the Baal worshipers that the Lord was the true God (1 Kings 18:17-40). When we lift our hearts in worship, we should realize we are standing in the presence of a holy God whose fire can consume the sin in our lives. However, there should be no fear of destruction from that divine fire—only an awesome fellowship in the presence of a holy God.

As our lives are cleansed by fire, so our work will be tried with fire. Everything that is not of eternal value will be burned. We will not need a bonfire to try our works and consume all that is wood, hay, and stubble. The very presence of God, the Consuming Fire, before whom we will give account of the deeds done, will consume all that are works of flesh, and our fleshly programs. Paul declared, "each man's work will become evident; for the day will show it, because it is to be revealed with fire; and the fire itself will test the quality of each man's work" (1 Cor. 3:13 NAS). Our motivation, our faithfulness, and our attitudes will be exposed to the light of the fire of His holiness.

The fire of God is a place of safety and security for the believer; it saves us from deception and uncleanness. It is there we can enjoy the light that casts out the darkness. To walk in the fire results in forgiveness, health, and stability. As temples of the Holy Ghost, we believers need to be continually cleansed, forgiven, and made whole. The Holy Spirit comes as fire to cleanse our temples and to make us holy as He is holy.

## RAIN

The Scriptures refer to the outpouring of the Holy Spirit as the early and latter rains. "Then shall we know, if we follow on to know the Lord: His going forth is prepared as the morning; and He shall come unto us as the rain, as the latter and former rain unto the earth" (Hos. 6:3). To a farmer, the latter rains are as equally important as the early rains for the maturing of the harvest. As a faithful husbandman, God watches over His harvest. "Behold, the husbandman waiteth for the precious fruit of the earth, and hath long patience for it, until he receive the early and latter rain" (Jas. 5:7b). God is not building His Church in a day. He is patiently working by His Spirit until we grow into maturity to become a glorious Church without spot or wrinkle. The life-giving rain that typifies the moving of the Holy Spirit is vital to that growth.

Rain speaks of the abundance of the Spirit's supply. The latter rain will bring an abundance of God's presence. "He shall come down like rain upon the mown grass: as showers that water the earth. In His days shall the righteous flourish; and abundance of peace so long as the moon endureth" (Ps. 72:6-7). We live in anticipation of the coming of the Holy Spirit to our hearts and to His Church as life-giving rain.

### BREATH (AIR)

The word for "spirit" in the Greek language is *pneuma*. It means breath. Breath is the element that depicts the Holy Spirit's *exclusiveness*. In the new birth experience, the Holy Spirit breathes the life of God into our spirits, causing us to live unto God. Thus, that life-giving breath belongs only to those who have been born-again. God sent the Holy Ghost to the Church, not to the world. He convicts the world of sin, but He came to the Church to reveal Christ to her and to prepare her to live with the Father.

The difference between the man who has only immortal life and the one who has both immortal life and the quickened spirit is his *destiny*. The first will live forever without God; the latter will live forever in the presence of God. The breath of the Holy Spirit gives life to our spirits when we are born again by the Spirit, when we accept the sacrifice of Jesus' blood for the forgiveness of our sins. He implants His seed (the Word) into our spirits and breathes His life into us, and we become children of God with eternal life. Christ is eternal life. If we have Christ living in us, we have life. Without Christ, we do not have life. We cannot live in God without the breath of God quickening our spirits.

## *WIND*

There are instances in both the Old and New Testaments where wind typifies the moving of the Holy Spirit. When Ezekiel found himself in the valley of dry bones, God told him to prophesy to the wind and say, "Come from the four winds, O breath, and breathe upon these slain, that they may live" (Ezek. 37:9). When the breath came into them, they lived and stood up as a great army. The picture of the wind that brought life to the dead bones is a type of the Holy Spirit who has power to create life within us. When Jesus was explaining salvation to Nicodemus, He said, "The wind bloweth where it listeth" (Jn. 3:8). Jesus told him that we can hear the sound of the wind, but we cannot tell where it came from or where it is going (v. 8). He used the simile of wind to describe the moving of the Holy Spirit.

On the Day of Pentecost, the Holy Spirit descended with the "sound from heaven as of a rushing mighty wind, and it filled all the house where they were sitting" (Acts 2:2). The Holy Spirit is not wind, but His coming was so powerful and awesome that it sounded like a rushing mighty wind to the disciples. This is the only description given in Scripture of the coming of the Holy Spirit on the Day of Pentecost. The disciples' lives were transformed as they experienced the omnipotent power of God in the Third Person of the Godhead coming to them as a mighty wind.

## RIVER OF GOD

Jesus declared, " 'He who believes in Me, as the Scripture said, "From his innermost being shall flow rivers of living water." ' But this He spoke of the Spirit, whom those who believed in Him were to receive…" (Jn. 7:38-39 NAS). Jesus referred here to the river as a type to describe the life-giving force of the Holy Spirit. A river is a source of water that sustains life abundantly. The psalmist described the life of a godly man as "a tree planted by the rivers of water, that bringeth forth his fruit in his season; his leaf also shall not wither; and whatsoever he doeth shall prosper" (Ps. 1:3). This beautiful simile of the fruitful life of the righteous symbolizes the power of the Holy Spirit as a river that continually brings abundant life to believers. When the river of God flows freely in our lives, we will bear fruit for the Kingdom and everything we do will prosper.

## DEW

Dew is that refreshing moisture so welcome after the heat of the sun has disappeared. These droplets settle in peace over the land and fill it with delight. The dew falls at night when all the creation is resting and the natural elements are at peace. Dew represents the *restfulness* in the Kingdom of God that the Holy Spirit came to give. When God provided Israel with daily manna in the wilderness, it fell with the dew upon the camp at night (Num. 11:9). Jesus referred to that manna when He proclaimed Himself to be the Bread of life (Jn. 6:32-35). In this type, the manna represented Jesus. The dew that fell with the manna symbolized the presence of the Holy Spirit. He will always be present where Jesus is present.

Job described this restful state when he wrote, "My root was spread out by the waters, and the dew lay all night upon my branch. My glory was fresh in me, and my bow was renewed in my hand " (Job 29:19-20). The prophet Isaiah foretold the Holy Spirit's desire to give us rest: "For with stammering lips and another tongue will He speak to this people. To whom He said, This is the rest wherewith ye may cause the weary to rest; and this is the refreshing: yet they would not hear" (Is. 28:11-12).

The Holy Spirit promises welcome rest not only to the individual believer, but to the corporate body of Christ as well. The psalmist declared, "Behold, how good and how pleasant it is for brethren to dwell together in unity!...As the dew of Hermon, and as the dew that descended upon the mountains of Zion: for there the Lord commanded the blessing, even life for evermore" (Ps. 133:1,3). Only the Holy Spirit can bring men together in unity in the Body of Christ. Unity is like the dew of heaven, full of pleasantness and refreshment. It is in unity that the Lord commands the blessing, the eternal life of the Spirit.

## WATER

Water is often used as an emblem of the Holy Spirit in the Scriptures, as we have seen in our study of the symbolism of rain, dew, and the river of God. Water is more necessary than food to man's life. We can survive without food for a considerably longer period than we can survive without water. The lack of water reduces life to an arid desert, a land without hope of fruitfulness  God's purpose is fruitfulness for all who receive the Spirit of God. When water symbolizes the Holy Spirit, the picture is always one of abundance, like rivers, springs, and wells that never run dry.

### Water From the Rock

God gave Moses instructions on how to receive life-giving water out of a rock. "Behold, I will stand before thee there upon the rock in Horeb; and thou shalt smite the rock, and there shall come water out of it, that the people may drink. And Moses did so in the sight of the elders of Israel" (Ex. 17:6). The miracle of receiving water out of a rock beautifully typifies for us the power of the Holy Spirit flowing out of Christ, who is our Rock. When Christ gave the Holy Spirit to believers, we received Him as living water out of our Rock, Christ Jesus.

## Water Springs

When the psalmist cried out, "All my springs are in thee" (Ps. 87:7b), he was acknowledging God as the only source of life. Water springs depict the very beginning of the source of life. Mountain springs feed the largest rivers at their starting points, the places where the rain and snows begin their long trek downward to the sea. The story of Caleb's daughter in the Old Testament illustrates the importance of water springs. When Caleb's daughter asked her father for a blessing, she said, "...for thou hast given me a south land; give me also springs of water" (Josh. 15:19a). She knew the life-giving value of water springs. Her father granted her request. Our father will grant ours as well when we ask for the power of the Holy Spirit to be our source of life.

We dare not look to any other source for life, which God's people have sometimes done throughout history. Jeremiah voiced God's lament that "My people have committed two evils, they have forsaken Me the fountain of living waters, and hewed them out cisterns, broken cisterns, that can hold no water" (Jer. 2:13). Looking for life from any source other than God is like molding broken clay cups that cannot contain refreshing, life-giving water for us.

## Wells of Salvation

Wells of salvation correspond to the rivers of living water that Jesus said would flow out of our innermost beings. Jesus told the woman at the well, "But whosoever drinketh of the water that I shall give him shall never thirst; but the water that I shall give him shall be in him a well of water springing up into everlasting life" (Jn. 4:14). The Holy Spirit, like the well, has an unlimited supply of life. Isaiah the prophet had this revelation when he declared, "Behold, God is my salvation; I will trust, and not be afraid: for the Lord JEHOVAH is my strength and my song; He also is become my salvation. Therefore with joy shall ye draw water out of the wells of salvation" (Is. 12:2-3).

## Valley of Baca

The valley of Baca represents a place of difficulties and tears. We probably would not think of this valley as a place of blessing. The Scriptures, however, teach:

*Blessed is the man whose strength is in thee; in whose heart are the ways of them. Who passing through the valley of Baca make it a well; the rain also filleth the pools. They go from strength to strength, every one of them in Zion appeareth before God.* (Psalm 84:5-7)

As we walk through difficulties in the power of the Holy Spirit, He transforms those problems into a well of life-giving strength for us.

We also can translate the Hebrew word for "well" as "a place of springs." Even our most difficult situations can become a spring, a source of life to us, as we discover how to abide in Christ in our suffering, drawing on the strength of the Spirit and experiencing His protection. Pain and suffering do not threaten the life of Christ. On the contrary, they become pathways to new springs of comfort and strength as we call on the Holy Spirit during those times of affliction. We learn to go from strength to strength.

## CLOTHING

When the Scriptures refer to the Spirit clothing individuals, they are describing the power of the Holy Spirit to *equip*. When God chose to use Gideon, for example, as a deliverer for His people, we read, "But the Spirit of the Lord came upon Gideon, and he blew a trumpet..." (Judg. 6:34). This verse can be translated as, "But the Spirit of the Lord *clothed* Gideon." God equipped Gideon for the task He gave him to do when the Spirit of the Lord came upon him.

Jesus told the disciples to tarry in Jerusalem until they be endued with power from on high at the coming of the Holy Spirit (Lk. 24:49). The word *endued* can be translated as *clothed* also. The Holy Spirit clothed the disciples with power to become witnesses to the gospel throughout the world. They were equipped by the Spirit to fulfill the will of God.

## EARNEST

The word *earnest* in the Greek refers to the first down payment, which assures the recipient of final payment in full. In modern Greek it means an engagement ring, the token of future marriage from the lover to his prospective bride.[4] Paul wrote to the Ephesians, "...ye were sealed with that holy Spirit of promise, which is the earnest of our inheritance until the redemption of the purchased possession..." (Eph. 1:13b-14). We have not received the fullness of our inheritance yet, but God gave us the Holy Spirit as a sample of what life will be like when we are fully redeemed. He is the down payment of our inheritance in Christ.

A little child slipped into his mother's kitchen where she was mixing a rich batter for a special homemade cake. The child stuck his fingers into that batter and then, licking them as he ran out the door, asked when the cake would be done. Having the Holy Spirit in our lives is like the wonderful taste of batter on our fingers; it makes us anticipate the finished cake. As the Holy Spirit brings us into Christ's presence, He gives us a foretaste of being received as Christ's Bride and enjoying everlasting love and communion with Him.

When Paul describes a people of God who are "sealed with the holy Spirit of promise" (Eph. 1:13), he is speaking of the Holy Spirit's work of producing a mark of identification, of ownership, an engraving of a glorious inner work, in His people. The Holy Spirit labels them as God's very own property, accepted by Him. A supernatural work has changed those people forever. They are not ordinary people anymore; they are no longer of this world. They have set their affections on things above, not on things of this earth (Col. 3:2). They are not so taken up, or interested in, or participants of this world's events. They are not shaken by every word of doom and gloom that comes along. They are no longer a part of a halfhearted, lukewarm congregation. They know that there is nothing worse than being in a church where God used to be or than in not knowing the purpose for which they were placed on the earth. Their heart cries out, "Even so, come quickly, Lord Jesus."

You might ask, "What happened to change them? What did the Holy Spirit do in that believer? What marked and sealed them forever as the Lord's possession?" It was simply this: The Holy Spirit gave them a foretaste of *the glory of His presence.* He came to them, opened their spiritual eyes, divided the veil of the flesh, and allowed them to experience a supernatural manifestation of His exceeding greatness. Isn't that why it is so necessary for God's house to be a place of prayer, purity, and power? Is that not what the psalmist was saying when he asked, "Who shall ascend into the hill of the Lord? or who shall stand in His holy place? He that hath clean hands, and a pure heart" (Ps. 24:3-4a). That is why we should not allow anything in our lives to hinder the Holy Spirit's work. We need the Spirit of God to pull back the veil of our flesh and give us a foretaste of our inheritance, an earnest of what we will one day receive in full.

God is sealing His people for His purposes in our day. We can go to meetings now where Jesus is so real that we can taste a little bit of Heaven in our souls. We come away with the sense of eternal reality, that an eternal work has been done inside of us. We feel we were not just challenged by a sermon, but were changed more into His image. God has put a holy fire in our soul and there is no more fear of the enemy—the world, the flesh, and the devil. There is a security in knowing that we have received a supernatural touch from God. We leave that service saying, "This isn't me. This is God's Spirit working inside of me."

You may have heard it said that God gives us a little heaven to go to Heaven in. I used to wonder what that meant. Now I think it simply means that He whets our appetite by letting us look into the glory of His Kingdom. We get a taste of His holiness, His love, His rest, and His peace. Then we are forever spoiled for this world because we have had a taste. Now we yearn for the fullness—or the cake, if you please—which we have only tasted. The Holy Spirit is the earnest of that fullness.

## SUMMARY

These emblems, taken together, provide a beautiful and comforting portrait of the Holy Spirit; the Holy

Spirit is not an emblem. As the Third Person of the God-head, He is a very desirable, divine Person. However, the life-giving qualities of these emblems accurately reveal to us many characteristics of this beautiful Third Person of the Godhead, as well as His lovely character and His great power to redeem the sons of men. These emblems show us His great desire to give abundant life to all who will receive Him.

## Notes

1. Ada R. Habershon, *The Study of the Types*, Grand Rapids, Michigan: Kregel Publications, 1980), pp. 11-13.

2. John Rea, *The Holy Spirit in the Bible,* (Lake Mary, Florida: Creation House, 1990), p. 21.

3. Ibid., p. 274.

4. Ibid.

# Chapter 4

# *The Fragrance of the Holy Spirit*

## *The Holy Anointing Oil*

God gave Moses detailed instructions for making a holy anointing oil for the children of Israel. This oil is one of the most beautiful and complete types of the Holy Spirit in the Scriptures. In this Old Testament reality, God foreshadowed the divine personality of the Holy Spirit as well as the redemptive work He came to do. A close examination of the anointing oil will reveal the Person of the Holy Spirit to us, in type, and teach us how He accomplishes His supernatural work in our individual lives and in the Church.

61

## CONTENTS OF THE COMPOUND

*Moreover the Lord spake unto Moses, saying, Take thou also unto thee principal spices, of pure myrrh five hundred shekels, and of sweet cinnamon half so much, even two hundred and fifty shekels, and of sweet calamus two hundred and fifty shekels, and of cassia five hundred shekels, after the shekel of the sanctuary, and of oil olive an hin: and thou shalt make it an oil of holy ointment, an ointment compound after the art of the apothecary: it shall be an holy anointing oil.* (Exodus 30:22-25)

God instructed Moses to make an ointment compound after the art of the apothecary. This holy anointing oil was no haphazard mixture of spices and oil; instead it was to be compounded as carefully as a pharmacist would prepare a medicine. God specified the ingredients and their amounts exactly, and instructed the people to never change the recipe throughout all generations. This unchangeability typifies the fact that the personality of the Holy Spirit does not change. It is true that, from one move of God to another throughout history, a particular emphasis or denominational flavor in teaching about the Holy Spirit has changed because of limited doctrinal understanding. Yet the Holy Spirit does not change; He is God and we must learn to know Him for who He is in His completion and perfection as the Third Person of the Godhead.

The contents and application of the anointing oil forshadow the anointing of the Holy Spirit that Jesus promised to believers after His resurrection from the dead (Acts 1:8). God instructed Moses to mix 500 shekels of myrrh with 500 shekels of cassia, 250 shekels of cinnamon, and 250 of calamus. When combined, they measured one quart of liquid spice. They were to be mixed with a hin of olive oil which, according to some scholars, was a six-quart measure. This seven-quart quantity of liquid spice and olive oil is significant because the number seven in the Scriptures represents perfection and completion. As God, the Holy Spirit's divine perfection had to be represented in type.

The four spices used to make the holy anointing oil each represent an aspect of the work of the Holy Spirit in our lives. Understanding the individual characteristics of each ingredient will give us a beautiful picture of how the Holy Spirit works. But the anointing oil was actually the result of mixing these ingredients to form a compound. By definition, a compound is a *distinct substance* formed by the chemical union of several ingredients. This typifies the work of the Holy Spirit as He forms an entirely new creation in us to transform us into the image of Christ. God's larger purpose in ordaining the anointing oil was to reveal these eternal realities of the Person and work of the Holy Spirit.

## Myrrh

*Myrrh* is a short, thorny, and ragged tree-shrub that is part of the family of balsam trees. Either by a natural process or by man's cutting the stems, a gummy substance oozes from the shrub-like tree. The pale yellow liquid gradually solidifies and turns dark red or even black. That is myrrh. So there were two kinds of myrrh that could be gathered from the same shrub. Pure myrrh, the freely flowing myrrh, oozes spontaneously. The other myrrh flows from incisions made in the bark. Merchants, selling it as a spice or medicine, considered the free-flowing gum a higher grade of myrrh than what they gathered from incisions in the tree.

Because of its strong, attractive fragrance, myrrh was a principal ingredient in the most costly ointments. Some scholars say it was a kind of frankincense or musk fragrance. The medicinal value of myrrh made it valuable as an ointment to dissipate the soreness of wounds. Doctors also used it as an antiseptic and in embalming. They made it a fluid by pressing and heating it. That process also released its strong fragrance. In the holy anointing oil, its importance as an ingredient is demonstrated by the large quantity prescribed.

The root word in Hebrew for myrrh is *marar*, which means bitter, or grievous. Although its fragrance is very desirable, its taste is very bitter. *Marar* also means "to drop on from a container above," as in a dispenser. It is a picture of an atomizer that "squirts" automatically as our need for it demands. As a healing ointment, myrrh represents the grace we need for bitter circumstances of our lives. For the times we encounter trials or step on rough places, the dripping of this soothing ointment is a picture of the dispensing of grace in our hearts when the Holy Spirit resides there. Perhaps the fact that the anointing oil contained twice as much myrrh as cinnamon and calamus reflects the greatness of our need for grace, more grace and much grace in our lives. In that way myrrh symbolizes the abundant provision of grace available to us in the Holy Spirit.

Although myrrh is bitter to the taste, its sweet aroma makes it very desirable. As the Holy Spirit dispenses the myrrh of grace to us in our difficult situations, He releases its fragrance in our lives. So even though our experiences are sometimes bitter, the fragrance of Jesus can be released in us when we receive His grace to walk through them. For example when Naomi came home to Bethlehem, having suffered the loss of her husband and two sons, she told the people to call her Marah (Ruth 1:20-21). She explained to them that the Almighty had dealt bitterly with her. Although Naomi's circumstances were bitter, the fragrance of her life in her devotion to God had influenced her daughter-in-law, Ruth, to follow her. Their lives demonstrated to many people the grace of God that was available to them in their bitter circumstances as they followed Him.

The fragrance of myrrh also characterized Jesus' life. The psalmist spoke prophetically of Jesus, "Thou hast loved righteousness, and hated wickedness; therefore God, Thy God, has anointed Thee with the oil of joy above Thy fellows. All Thy garments are fragrant with myrrh and aloes and cassia..." (Ps. 45:7-8 NAS). Jesus was acquainted with sorrow and grief, but He was anointed with the oil of joy as well. He was "despised and rejected of men" (Is. 53:3), but the fragrance of His life revealed the Father's love and drew men to follow Him.

God wants His people to be equipped with the divine ability to rise above sufferings and persecutions and to enjoy the sweet smell of the myrrh of grace in their lives. Freely dispensed, it has the power to remove the soreness from wounds that resulted from consequences of past sin, our own sin nature, or mistreatment by other people. Then, when we are persecuted, we can turn the other cheek as Jesus taught us to do, and release the fragrance of meekness and grace in our lives. Our witness is not so dependent upon how we act in life, but upon how we *react* in life's situations. If our reactions reflect grace, it is evidence of the Holy Spirit producing the fruit of the tree of life in us and making us Christ-like.

Myrrh characterized not only Jesus' life, but also His death. When the wise men came to visit baby Jesus, one gift they presented to Him was myrrh. It spoke prophetically of Jesus' suffering on the cross. Surely there could be no more bitter agony than that which the sinless Christ suffered when He took the sin of the whole world upon Himself. Surely no sweeter fragrance was ever released than that of the salvation for lost mankind bought by the suffering of Jesus. John wrote that Jesus was "full of grace and truth" (Jn. 1:14). The grace of God that proved sufficient in the ultimate sacrifice made by the Lamb of God is sufficient for our trials as well.

When Jesus tells us to take up our cross and follow Him (Lk. 9:23), He furnishes us with the grace to carry it. We were born again to die to sin and the self-life. The Holy Spirit shows us the truth about ourselves and gives us the grace to take our sin nature to the cross. In type, the bitter but healing oil of myrrh, freely dispensed, is grace to die to self. As we choose to die to our wills and desires, that myrrh of grace yields its sweet fragrance in our lives.

### Cinnamon

*Cinnamon* is much more rare than myrrh. It is the aromatic, inner rind of the *laurus* cinnamon. Native to Ceylon (India), it is a tree that grows about twenty feet high with stiff, evergreen leaves. The harvester gathers cinnamon from the inner bark of the tree. It also has profuse white blossoms succeeded by a nut. The bark of the tree yields an oil, which is a golden yellow color. Cinnamon is a delightful spice that has a good taste and a pleasant aroma.[1]

To refine the oil of cinnamon, however, requires fire. The apothecary boils the plant to separate the inner rind from the coarser shell of the plant and then further refines that rind, by fire, to produce the oil of cinnamon. In much the same way the Holy Spirit works in our lives to burn the coarseness from us, refining us to bring forth the fragrance of Christ in our attitudes and dispositions. The Holy Spirit will sometimes take us through difficult circumstances to burn out those ungodly things in our natures that we inherited from Adam. As we yield to His fire, He brings us to a maturity that allows others to see the life of God within us, unhindered by the coarseness of our outer "shell."

Where there is grace there is also fire. John the Baptist declared that Jesus would "baptize you with the Holy Ghost, and with fire" (Mt. 3:11). The fire of the Holy Ghost purges the sin from our lives and causes us to shed the nature of the old man. I have known people who have lived sinful lives and who were haunted by their pasts. Their consciences condemned them and their sin had left deep scars on their lives. But when the Holy Spirit filled their lives and they allowed His divine fire to burn out the sin, the myrrh of His grace healed their scars and their faces began to shine. A sweet fragrance of peace and joy filled their lives, erasing the scars. The refining processes of the Holy Spirit as typified in the refining of cinnamon can change our lives for eternity, and allow us to enjoy the presence of God continually.

## Calamus

*Calamus* is a very sweet cane plant or reed that is also rare. It grew in distant places, probably Asia minor and Greece (Ezek. 27:19). A chief characteristic of this reed-like plant is the unusually sweet fragrance it exudes, especially when it is bruised.[2] The more it is broken and bruised, the sweeter the fragrance it releases. Isaiah declared of Jesus, "He was bruised for our iniquities" (Is. 53:5). In His suffering, Jesus revealed the meek and gentle nature of the lamb that does not retaliate when someone injures him. Proud, independent, self-centered, undisciplined people do not reflect the spirit of the lamb. That lamb-like spirit, like the sweet fragrance of the bruised calamus, is found in us as we allow the Holy Spirit to fill us. Then He changes our reactions and melts our hearts so that in our crushing sorrows we release a sweet fragrance that delights the heart of God. The Holy Spirit produces in us the spirit of God's family, which is the nature of the Lamb.

The lamb-nature is the spirit of the Bride that the Holy Spirit is preparing for the Son. The writer of the Song of Solomon describes the bride as a garden filled with spices. "Thy plants are an orchard of pomegranates, with pleasant fruits; camphire, with spikenard...calamus and cinnamon...myrrh and aloes, with all the chief spices" (Song 4:13-14). Solomon's bride is a beautiful picture of the Bride of Christ. As the Holy Spirit fills our lives with Himself, we become like gardens that produce the fragrance, beauty, and fruitfulness of these fruits and spices. Though rare, calamus was found here in the lily beds of the bride's garden. Yet only the Holy Spirit can produce the sweet fragrance of the meekness that comes from our being bruised in life's situations.

## Cassia

The fourth spice, *cassia*, is an aromatic white plant or tree native to Arabia. Doctors used it as a purging medicine. Its small leaves still provide the medicine known as senna leaves. The ancients, however, burned it on their altars with frankincense. The word itself means "to split, to scrape off, to purge, or to separate. "Like cinnamon, cassia is gathered from the inner bark of a tree. It strongly resembles cinnamon in its taste and scent, but is more pungent and of coarser texture. Its bark is less delicate in taste and perfume than that of cinnamon.

In Hebrew, the primitive root word for cassia is *qadad*, which means "to shrivel up." From that definition we derive the connotation of "contracting or bending the body or neck in deference; bowing down the head, stooping; doing homage to men of rank." As a part of the anointing oil, cassia further typifies the cleansing work of the Holy Spirit in our lives. He teaches us to defer to others and to esteem others better than ourselves (Phil. 2:3).

The Holy Spirit comes so we can "put off the old man," and experience a circumcision of heart from the world, the flesh, and the devil. He comes to separate the wheat from the chaff within us. Other biblical terms for this purging work of the Holy Spirit are pruning, refining, and sanctifying. These processes, typified in all four spices, describe the ultimate goal of the Holy Spirit to rid us of our carnal nature, the nature that is not like God. He then creates in us the lamb-nature of Jesus and releases the beautiful fragrance of the anointing in our lives.

## COUNTERFEIT

According to God's instructions, this holy anointing oil could not be duplicated or in any way counterfeited without incurring God's judgment.

*Upon man's flesh shall it not be poured, neither shall ye make any other like it, after the composition of it: it is holy, and it shall be holy unto you. Whosoever compoundeth any like it, or whosoever putteth any of it upon a stranger, shall even be cut off from his people.* (Exodus 30:32-33)

God had given specific instructions for the use of the anointing oil as well as for its composition. If a person violated those instructions for any reason, that offender was to be punished.

In the Church today we must be careful not to substitute our programs and promotions, our emotional responses to enthusiastic music, or other carnal or religious forms for the true working of the Holy Spirit. We must seek the reality of God's presence in our services according to the instructions He has given in His Word. As the holy anointing oil was to be prepared and used according to God's instructions, so must we relate to the Holy Spirit in a way that our hearts and motives are right before God.

There was a certain man named Simon in the Book of Acts who had wicked motives for wanting to receive the Holy Spirit. He wanted to buy the power of the Holy Spirit for personal gain, to have power over men's lives. The precious Holy Spirit cannot tolerate such selfish motives. Peter sternly rebuked Simon, "Thy money perish with thee, because thou hast thought that the gift of God may be purchased with money. Thou hast neither part nor lot in this matter: for thy heart is not right in the sight of God" (Acts 8:20-21).

We must never consider "using" the power of God for personal aggrandizement. God gave us the Holy Spirit to reveal Jesus to us and to bring us into relationship with the Father. It was through extreme suffering that the Godhead made possible our reconciliation to God. Jesus was the Lamb slain from the foundation of the world for our sins (Rev. 13:8). As we allow our hearts to be melted in gratitude for Jesus' sacrifice, we will experience right relationship with God and be genuinely motivated to share the good news of that relationship with others. That is God's purpose for giving us the power of the Holy Spirit.

## CONDEMNED FOR STRANGERS

God commanded not only that the anointing oil not be counterfeited; but also that it not be put upon a stranger. The penalty for both offenses was the same; the offender would be cut off from his people (Ex. 30:33). The people of Israel understood that a person who was not a part of God's chosen people did not qualify for having the anointing oil applied to him; he was a stranger.

In applying the anointing oil even to God's people, they needed to follow a certain order. For example, the priests used the oil as part of the cleansing required for those who suffered with leprosy. Oil was not to be applied, however, until after the blood was applied to the leper. According to the Mosaic law, when a person had leprosy, only the priest could apply the blood of cleansing to him (Lev. 14). This procedure required the sacrifice of a lamb. Its blood was then applied to the person's ear, thumb, and toe. Afterward he could have the oil applied to those same places on top of the blood. This was the order of the process required for him to be restored to his home.

Leprosy was a state of uncleanness and represents to us today the sinful condition each of us is born into.

Our sin is forgiven only when we apply the blood of Jesus to our hearts by asking for His forgiveness. To be cleansed from sin we must first accept the sacrifice of the shed blood of Jesus, the Lamb of God. Then we become part of the family of God; we are no longer strangers and we can have the oil applied where the blood was applied. We have said that the anointing oil represents the Holy Spirit in type. So we understand the order of its application to represent another order—that after the blood of Jesus is applied to our sins, we become eligible for the baptism of the Holy Spirit. An unsaved person cannot receive this baptism. It is not for strangers, but for blood-washed children of God.

## *COSTLY*

God chose to use *myrrh, cinnamon, calamus,* and *cassia* to be a part of the anointing oil. He did not select these particular spices because they were common or easily accessible. On the contrary, they were rare and had to be imported from a great distance. Thus it was very costly to compound such rare spices in large quantities into a holy anointing oil. This fact symbolizes the beautiful truth of how costly it was for the Godhead to send to earth the Holy Spirit as a servant to prepare a bride for the Son of God. The Godhead was willing to make this sacrifice to fulfill God's eternal plan that many sons be birthed and brought to maturity in His Kingdom. God is still intent on building a glorious Church through which the fragrance of His divine life will permeate to the world. He will reveal the lamb-like spirit of Christ through His Church for all to see.

As there was great cost involved for God to provide salvation for us, so there is cost involved for us to follow Him. Although salvation is a free gift to all who believe on Jesus, it costs us to choose His will instead of ours. Each of us must consider the cost for being filled with the Holy Spirit. In order to be continually filled with the Holy Spirit, we must allow the Holy Spirit to empty us of our flesh-life, which militates against the life of God. The Spirit of the Lamb must displace our Adamic nature with its carnal mind and self-centered desires. If we do not consider the cost involved in knowing the Third Person of the Godhead, we will not be prepared for the return of the Bridegroom. In the parable of the ten virgins who were waiting for the return of the Bridegroom, each virgin had a measure of the Holy Spirit, as typified by the oil in her lamp. However, the five wise virgins took extra oil with them, while the five foolish virgins did not. When the bridegroom finally came at midnight, the foolish virgins were out of oil. They asked the wise virgins to give them some of theirs, but the wise virgins replied that they would need their oil to meet the bridegroom if he delayed (Mt. 25:1-13).

Jesus called the five virgins who did not take enough oil, foolish. They were not careful to prepare their lamps for the long wait. They themselves had not considered the cost for being ready for His coming, but were willing for others to pay it for them. That is not the way of the Kingdom, however, so they missed His coming. We do not know all that lies ahead of us in our journey through life. But if we count the cost and allow ourselves to be filled with the oil of the Holy Spirit, we will have some to spare for the unexpected—and we will still be walking in the light when Jesus, our Bridegroom, returns.

## *CONSECRATION*

The holy anointing oil was used to consecrate people and places that were to be separated unto the Lord. God commanded Moses to anoint the tabernacle, the ark of the testimony, the table and all its vessels, the candlestick and its vessels, the altar of incense, the altar of burnt offering, and the laver with this oil. This act of anointing would sanctify them, or set them apart, to be used only for God's purposes. The anointing oil also was to consecrate Aaron and his sons, "that they may minister unto Me in the priest's office" (Ex. 30:30). They were set apart to minister unto the Lord.

In that same way Jesus "hath made us kings and priests unto God and His Father" (Rev. 1:6a). We are consecrated by the Holy Spirit to minister unto God. Paul wrote to the Corinthians, "Know ye not that ye are the temple of God, and that the Spirit of God dwelleth in you?" (1 Cor. 3:16) The anointing of the Holy Spirit sanctifies us and makes us holy, setting us apart for the purposes of God. The altar of our hearts should be a place for the light of the Holy Spirit to dwell. As He transforms us into the image of Christ, He gives us grace to turn from sin and the carnal nature.

Too often when we receive the baptism of the Holy Spirit we expect to become a great preacher or have a great ministry. That is not why He filled us with the myrrh of grace. That is not why He allowed us to be bruised. He wants instead to smell the fragrance of His presence in our lives as we minister to Him. Let's allow the sweet fragrance of Christ to flow out of our lives, and others will be drawn to Him, not to us. We are consecrated, set apart, unto Him through the anointing of the Holy Spirit.

## THE TYPE FULFILLED

I can imagine Moses looking up at God and musing on all he did to compound that anointing oil. Could he have known that it was just an object lesson, a type of what God would really do one day in sending His Holy Spirit to earth to fill His people? Moses had followed God's instructions to mix myrrh, cinnamon, cassia, and calamus in olive oil and seal it in a bottle to be used in consecration. He did it all just to typify the reality of the coming of the Holy Spirit. As a servant of God, it was his lot to simply obey and prepare the holy anointing oil as God had commanded him, sealing it up to be used as God ordained.

On the Day of Pentecost, Peter stood up and said, "But this is that which was spoken by the prophet Joel; And it shall come to pass in the last days, saith God, I will pour out of My Spirit upon all flesh..." (Acts 2:16-17). It was as though Peter reached up to Moses' shelf for that anointing oil and started splitting and cracking open those vials over people's heads. It was the day of the reality of the outpouring of the Holy Spirit, the day of the bursting of the bottles. What Moses had prepared in type became a reality when God sent the Holy Spirit to earth to do His work of redeeming a glorious Church. He came to fill every heart that was seeking Him. Having had the blood of Jesus applied for the forgiveness of sins, the fragrance of that holy anointing oil would permeate their lives as the Holy Spirit filled them with His power. They would become a demonstration of the life of Christ in the earth.

As the power of the Holy Spirit fills the Church, we will experience the dispensing of myrrh, receiving the grace to go to the cross and exchange the self-life for the Christ-life. We will endure the fire of God purging our sin and stripping away the things that previously bound us to the world. A sweet fragrance will begin to rise from us, and others will be drawn to that sweetness. As the Church consecrates herself to minister unto the Lord, the fragrance of His presence will draw people to Himself. We must learn to individually yield and surrender to Him so each of us can be a part of the glorious Church that is filled with the Holy Spirit corporately. As we do, we will know Him personally and He will bring us, restored to the image of God, home to the Father. We will then know the unspeakable joy of being presented to our Savior and Bridegroom as His Bride.

To know the Holy Spirit is to have relationship with Heaven's Divine Administrator of the purposes of God on earth. The revelation of Himself as a Person leads to the fuller revelation of His purposes in our lives as individual believers and as the Church. Our destiny will unfold as we learn to follow Him.

### Notes

1. The New Westminster Dictionary of the Bible, ed. H.S. Geyman, (Philadelphia, Pennsylvania: Westminster Press, 1970), pp. 176

2. Ibid., pp. 134

# Chapter 5

# *Seven Offices of the Holy Spirit*

## *Part I: Heaven's Divine Administrator on Earth*

The Holy Spirit, as a divine Person, functions in seven different spheres of service that can be called "offices." Through these offices this Third Person of the Godhead executes specific duties to fulfill the eternal plan of God. This comprehensive authority structure can be illustrated in the office of the President of the United States. He is the chief executive of this nation, the chief administrator, the chief diplomat, and the one ultimately responsible for the welfare of the nation. Should our country go to war, he serves as Commander-in-Chief of the nation's armed forces. He is directly responsible for many areas of government, and ultimately responsible for all governmental decisions.

In the same way God has designated the Holy Spirit to a chief executive capacity with respect to the seven areas of authority that affect the spirit, soul, and body of individual believers. The offices of the Holy Spirit reveal His governmental authority over the Church. These impact each of our lives individually while building the Body of Christ corporately. Under these offices are at least 66 specific services that the Holy Spirit executes for the Body of Christ. In our study we will list these services as they relate to each particular office.

Of these seven divine offices that the Holy Spirit administrates, the first four reveal the work of the Holy Spirit in *creating the divine life of God in us.* Anyone who lives without that divine life merely exists. We discover the reality of life only in knowing Christ, for Christ is Life. That is what John meant when he wrote, "He who has the Son has life; he who does not have the Son of God does not have life" (1 John 5:12 NIV). The Holy Spirit is the source of that divine life.

The other three offices reveal the divine power the Holy Spirit gives us as He *governs our lives* and fully develops the character of Christ in His Church (see Chapter 6). He is the only One who can bring us to

Christian maturity and true holiness. As we learn to yield in obedience to the Holy Spirit, our lives become victorious and we can reign in life as God intended.

## *THE SPIRIT OF LIFE*

*For the law of the Spirit of life in Christ Jesus hath made me free from the law of sin and death...And if Christ be in you, the body is dead because of sin; but the Spirit is life because of righteousness. But if the Spirit of Him that raised up Jesus from the dead dwell in you, He that raised up Christ from the dead shall also quicken your mortal bodies by His Spirit that dwelleth in you.* (Romans 8:2,10-11)

When the Scriptures refer to the Holy Spirit as "the Spirit of..." they signify that He is the executor of the office named. For example, as the Spirit of Life, the Holy Spirit makes us alive to God by creating the *life* of Jesus in us. Jesus said, "I am the *way,* the *truth,* and the *life*" (Jn. 14:6a). Jesus is life and the Holy Spirit is the Spirit of Life. The Holy Spirit has come to give to us the things of Jesus that pertain to life (Jn. 16:14). All of the divine qualities of Jesus' life—His peace, His joy, His righteousness—reside in the Spirit of Life.

As God's divine administrator of the heavenly estates, the Holy Spirit desires to create in us the life of Christ. In personal salvation, the life of Christ is birthed in us. The Holy Spirit takes the living seed of God, the Word, and impregnates our spirits with the life of Christ. This is what Paul declared as "Christ in you, the hope of glory" (Col. 1:27). To experience that reality requires personal acceptance of Christ as the Savior who forgives sins by the power of His shed blood on Calvary. Jesus called this supernatural happening, "being born again of the Spirit" (Jn. 3). We experience peace and freedom from guilt when we are born again and begin to experience life as God intended for a child of the King to live it. To be a Christian, then, is to allow Christ to live His life through us. It is the Holy Spirit who performs this supernatural work, who makes the Word become flesh in our lives.

Then, when we are baptized into the Holy Spirit, we come into a fuller relationship with the Spirit of Life. He operates in us as a dynamo of power to propel the force of His life through us. Jesus said, "But ye shall receive power, after that the Holy Ghost is come upon you" (Acts 1:8a). Every aspect of the life-giving force within our inner man functions by the power of the Holy Spirit.

As the Holy Spirit creates the life of God in us individually, He begins to unite our lives with those of other believers in the Church. A church is alive to God when the Spirit of Life breathes revelation to people's hearts from the written Word as it is taught by an anointed minister. There is divine life in the Word, and as we receive it under the anointing of the Holy Spirit, we receive a quickening, life-giving power in our spirits. Without the Spirit of Life anointing the written Word, the letter of the law will kill. It is the Spirit that gives life (2 Cor. 3:6). There are churches condemned under legalism and religious forms because they do not have the quickening power of the Spirit of Life. The Holy Spirit is not given His proper place of authority in the lives of those ministers and believers. It is imperative for us to learn to yield to the Spirit of Life both individually and corporately so we might experience true life in Christ.

## Services of the Spirit of Life

These are the services of the Holy Spirit as He functions as the Spirit of Life: In creation He hovered over the earth and brought order out of chaos and light out of darkness. He breathes the life of God into believers and impregnates them with the living Word. He lifes the Word. He anoints us and He baptizes the believer into the Body of Christ. He produces the life of Christ in and through the Spirit-filled person. He seals us and He works resurrection power in and through us. He bears witness with our spirit that we are children of God.

## II. THE SPIRIT OF TRUTH

*But when the Comforter is come, whom I will send unto you from the Father, even the Spirit of truth, which proceedeth from the Father, He shall testify of Me.* (John 15:26)

*Howbeit when He, the Spirit of truth, is come, He
will guide you into all truth.* (John 16:13a)

We cannot know God without knowing the Spirit of
Truth. We cannot receive anything God has for us in
the light of the Word if the Holy Spirit does not illumine it to us. Jesus said He had many things to say to
the disciples, but that they could not bear them yet (Jn.
16:12). Yet He also said that when the Spirit of Truth
was come, He would receive the things of Jesus and
show them to them (Jn. 16:15). Truth is a Person: Jesus
Christ (Jn. 14:6). As we walk with the Spirit of Truth,
communing with Him and yielding to Him, divine truth is
ever expanding in us, bringing us to a mature relationship with God.

We do not understand truth in the same degree we
did when we were first born again that we do after we
have walked with God for several years. When a three-
year-old asks his father where babies come from, his
father will not give him the same kind of answer that
he would give his teenage son. In the same way, when
we were first born again we did not understand truth as
one who has walked with God for many years would
understand it. Our relationship with our heavenly Father grows as we mature enough to develop a capacity
to receive divine truths.

Even after we intellectually grasp the concept of a
truth, we do not fully possess it until we can see it changing our lives. When the children of Israel entered the

Promised Land, they did not immediately possess all of it. They took possession of the land one city at a time through divinely led conquest. Like the children of Israel who fought with giants in the Promised Land, we must fight the enemies of truth, routing unbelief and doubt from our minds and hearts to possess that truth for ourselves. That can be done only by continually yielding to the Spirit of Truth within us.

## Process of Revelation

The Spirit of Truth takes us through a divine learning process to make revelation a reality that changes our lives. That process results in the *unveiling* of the Christ who is *in* us. The Spirit quickens the Word that is "sharper than any two-edged sword, piercing even to the dividing asunder of soul and spirit" (Heb. 4:12). That Word reveals the veil of flesh in our lives that keeps Christ so hidden that we do not know Him as we should. "Line upon line" the Spirit of Truth works to remove that veil of flesh to reveal Christ in us until His glory, His divine Presence, fills us. Paul declared that we are the temple of the Holy Spirit (1 Cor. 3:16). As the Holy Spirit fills our temple, the mind of Christ becomes our mind, His emotions become our emotions, and His will becomes our will. My will becomes His will, and we become the will of God. It is God's desire for His manifest presence to completely fill His temples.

The first step toward revelation in this divine process is to receive *information*. We must first receive a basic truth in our minds and hearts in order for the Holy Spirit to bring it to our remembrance. When that information begins to be a light to our spirits, it becomes *illumination*. We understand, in a way we never understood before, the truth that was once only information to us. Then it becomes our responsibility to walk in that truth. As the Holy Spirit continues His process of bringing us to revelation, we find ourselves responding to the truth with His joy. The Holy Spirit receives the Word with joy and, as we receive it from Him, it becomes *inspiration* to us. New desires to obey the Word fill our hearts.

The written Word of God (*logos*) can be viewed as a transcription of God's voice. When that transcribed Word moves from our heads to our hearts, it becomes a living Word to us (*rhema*). That living Word is *revelation*. Revelation makes the truth become a living Person to us. When we are born again, Jesus' life comes to reside in our spirits. Then, through the revelation of His Word to our spirits, His life begins to mature inside us. As we respond to revelation, we yield our wills, minds, and emotions to His divine character of holiness and righteousness, and the life of Christ is unveiled within us. When the Holy Spirit breathes a revealed truth into our spirits, it becomes our life. We actually experience what we had one day only heard with our ears as information. Our obedience to that revelation enables the Holy Spirit to keep giving us new revelation. Once revelation begins to flow in us, it keeps flowing until we resist it.

After revelation begins to work in our hearts, the next step in this divine process is *realization*. Realization is understanding that we are being changed through our obedience to the revelation that has become a part of our life. Other people can observe this change in us. Our spirits are sensitive to the truth that has become a living reality in us, and we are careful not to disobey it. A consistent walk in greater depth of revelation then brings a gradual *transformation* to our lives. We are changed from glory to glory into the image of the Son through our obedience to that revelation. The final step the Spirit of Truth works in us is the *manifestation* of Jesus' character in our lives. Maturity is the beauty of Jesus seen in people who have allowed the Spirit of Truth to touch their lives in every area of their soul and spirit. They, in obedience to God, have continually turned from sin and allowed the nature of Christ to be fully unveiled in them.

## *The Character of Truth*

The Spirit of Truth does more than just reveal concepts of truth to us. He makes us people who are truthful; that is, He makes us people who are full of truth. If we do not live the truth, what we speak is not truth. When what we speak becomes an experienced reality in our lives, then we are people who speak truth. As someone has well said, "Show me your wounds and I will believe your message." The way we live our lives gives substance and credibility to our words. As we yield to the Spirit of Truth, we cannot continue to be dishonest. He cleanses us from exaggeration, prefabrication, white lies, and other more "acceptable" forms of dishonesty.

The Holy Spirit causes us to speak truth in every situation. He does not tolerate gossip, backbiting, and other sins of the tongue that cause division and dissension in the Body of Christ. The Old Testament Scriptures include those who cause dissension among brethren in the list of seven things that God hates (Prov. 6:19). The New Testament instructs us to speak the truth to each other in love (Eph. 4:15). It requires a deep work of the Holy Spirit to cleanse us from sins of the tongue and to cause us to speak truth from our hearts in every situation of life. The Bible teaches that those who do not receive the love of the truth will be deceived (2 Thess. 2:10-12). We must learn to know and love the Spirit of Truth if we want to escape that fate.

## Services of the Spirit of Truth

As the Spirit of Truth, the Holy Spirit illuminates, inspires, reveals, writes, and corrects. He speaks expressly (preaches), speaks mysteries (prophesies), searches, counsels, and instructs (as the Teacher). He also demonstrates the Word, receives the Word with joy, brings things to our remembrance, convicts, makes God's promises alive to us (*logos* to *rhema*), renews the spirit of our mind, and shows us things to come.

### III. THE SPIRIT OF ADOPTION

*For ye have not received the spirit of bondage again to fear; but ye have received the Spirit of adoption, whereby we cry, Abba, Father. The Spirit itself beareth witness with our spirit, that we are the children of God.* (Romans 8:15-16)

It is my earnest conviction that we need to be delivered from five areas of carnal thinking before we can understand and be a part of what God is doing in the earth. These areas include tradition, prejudice, denominationalism, culture, and custom. Our carnal minds have been trained to think in certain ways that differ greatly from each other, even from one geographic location to another. We view the Scriptures through minds that have been prejudiced according to our racial and religious backgrounds as well as to our cultural environments. Although it is not our purpose here to explore each of these areas of bondage, we mention them because of our present topic: *adoption*.

Our Western custom regarding adoption of children has clouded our biblical understanding of adoption because it is quite different from Eastern custom. Our practice of adoption can be defined simply as, *"to take by choice into relationship.*" In our culture, adoption involves taking an infant or child from someone else's family, giving them our surname, and legally making them our child. We change their environment, and they will undoubtedly adopt many of our characteristics simply by living with us. We can even influence their choices, and they will share our outlook on life and our attitudes about many of life's situations. However, the traits they received by heredity cannot be changed because their bloodline was not affected by adoption.

In Bible culture, adoption did not refer to people receiving an infant into their home to raise as their child. The ancient Romans and Greeks both had the same adoption practices. They adopted none but sons who had been born to them. When a son grew to maturity and was equipped to bear the family name responsibly, he was declared to be "a son" by his father and adopted as an heir of the family estate. Adoption was a recognition of *mature sonship* (Gal. 4:1-2). It did not take place at birth. The declaration of adoption in that culture took place at maturity; it signified heirship and throneship, rulership and joint-ownership. It had nothing to do with "babyship," as we understand adoption in our Western culture.

It is written of Jesus that He "increased in wisdom and stature, and in favour with God and man" (Lk. 2:52). These few words about Jesus' life as a young man reveal the maturing process that prepared Him to be a Son. The prophet Isaiah declared, "For unto us a child is born, unto us a son is given: and the government shall be upon His shoulder..." (Is. 9:6). Although Jesus was the incarnate Christ child born to a virgin, Mary, He was required to grow to maturity to become the Son that "is given."

What was the first thing the Father said audibly (to the world) about Jesus at His water baptism? He declared from Heaven for all to hear, "This is My beloved Son" (Mt. 3:17). That declaration held far more significance than just being a simple reiteration of Jesus' identity. It meant that Jesus had qualified for sonship in the Father's eyes, that He had satisfied His requirements for sonship. Then, when Jesus went to the mount of transfiguration, God declared again, "This is My beloved Son, in whom I am well pleased" (Mt. 17:5). Jesus did nothing that the Father did not tell Him to do. He lived to please His Father only. We must follow Jesus' example if we are to be called sons of God. He is not a son in the biblical sense who has not absorbed his father's spirit, heart, vision, and purpose, desiring to please him in all things. That maturity qualifies him for sonship; He can run his father's business.

As children of God, we are born into the family of God. However, God didn't just change our environment;

He also changed our bloodline. He delivered us from the power of darkness and translated us into the Kingdom of His dear Son (Col. 1:13). He birthed us into His family. To become adopted sons, though, and heirs to the throne, we must come to maturity—increasing in wisdom and stature and receiving God's favor. Paul teaches clearly throughout the Christological epistles that we are expected to become sons with knowledge. He taught that ministries were given to the Church for the perfecting of the saints, "until we all attain to the unity of the faith, and of the knowledge of the Son of God, to a mature man, to the measure of the stature which belongs to the fulness of Christ" (Eph. 4:13 NAS). The Spirit of Adoption who lives inside us enables us to come to mature sonship. He trains, nurtures, and disciples us until we come to full stature.

Paul referred to this work of the Holy Spirit when he declared, "For all who are being led by the Spirit of God, these are the sons of God" (Rom. 8:14 NAS). The discipline of being led by the Holy Spirit, learning to hear and obey Him in all of life's situations, is the prerequisite for being called sons of God. As we yield to the Spirit of Adoption, He trains us as sons. As we continue to obey Him, He makes us heirs of God and joint heirs with Jesus Christ. One day He will let us rule with Him—when we are mature enough to reflect our Father's spirit, heart, vision, and purpose.

The Spirit of Adoption who changes our natural heredity into a divine heredity and places us in a new environment, lives inside us. We must learn to cooperate with Him in this process of adoption. We need *not* say as the world does, "Once an alcoholic, always an alcoholic," or "Once a harlot, always a harlot." Jesus shed His blood to buy us back with the supreme price of His life. When we are born into the family of God we are given a new bloodline; we have a new heredity. Our heredity becomes the same as that of the heavenly Father who is holy. The Spirit of Adoption living within us has the power to transform us into mature sons as we surrender our lives to Him.

### Services of the Spirit of Adoption

As the Spirit of Adoption, the Holy Spirit calls us, fills us with Himself, brings us to maturity, and brings us to sonship with knowledge and a submission to His leadership, ownership, throneship, and authority. Also, He glorifies us. It will be sons with knowledge who will reign with Him.

### IV. THE SPIRIT OF HOLINESS

*Concerning His Son Jesus Christ our Lord, which was made of the seed of David according to the flesh; and declared to be the Son of God with power, according to the spirit of holiness, by the resurrection from the dead.* (Romans 1:3-4)

The concept of holiness may be one of the most misunderstood truths in the Bible. How we respond to the word *holy* depends much on our cultural and religious backgrounds. We may disdain the idea of holiness altogether, or we might react in fear when we think of it. Man has tried to define holiness in a religious way, by establishing laws with many requirements of do's and don'ts. Therefore, some Christians think only of certain external codes of living when anyone mentions the word *holiness*. The Pharisees are a good example of people who kept religious forms to represent holiness. But Jesus condemned them sternly for their hypocrisy. They did not understand that true holiness cannot be legislated by codes and regulations. Any attempt at such legislation results in legalism.

Holiness is a Person. The nature and character of the Godhead reveals true holiness. Christ Himself has become our righteousness (Jer. 23:5-6). We dare not teach that the mere following of external regulations has the power to make us right with God. We are not saved by works, but by grace through faith in the blood of Jesus (Eph. 2:8). Holiness is not man-made; it is God-made. When God makes us holy, we are pure, clean, and without guile. To be a person without guile means to have a heart that is free from bitterness, vindictiveness, and retaliation. Jesus said, "Blessed are the pure in heart: for they shall see God" (Mt. 5:8). Holiness is the nature of God, not our human nature, demonstrated in our lives. True holiness is manifested by

Christ-like character, not by external life styles. It is the work of God done through us, not our dead works. It is His righteousness, not our self-righteousness. The righteousness of man is as filthy rags in the eyes of God (Is. 64:6). The Holy Spirit must save us from the hypocrisy of our self-righteousness to make us truly righteous.

As the Spirit of Holiness, the Holy Spirit brings judgment, fire, and burning into our lives. He searches out and condemns sin, destroying all the impurities of the soul and spirit (Is. 10:16-18). Yet He deals with us gently, according to His nature, and gives us grace to walk in His holiness. He not only imputes righteousness to us as a declaration that we are righteous, but He also imparts His righteousness into our hearts so holiness becomes a way of life for us.

It is so important to live our lives in such a way that others will desire the Christ-like character they see in us. When people admire the sweetness and peace of God they see in a person's life, they will desire those qualities for themselves. It is not a code of behavior that establishes Christians in holiness, but the character of Christ worked into their minds and hearts. Standards of conduct will differ even between localities of Christians, according to the general guidelines taught in those places. If we are unsure whether or not we are reflecting true holiness in a situation, we can ask the following questions:

- What is the moral implication of this behavior or attitude?

- Does it tempt someone to sin?

- Does it cause me to be less like Christ?

- What does the Word of God teach about it?

Concerning dress, for example, the moral question involved is modesty. Immodest dress can tempt people to the sin of lust. If the way a lady dresses makes a man want to be a gentleman and evokes his respect, then she is dressing correctly. But if a man has to pray for grace while he is in her presence, and look the other way to avoid sinning, then she has sinned. On the other hand, a woman can wear her dresses to her ankles, her sleeves to her wrist bones, and her collars up to her chin, and still not be holy. Although she is modest, her heart may be critical, cynical, cantankerous, and judgmental. True holiness is a condition of the heart reflected in every area of our lives. Only the Holy Spirit can teach us to be truly holy as He forms the character of God in our hearts.

## Services of the Spirit of Holiness

As the Spirit of Holiness, the Holy Spirit fans, sweeps, and cleanses our temples. He washes us with the Word, blood, and Spirit. He sanctifies as well as convicts and corrects. He burns as a fire. He brings us His righteousness, and He brings us into fellowship with God.

## SUMMARY

The first four offices of the Holy Spirit reveal His power to establish the life of God in the believer. Heaven's Divine Administrator first creates God's divine life in us through the office of the Spirit of Life. Then He develops that new life in us, working as the Spirit of Truth to bring us to a more perfect revelation of God. He continues to work patiently in us as the Spirit of Adoption until we can be called sons with knowledge, having the life of Christ manifest in us. Our growing relationship with God brings us to a realization of holiness as He works in us as the Spirit of Holiness. True holiness is a result of the Holy Spirit changing our hearts until holy living becomes a way of life for us.

As we begin to grasp an understanding of this creative work of the Holy Spirit in our lives, we should see our great need to be properly related to this Third Person of the Godhead. He is faithful to bring us to an awareness of our need for relationship with Him. Then as we yield to Him, as we allow Him to govern our lives, He will work in our hearts to fulfill His predestinated purposes for us.

# Chapter 6

# *Seven Offices of the Holy Spirit*

## *Part II: Governing the Life of Believers*

Believers who choose to yield their lives to the Holy Spirit will soon discover His divine governing power in their life situations. God intends for the relationship of the Holy Spirit with believers to go beyond first creating the life of God within them and nurturing it until they become fully developed sons of God. By His divine power, the Holy Spirit desires to *govern* our lives so He can fulfill all the purposes of God in us individually and, subsequently, in the Church. As we mature in our walk with God, we recognize our increasing dependency on the Holy Spirit. Paul warned the church at Galatia that they could not perfect their lives through the efforts of the flesh or by fulfilling the code of the law (Gal. 3:3). Only faith in the work of the Holy Spirit would bring them to maturity in their walk with God. Likewise, if we are to become the people of God who fulfill God's dream for a family—sons and daughters in His image—we must learn to walk in submission to the governing power of the Holy Spirit.

## V. THE SPIRIT OF GRACE

*Of how much sorer punishment, suppose ye, shall he be thought worthy, who hath trodden under foot the Son of God, and hath counted the blood of the covenant, wherewith he was sanctified, an unholy thing, and hath done despite unto the Spirit of grace?* (Hebrews 10:29)

The Spirit of Grace governs the attitudes and actions of the believer who has learned to walk in dependence on the Holy Spirit. Scholars have accurately defined the grace of God in many different ways. Some have written entire books to discuss the comprehensive meaning of grace. Theologians tell us that grace, simply defined, is *God's unmerited favor, His undeserved kindness.* Another common phrase used to describe grace is *divine love in action.* Dr. Sam Sasser, in his course entitled "Grace, the Making of Character," beautifully defines grace as "God's ability to give us new desires and then, nurturing those desires, bring them forth in our lives until His will is accomplished."[1] Grace in the broadest sense is that quality of God's love that works in every area of our lives where we are deficient and have need. We are so inadequate in many areas of our lives that we must have God's love action to help us and rescue us. The Scriptures admonish us to "draw near with confidence to the throne of grace, that we may receive mercy and may find help in time of need" (Heb. 4:16 NAS).

For our study, we will consider the Spirit of Grace to be the One who *gives us the divine enabling to do all the Scriptures require of us, to obey God fully.* For example, we need grace to walk in the light with our brothers and sisters as God's Word commands (1 John 1:7). We need divine grace to be able to give up bad habits, to return good for evil, and to turn the other cheek. We need the Spirit of Grace to help us in the mundane things of daily life, and not just hard situations and difficult relationships.

Human nature is *not* basically good, as the humanists insist. It is basically sinful. Our natural personality is self-centered, filled with pride, laziness, dishonesty, and selfishness. The Spirit of Grace helps us in the painful process of coming to the cross to exchange our sinful nature for Christ's sinless nature. As we yield to the work of the Holy Spirit, He forms the character of

Christ in us and we begin to respond to life differently. We find ourselves doing the unselfish tasks we would not otherwise have done. Because of God's grace working in us, we can respond lovingly even in unloving circumstances. The most satisfying experience of our lives is learning to love people we could not have loved without the grace of God. We experience true freedom when the Spirit of Grace delivers us from our selfish human nature and enables us to walk in the nature of Christ.

When, on one occasion, Jesus read the Scriptures in the synagogue, the Bible says all the people wondered at the "gracious words which proceeded out of His mouth…" (Lk. 4:22). A literal Greek translation of that verse reads that "He gave the message of grace."

That message of grace was the wonderful declaration of the prophet Isaiah:

*The Spirit of the Lord is upon Me, because He hath anointed Me to preach the gospel to the poor; He hath sent Me to heal the brokenhearted, to preach deliverance to the captives, and recovering of sight to the blind, to set at liberty them that are bruised, to preach the acceptable year of the Lord.* (Luke 4:18-19)

When the Spirit of Grace operates in us, the divine love of God works in these ways to heal us and set us free. Then He works through us to share the gospel and bring that liberating message of grace to other lives.

I don't pretend to know all about grace. I just know it is the love-action of God that has been there to rescue me every time I have needed it. I have felt the grace of God sustaining me in my grief each time I walked behind 11 members of my family to the cemetery. In November of 1991, my 31-year-old grandson, David, had a freak accident that resulted in his death. A gas grill exploded in his face and severely burned his lungs. I spent four days with him after the accident and talked with him about His heavenly Father's love. He and I rejoiced that he was chosen by His Father before the foundation of the world (Eph. 1:4) and that he had chosen to be chosen; we were grateful that we knew Jesus as our Savior. As we took communion together, we both knew that he was ready to meet his God. He died a few days later.

When I stood by my grandson's casket, my natural mind wanted to scream, "What a waste!" David was a university graduate, a young entrepreneur with 65 employees under him. But instead of expressing my grief, I declared, "Satan, I have something to say to you Just in case you had anything to do with this, you didn't win! I know where my grandson is. And you don't have anything better to offer than Heaven." In that moment the Holy Spirit flooded my spirit with great grace and great peace. Three weeks later in a Sunday morning worship service, the Father witnessed to me that my grandson was worshiping with us. God gave me the understanding that David knew more about worship now than I did, though I have been teaching worship for years. The Spirit of Grace is sufficient to sustain us in the most difficult situations we will ever face in this life.

## *Services of the Spirit of Grace*

As the Spirit of Grace, the Holy Spirit lifts up a standard against the enemy, provides help in our time of trouble, and gives us liberty. He is our Advocate and our Comforter, our Paraclete who comes alongside to help. He causes us to rest, bids us (compels us), hinders us (suffers us not), helps our infirmities, drives us (as He did Jesus into the wilderness [Mk. 12:12]), and carries us out (Ezek. 37:1) as more than conquerors.

## VI. SPIRIT OF SUPPLICATION

*And I will pour upon the house of David, and upon the inhabitants of Jerusalem, the spirit of grace and of supplications....* (Zechariah 12:10)

We do not use the word *supplication* very often in our vocabulary today. Supplication is by definition "an entreaty, a humble earnest prayer in worship, a petition." In its broadest meaning, the word embraces the entire realm of prayer. As the Spirit of Supplication, the Holy Spirit executes the office of prayer, governing the communication department between our spirit and God. God is Spirit and our inner man is spirit. The Spirit of Supplication comes to establish us in a prayer relationship with God so we can commune freely with

Him. Communion with God doesn't mean just saying prayers at certain times. It involves living a life of prayer (see Chapter 9).

There are times when we pray alone, quietly waiting in the presence of God. But that is not the only time we pray. Prayer is talking to God even when we can't talk aloud. My spirit can talk to God in the middle of a store. I can pray about many things as I walk through my day without physically being in a designated place of prayer. We need to learn to cultivate a spirit of prayer as we live our lives in ordinary daily situations. Then our praying will be effective when we do get to the place of prayer. Learning to yield to the Spirit of Supplication will bring us into vital relationship with the Holy Spirit.

## The Lord's Prayer

When Jesus taught His disciples to pray what we call "The Lord's Prayer," He revealed the nature of the Spirit of Supplication. In this model prayer, He first instructs us to come reverently to our heavenly Father, hallowing His name. Then, having come to Him in a proper attitude, we are to ask for His Kingdom to be established and His will to be done in our lives and on this earth. After that, He teaches us to ask for our daily bread, and for protection from evil. He shows us that these are legitimate needs that we can expect our heavenly Father to meet.

Then, in this same prayer, He instructs us to forgive those who sin against us and to ask God to forgive us our trespasses. One of the greatest privileges on earth is to forgive another's offense against ourselves. Once a little girl was heartbroken because she felt her daddy had made a mistake. She didn't think adults made mistakes. So she asked her daddy, "Why do adults make mistakes?" Her daddy replied kindly, "I guess so children can forgive them." Her face brightened and with a smile of relief she threw her arms around her daddy and cried, "I forgive you." If no one ever offended us, we would never know the joy of forgiveness. We must extend the forgiveness we have personally received from God to those who trespass against us. For, if we do not forgive, the Scriptures teach that our heavenly Father will not forgive us (Mk. 11:26). God can give us a forgiving spirit that will not harbor resentment against another. Understanding that we are all imperfect and that we desperately need forgiveness ourselves helps us to forgive each other.

Finally, Jesus ended this model prayer by acknowledging God's eternal power and glory. As we ascribe to God the Kingdom, the power, and the glory forever, we gain the eternal perspective from which God views all of life. He is God, and we are His children who are destined to worship Him throughout eternity. These basic principles of prayer outline for us our dependence on God to meet all our needs. They also teach us our proper attitude toward God and our fellow man.

Only the Holy Spirit can help us to follow these principles, so we can learn to please God in all we do.

Even with these instructions regarding prayer, we find that there are occasions when we don't know how to pray about a particular situation or difficulty. As we learn to yield to the Holy Spirit, He prays through us in the office of supplication. When the Holy Ghost prays through us, we can be sure He is praying according to the predestined purpose of God. That is why the baptism of the Holy Spirit with its heavenly prayer language is so important for each believer. Praying in other tongues is a means of divine communication that the Holy Spirit initiates. (This topic is covered in Vol. 2.)

We cannot receive the promise that all things work together for good to those who love God, to those who are called according to His purpose (Rom. 8:28), unless we are experiencing the reality of the Holy Spirit praying His will through us. He searches our heart and makes intercession for the saints according to the will of God (Rom. 8:26-27). It was a glorious hour in my life when the Holy Spirit revealed to me through this passage of Scripture that the three members of the Godhead are in agreement in prayer when we pray in the spirit. The *Holy Spirit* is groaning, praying to the *Father* in the spirit while *Jesus*, the Word, searches our hearts and intercedes for us, the saints. We know that the purpose of God they agree upon in prayer by the Holy Spirit will work out for our good according to His loving purpose.

*Applications of Prayer*

In his practical little epistle, the apostle James lists seven *applications* of prayer in which he clarifies for us how to pray in certain situations. Careful attention to his instructions will help us gain the answers we need when we are in these situations. God's pattern always works when we walk in the understanding of His ways. James gives us some very needed understanding in this passage.

**"*Is any among you afflicted? let him pray*"** (Jas. 5:13a). This is *personal* prayer. The word *afflicted* means to leave lame tracks. In the Old Testament a man could not qualify for being a priest if he was afflicted because he would automatically leave lame tracks. In the spiritual application, a crippled person is one who does not walk with God in the way he should walk. James instructed men to pray for themselves if they were lame or afflicted. Pray for yourself if you are not keeping God's commands and settle the issues between you and God. Do not ask someone to lay hands on you to pray for your affliction or sin. God will hear your repentant prayer and answer it.

**"*Is any sick among you? let him call for the elders of the church; and let them pray over him, anointing him with oil in the name of the Lord*"** (Jas. 5:14). The *elders* are to anoint the sick with oil and expect God to heal them. Notice that the one who is sick is to call for the elders. People sometimes become offended when no one comes to pray for them when they are sick. They fail to understand that, according to this teaching of James, they have a responsibility to call for the elders to pray for them.

*"And the prayer of faith shall save the sick..."* (Jas. 5:15). Prayer must always be accompanied by *faith*, the belief that God wants to heal and that He will. As we believe and obey the command of the Word to anoint the sick with oil and pray for their healing, God will answer our prayer. Faith must energize all our praying if we want to realize the answers we seek. When the Holy Spirit prays through us, we know we are praying in faith. His prayers always get answered.

*"Confess your faults one to another, and pray one for another, that ye may be healed"* (Jas. 5:16a). We are instructed here to pray for one another and to openly *confess* our faults to one another, with the promise that in doing so we shall be healed. There is a power in confession that brings release from our faults and allows us to be healed of their bondage. John concurred with this principle when he wrote, "But if we walk in the light, as He is in the light, we have fellowship one with another, and the blood of Jesus Christ His Son cleanseth us from all sin" (1 John 1:7).

*"The effectual fervent prayer of a righteous man availeth much"* (Jas. 5:16b). God honors the *prayers of the righteous,* especially when fervency of desire accompanies it. David knew that if he regarded iniquity

in his heart, God would not hear him (Ps. 66:18). When we pray to a holy God, we must approach Him with clean hands and a pure heart (Ps. 24:3-4). We also must have an intensity of desire like the blue flame of a welding torch that will melt what it touches. Then we can expect to receive what we need from God.

*"Elias* **[Elijah]** *was a man subject to like passions as we are, and he prayed earnestly that it might not rain: and it rained not..."* (Jas. 5:17). The term *earnestly* means sincerely, without hypocrisy and from the depth of our heart, not just from our lips. Although Elijah was a prophet appointed by God, he could not simply command that it not rain. He had to pray earnestly to accomplish God's purposes. He was a righteous man, but it was not by his righteousness alone that judgment was brought upon a wicked people. It was through his earnest praying that God's will was accomplished. Knowing the will of God is not enough. After we know the will of God for a particular situation, we need to pray until we see it fulfilled.

*"And he prayed again, and the heaven gave rain..."* (Jas. 5:18). Elijah got into the position of travail and prayed earnestly for it to rain as God had promised. He sent his servant seven times to look for clouds in the sky that would suggest the coming of rain. When there was no sign of rain, he prayed *again*. Finally, the servant returned with the good news that he had seen a cloud the size of a man's hand. Elijah did

not stop praying until he had received what God had promised to do.

There is an extreme teaching regarding faith that says we must ask God only once for our petition. If we ask again, according to this teaching, we are guilty of unbelief. Those who teach that erroneous idea fail to consider God's requirement given in the Scriptures to *persevere* in prayer (Lk. 18:1). Granted, we never have to twist God's arm or beg Him to answer our cry. But there are times when we must persevere in our asking because of supernatural hindrances that delay answers to our prayers. The prophet Daniel experienced such a delay. When the angel arrived with the answer to Daniel's prayer three weeks after he had first prayed, he explained to Daniel that the delay was caused by supernatural resistance he encountered in the heavens when on his way to bring the answer. God requires us to pray until we receive the answer He has promised to give us. How many answers have we forfeited because we did not persevere in the place of prayer?

Although James' comprehensive teaching on prayer covers only a few short verses, we will profit much by applying these simple principles to our prayer lives. God's order must be followed if we expect to see answers to prayer. His desire is to hear and answer our prayers, and His instructions are clear. Even the disciples asked Jesus to teach them how to pray. We can do the same. By reading the Word and expecting to receive help from the Holy Spirit, our prayer lives can be so transformed that we walk with Him in an effective relationship of prayer.

## Services of the Spirit of Supplication

As the Holy Spirit establishes in us His office of supplication, He prays "His prayers"; intercedes; groans under the weight of "His glory"; and petitions. He also praises; worships; produces thanksgiving; makes God's house a house of purity, power, and prayer; and establishes heart communion between man and God.

## VII. THE SPIRIT OF GLORY

*If ye be reproached for the name of Christ, happy are ye; for the spirit of glory and of God resteth upon you: on their part He is evil spoken of, but on your part He is glorified.* (1 Peter 4:14)

We do not often hear the word *glory* in conversation. Yet in the Bible it is a vital and rich term that provides perspective for our values and calls us to deepening worship of our God. In the Old Testament, the glory of human achievement is an ascribed glory. It exists in the eye of the beholder. But the glory of God is objective. It is rooted in His very nature, not in the evaluation of others. When God's glory is unveiled and recognized, all those things in which human beings take pride fade to nothingness.[2]

When Moses begged God to show him His glory, the Bible reports, "And He said, 'I will make all My goodness pass before thee, and I will proclaim the name of the Lord before thee; and will be gracious to whom I will be gracious, and will shew mercy on whom I will shew mercy' " (Ex. 33:19). This passage links the glory of God with His loving character. God displayed His great redemptive power in the exodus (Num. 14:22), even as He displays His creative power when "the heavens declare the glory of God" (Ps. 19:1). But *glory* implies more than God's disclosure of who He is. It implies an invasion of the material universe, and expression of God's active presence among His people. God's objective glory is revealed by His coming to be present with us, His people, and to show us Himself by His actions in our world.[3]

The New Testament Greek word for glory is *doxa*. It has at least five different meanings. Each aspect of the word expands our understanding of the glory of God as more than a cloud or something so mystical we cannot relate to it. First of all, *doxa* expresses the majesty and splendor of God. It also means to ascribe to Him the honor and credit for His operation through us. The "glory of God" carries the idea of the reputation of God as well. As believers who desire to live for the glory of God, we have been given charge of His reputation. Still another aspect of the word *glory* involves the Spirit of Glory resting upon us in our trials and testings, changing our character into the character of Christ. Finally, the meaning of glory which we perhaps love the most, refers to the "manifest presence of God." That manifest presence is different from His omnipresence or even His abiding Presence, as we shall learn in our study. At times, because of our limited understanding, we have made the glory of God into something mystical. We have referred to it as the "cloud," for example, that led the children of Israel. But the glory of God as we have just described it is much more than a cloud; it is the awesome majesty of the presence of God.

What, then, is our response to the glory of God? We are to ascribe to the Lord glory (1 Chron. 16:28) and to glory in His holy name (1 Chron. 16:10). We are to worship Him by recognizing His presence and praising Him for those qualities that His actions on our behalf unveil. We say with the psalmist David, "But You are a shield around me, O Lord; You bestow glory on me and lift up my head" (Ps. 3:3 NIV). We glorify God by offering Him our praise and by being channels through which the Holy Spirit, who lives within us, can communicate God to those around us.[4]

### God's Glory Revealed in Suffering

The glory of God will be revealed in us as we are victorious in the trials we must endure. Paul understood this when he wrote, "For I reckon that the sufferings of this present time are not worthy to be compared with the glory which shall be revealed in us" (Rom. 8:18). He explained to the Corinthians that believers are changed from glory to glory by the Spirit of the Lord (2 Cor. 3:18). Then he described many difficult trials he was experiencing, and declared: "For momentary, light affliction is producing for us an eternal weight of glory far beyond all comparison" (2 Cor. 4:17 NAS). It is God's desire that His glory be revealed in us through our trials. God permits trials to come into our lives to test us. God's kind intent is for these trials to change us into the image of Christ. When Peter wrote to Christians concerning the "fiery trial which is to try you" (1 Pet. 4:12), he urged them not to think it strange that they should have to suffer in that way. He exhorted them to rejoice as partakers of Christ's sufferings so "that when His glory shall be revealed, ye may be glad also with exceeding joy" (1 Pet. 4:13b). Peter considered the glory of God to be far more worthy of consideration than the sufferings of this life that test us. We will respond lovingly, as Christ did, in painful situations as we become more like Him. The Spirit of Glory enables us to be victorious in the suffering we must endure.

God allowed Job to experience severe trials in his life. Through Job's right responses to these painful experiences, he came into a deeper relationship with God. He acknowledged that fact when he cried, "I have heard of Thee by the hearing of the ear: but now mine eye seeth Thee" (Job 42:5). From trial to trial, from victory to victory, the Spirit of Glory is changing us. Fiery trials come to test our patience and to form godly character in us. These trials make us dependent on the Holy Spirit to help us respond in a godly way in them. The Spirit of Glory rests on us in our suffering if we yield to Him without rebelling against the trial.

I knew a young married couple who attended Asbury College. He was a beautiful preacher and she was a wonderful singer and organist in a Methodist church in Charlotte, North Carolina. They had been married about four years when she gave birth to their little daughter. This baby was the answer to their earnest prayers for a child and she quickly became the darling of their hearts, filling their home with love and joy. When she was about two years old, a beautiful little girl so loved by everyone, tragedy struck. One afternoon as her mother was ironing, this little child fell to the floor and silently lay there. Alarmed, her mother ran and picked her up and took her immediately to the hospital. Their precious daughter was diagnosed as having spinal meningitis. She died that night about midnight.

Everyone in the church there predicted that the bereaved young mother would be devastated. They feared that she would not make it, for her life had seemingly been wrapped up in that baby they had wanted so badly. As the sun was lowering on the cemetery in Charlotte two days later, they laid that little body to rest. In that moment friends heard a voice softly singing, "What a friend we have in Jesus, all our sins and griefs to bear…"[5] It was the voice of the little girl's mother. She didn't collapse in her hour of deepest grief. The Spirit of Glory rested on her, strengthening her in her great loss.

God used the personal triumph of that couple to bring revival to their church. They had studied at Asbury College and knew what an old-fashioned revival was. They had been praying for God to revive their church. Now, God didn't take that baby's life to bring revival; He is not unkind. But as a result of that tragedy, the church began to call upon God and He came to them with His Presence. As this couple gave testimony to the sufficiency of the grace of God, the glory of God shined through them in their deep suffering.

## Martyr's Grace

When angry men were stoning Stephen to death, "...he, being full of the Holy Ghost, looked up steadfastly into heaven, and saw the glory of God, and Jesus standing on the right hand of God" (Acts 7:55). The Spirit of Glory gives us the power to die a martyr's death. Many people from throughout the ages will one day wear a martyr's crown, having experienced that strong love for God that chooses to die for truth rather than recant. As we yield to the Holy Spirit, the Spirit of Glory will govern our lives in the most difficult circumstances, and bring us into a cherished relationship with God.

## The Presence of God

It is worth whatever suffering we must endure to have the manifest presence of God. As we have mentioned, the Bible teaches three different aspects of the presence of God. First, it teaches *omnipresence,* which means God is present everywhere. God asked the prophet Jeremiah, "Can any hide himself in secret places that I shall not see him?...Do not I fill heaven and earth?..." (Jer. 23:24). And the psalmist David asked God the question, "Whither shall I go from Thy spirit? or whither shall I flee from Thy presence?" (Ps. 139:7) These Scriptures, along with many others, testify to the omnipresence of God.

Secondly, the Bible teaches God's *abiding presence.* Jesus taught, "Abide in Me, and I in you. As the branch cannot bear fruit of itself, except it abide in the vine; no more can ye, except ye abide in Me" (Jn. 15:4). As believers we must learn to cultivate that abiding relationship with God. Out of that relationship will come fruitfulness from our lives. We learn to abide in Him through reading His Word and praying, through both private and corporate praise and worship, and through obedience to His commands.

Thirdly, the Scriptures teach God's *manifest presence*; that is, the presence of God in a certain place at a given moment in time manifesting Himself to His people. When Jacob was fleeing from his brother Esau, he experienced the manifest presence of God in a dream. When he awoke, he was afraid because of the awesome presence of God. He declared, "Surely the Lord is in this place; and I knew it not" (Gen. 28:16). Abraham also experienced the manifest presence of God one day as he sat in his tent door in the heat of the day. The Bible says, "And the Lord appeared unto him in the plains of Mamre" (Gen. 18:1a). Abraham spoke with Him and served Him a meal, begging Him to stay a little longer. Then God reconfirmed to him the promise of a son and revealed His purposes regarding Sodom to His friend, Abraham.

A New Testament example of the manifest presence of God occurred when the disciples prayed during a time of persecution. They cried out, "And now, Lord, behold their threatenings: and grant unto Thy servants, that with all boldness they may speak Thy word, by stretching forth Thine hand to heal; and that signs and wonders may be done by the name of Thy holy child Jesus" (Acts 4:29-30). God manifested His presence in a mighty way in answer to their cry. "And when they had prayed, the place was shaken where they were assembled together; and they were all filled with the Holy Ghost, and they spake the word of God with boldness" (Acts 4:31).

God manifests His presence through His people, whom the Bible calls "earthen vessels" (2 Cor. 4:7), by the anointing of the Holy Spirit through supernatural gifts. A prophetic anointing on the preached Word, for example, makes us conscious, with our natural senses, that He is there. He also manifests His presence in our praises to Him, in healing power and in many other ways. God will fill the Church with the glory of His manifest presence. Then the pain of our trials will be eclipsed by the wonderful presence of God in His manifest glory.

## Services of the Spirit of Glory

As the Spirit of Glory, the Holy Spirit forms the goodness of God in us: His honor, His reputation, His transfiguration, and His manifest presence. He changes us from glory to glory; He fulfills the Father's purpose in us (Rom. 8:26-29). He forms in us the exchanged life (Christ's life for the self-life). He wars with the flesh, lusts against it, and crucifies it. He makes us partakers of His glory; He baptizes us into the "baptism of suffering"; and He provides glory for suffering.

### SUMMARY

In summarizing the seven offices of the Holy Spirit, we may conclude the following: The Holy Spirit, as He appropriates the life of Christ our Lord for, to, in, and through us, is the One who is all-sufficient in strength; the One who lifes us in God and brings us into worship. He reveals truth to us and He adopts us into the family of God, bringing us to mature sonship prepared for rulership, throneship, and joint heirship. He enables us to exchange our sinful nature for the holiness of God through His provision of grace, more grace, much grace, and abundant grace. He makes our supplications effectual. He also causes us to be victorious in suffering, changing us and fitting us into God's eternal plan. The power of the Holy Spirit moves through these seven offices, administrating each as it is needed, to redeem a people to be a Bride for the Son. Only as each of us becomes personally acquainted with the Holy Spirit do we become a part of the fulfillment of God's will. We must yield our lives to this Third Person of the Godhead and learn to walk with Him in order for Him to change us into the image of Christ.

## *Notes*

1. Sam Sasser, *Grace: The Making of Character*, Fountain Gate Publishing, (Plano, Texas: 1991) p. 33.

2. *Vine's Expository Dictionary of Old and New Testament Words*, (Old Tappan, New Jersey: Fleming H. Revell, 1981) pp. 310-312.

3. Ibid.

4. Ibid.

5. "What a Friend We Have in Jesus," Joseph Scriven and Charles Converse.

# Chapter 7

# *Sevenfold Power of the Holy Spirit*

## *The Omnipotence of God Revealed*

In order to speak comprehensively of the power of the Holy Spirit, we need to define divine omnipotence in human terms, which is no small task. There are seven Greek words used throughout the New Testament that describe different aspects or manifestations of the omnipotent power of God. An understanding of these terms will help us to comprehend the transcending power and ability of the Holy Spirit to transform every life and situation that He touches, and to fulfill the highest purposes of God in the earth. Studying the power of God should inspire wonder and awe in our hearts and cause us to bow in worship before Him. How can we comprehend the greatness of the God who desires fellowship with man so earnestly that He uses all His divine power to redeem us and bring us into relationship with Himself? Such divine love is what the Holy Spirit came to reveal to us as He works to transform us into the image of Christ.

The Scriptures reveal many acts of the awesome power of God. We first glimpse His omnipotent power in the creation of the universe. The power of the Holy Spirit in creation brought forth something out of nothing through the Word of God. The Scriptures teach us that mankind can recognize God simply by beholding the awesome wonders of His creation (Rom. 1:19-20). Another manifestation of the power of the Holy Spirit is in His military strength and might, the kind we would expect to see in an army. The hosts of Heaven are endued with this kind of power. When Joshua was preparing to take the children of Israel into the Promised Land, God appeared to him as a mighty warrior. Joshua did not recognize Him at first and he asked, "Art thou for us, or for our adversaries?" (Josh. 5:13c) The reply came, "Nay; but as captain of the host of the Lord am I now come. And Joshua fell on his face to the earth, and did worship..." (Josh. 5:14). This divine military power gave the Israelites victory over the giants of the land.

The resurrection power of the Holy Spirit is that power that raised Christ from the dead. Resurrection power is greater than the power of death. Christ conquered death, hell, and the grave through the resurrection power of the Holy Spirit. Paul wrote of this power, "But if the Spirit of Him that raised up Jesus from the dead dwell in you, He that raised up Christ from the dead shall quicken your mortal bodies by His Spirit that dwelleth in you" (Rom. 8:11). It is that resurrection power that gives us ultimate victory over death.

The Holy Spirit also is that dynamic force that equips a person for service. The Spirit makes a believer effective in destroying supernatural forces of darkness through miraculous and wonderful works. It is also the power of the Holy Spirit that brings a moral strength to man that can elevate as well as calm an individual soul or a society that follows after godliness. The Holy Spirit is the power of Christ visibly operative in an assembled church that has Christ as its Head. This kingly power of God is discerning; it acts in divine knowledge upon the minds of men in manifold wisdom, revealing Jesus to those who believe. The power of the Holy Spirit moves in healing for the sick and in working of miracles. He is the divine Power of God who is able "to do exceeding abundantly above all that we ask or think, according to the power that worketh in us" (Eph. 3:20).

Having declared all that, we must still acknowledge our finite limitation in describing the omnipotent power of the living God. Do we really know Him? There are those who have attributed only one or two of these aspects of power to the Holy Spirit. Perhaps they think He came to give them the gift of tongues, or to bring deliverance from demonic oppression. Though these are aspects of His power, they do not comprehensively represent His Person. We dare not limit our understanding of His work to one or two manifestations of His power. If we do, what will happen when we discover we need Someone to exchange our sinful Adamic nature for a Christ-like nature? Who will deliver us from anger, malice, and jealousy? Who will transform our minds to give us the mind of Christ? Who will take our moral weakness and give us strength to love God and serve Him? We need to know the Holy Spirit in all the omnipotent power of His Person. Then we must allow His divine power to work in and through us so His complete will and purpose can be accomplished.

## I. ARCHĒ

The Greek word *archē* describes the divine power that can create something out of nothing. It is that power that brings forth something from itself as the source or beginning. We recognize in the root form of the word *archē* the English electrical term *arc* that defines a natural power source. That electrical arc that is the point of ignition for man's machinery gives us an accurate picture of this divine creative power of the Holy Spirit.

## In Creation

God's creative power set the universe in motion with His Word. "In the beginning was the Word, and the Word was with God, and the Word was God...All things were made by Him; and without Him was not any thing made that was made" (Jn. 1:1,3). When God created the world, He simply spoke it into existence through His divine power. "And the Spirit of God moved upon the face of the waters. And God said, Let there be light: and there was light" (Gen. 1:2b-3). It is this omnipotent power of creating a "beginning" that man's mind cannot comprehend, for we are incapable of creating in that sense.

The Scriptures teach us that "through faith we understand that the worlds were framed by the word of God, so that things which are seen were not made of things which do appear" (Heb. 11:3). Only by believing can we grasp the greatness of God's creative power. Again, concerning the beginning of creation, we read, "And, Thou, Lord, in the beginning [*archē* ] hast laid the foundation of the earth; and the heavens are the works of Thine hands" (Heb. 1:10). As created beings, we are a result of this *archē* power of God that initiated life as we know it.

## The Incarnation

The Incarnation of the Son of God is also an example of this creative power resident in the Holy Spirit. In the Scriptures the angel told Mary that "the power of the Highest shall overshadow thee" and "the Holy Ghost shall come upon thee" (Lk. 1:35). Both statements are synonymous expressions (Mt. 1:18-20; Is. 7:14; Lk. 1:35). One depicts the Divine source and the other, His holiness. The sinlessness of Jesus was not due to the sinlessness of His mother, but to the divine origin of His human nature, the Spirit of God (Heb. 10:5).[1] And "the Word became flesh, and dwelt among us..." (Jn. 1:14 NAS). The *archē* power of the Holy Spirit made possible the Incarnation of Christ—God becoming man.

## New Creation

Concerning the beginning of our Christian lives, John declares, "If that which ye have heard from the beginning [*archē*] shall remain in you, ye also shall continue in the Son, and in the Father" (1 John 2:24b). The *archē* power of the Holy Spirit is like the switch that starts the ignition; it brings man into contact with God. The Spirit initiates a good work in us by His divine power, and then continues to perfect that work in our lives. Peter declared that we are born again "not of corruptible seed, but of incorruptible, by the word of God, which liveth and abideth for ever" (1 Pet. 1:23). Christ literally comes to live within us, through His incorruptible life, when we are born again. Paul the apostle taught, "Therefore if any man be in Christ, he is a new creature: old things are passed away; behold, all things are become new" (2 Cor. 5:17). Accepting

Jesus as our Savior ignites the *archē* power of God in our spirits, which creates eternal life. Because the creative power of God has come into the life of a believer, "Christ in you, the hope of glory" (Col. 1:27) becomes a living reality.

### In Prayer

I believe the Holy Ghost wants us to live so we can touch the presence of God at all times. As we come to the place of prayer, we need this *archē* power to ignite faith in our hearts and bring our thoughts and desires into the presence of God. Every effective prayer has the divine power of God as its source. As we learn to yield to the Holy Spirit's power to inspire our prayer lives, we will know much more effectiveness in receiving answers to our prayers. The creative power of the spoken word on our lips, when energized by the power of the Holy Spirit, will bring supernatural results. It is through this kind of prayer that God accomplishes His will.

### II. EXOUSIA

*Exousia*, another Greek word translated into English as *power*, particularly denotes *the ability to decide and perform an action without hindrance. Exousia* is the decisive authority of God. This word is usually used with *archē*, the power that sparks *exousia*. By connotation *exousia* reflects the power and the right to influence and enforce, the kind of right that government officials exercise. It depicts authority as well as divine ability to perform a task. Nothing happens even in this fallen world without the operation of *exousia*, the divine authority of God.

When the scribe asked Jesus what right He had to forgive sins, Jesus replied, "Whether is it easier to say to the sick of the palsy, Thy sins be forgiven thee; or to say, Arise, take up thy bed, and walk? But that ye may know that the Son of man hath power [*exousia*] on earth to forgive sins..." (Mk. 2:9-10). The authority and jurisdiction to forgive was part of the power of God manifested in Jesus on earth. The scribes knew that God had the power to forgive sins. But, instead of concluding that Jesus was the Son of God because He demonstrated the power to forgive sins, they called Him a blasphemer. By denying the *exousia* power of God, they revealed a wicked heart of unbelief that could not enter the Kingdom of God.

It is this decisive aspect of *exousia* power that enables us to enter the Kingdom of God. "But as many as received Him, to them gave He power to become the sons of God, even to them that believe on His name" (Jn. 1:12). We cannot become sons of God without first receiving the power to do so. It is the power of the Holy Spirit that convicts men of sin (Jn. 16:8) and causes them to confess Jesus as Lord (1 Cor. 12:3). The word *convict* means cognitive process, for example to reprove, refute, or convince. It also signifies a moral process beyond the mental activity, a moral conquest of our mind and our actions. The Holy Spirit endows the Christian life from beginning to end with moral character. We live the life exemplified by Christ through the empowering of the Spirit. Thus the Christian life is inherently and essentially supernatural.[2] We are free to reject or accept this supernatural *exousia* power for our lives. If we reject it, then we cannot know God, for it is this power of His that gives us the ability to know Him. Everything we have we receive from God, who offers us His *exousia* so we may become His children.

After becoming children of God, we begin to realize our need for fellowship with other Christians. God ordained the existence of a body of believers known as the Church to reflect the life of Christ in the earth. "And He gave some, apostles; and some, prophets; and some, evangelists; and some, pastors and teachers; for the perfecting of the saints, for the work of the ministry, for the edifying of the body of Christ" (Eph. 4:11-12). As the Holy Spirit gives these ministries, He enables these people through divine *exousia* to lead others to grow in God. Paul declared to the Corinthians, "For though I should boast somewhat more of our authority [*exousia*], which the Lord hath given us for edification, and not for your destruction, I should not be ashamed" (2 Cor. 10:8). God gave Paul his authority and ability to edify the Church. Thank God for His divine enabling that He gives to us to become a glorious Church, transformed into the image of His Son.

## III. ISCHUS

*Ischus* expresses the boisterous, valiant, almighty force of divine power *with its ability to penetrate opposition.* Military force demonstrates this kind of power. We could call this the "bulldozer breath." The Book of Acts refers to the force of the preached Word of God as *ischus* power: "So mightily grew the word of God and prevailed" (Acts 19:20). It was this supernatural power of the preached Word that convinced thousands of people to turn to Christ for forgiveness of their sins. Later the apostle John declared, "I have written unto you, young men, because ye are strong [*ischus*], and the word of God abideth in you, and ye have overcome the wicked one" (1 John 2:14b). The meaning of power in this text is divine strength to conquer supernatural foes. Jesus admonished the disciples to ask for this mighty strength that they not be overthrown in the approaching disasters of the last time and that they be able to stand before the Son of Man (Lk. 21:36). God's *ischus* power would deliver them and bring them to their goal.

## IV. DIDŌMI

The root meaning of the Greed word *didōmi* translates as *"the power to give."* Concerning God giving

Jesus to the world, this *didōmi* power reveals the realistic character of love as a gift, not just as a disposition. There is the power of *action*, not just of feeling, in love. God's love gave Jesus specific works to accomplish while on earth. It was the love of God reaching out to man that healed the sick, fed the hungry, and raised the dead. His love compelled Him to give life to those who asked for it, and ultimately to lay down His own life so He might have many brethren.

Jesus declared, "All that the Father gives Me shall come to Me, and the one who comes to Me I will certainly not cast out" (Jn. 6:37 NAS). It was neither Jesus' strength of personality nor monetary benefits that drew His disciples to Him. It was the supernatural power of God that *gave* men as disciples to Jesus. Even though many turned away when Jesus declared Himself to be the bread of life, there were still those who received the power of God to choose to follow Him. When Jesus asked His disciples if they would turn away also, Peter declared, "Lord, to whom shall we go? You have words of eternal life" (Jn. 6:68 NAS). They received the *didōmi* power of God that caused them to give their lives to following Jesus. Jesus prayed, "I manifested Thy name to men whom Thou gavest Me out of the world; Thine they were, and Thou gavest them to Me, and they have kept Thy word" (Jn. 17:7 NAS). Jesus, clearly acknowledged here that it was the love of God that gave men the power to become disciples of Christ.

Jesus' death reveals the ultimate power of that "giving" love, that was willing and able to suffer the supreme sacrifice for the salvation of mankind. Jesus' death proves the boldness of conviction and courage, the determined power to win and to conquer that is inherent in godly love. Some have spoken of the love of God as "tough love," describing the fiber of determination and longing that characterizes His love. He will not be denied the object of His affections, despite those who deny Him. Still, His great love is pursuing man as the "Sheriff of the skies," desiring to arrest man's attention from his destructive course of sin, and turn his feet toward everlasting life.

Among the Jews, *didōmi* power was the word often used to refer to the death of martyrs. Martyrs were those people who were forced to die a torturous death if they did not recant their faith in Christ. They possessed a supernatural power to lay down their lives for what they believed. It is this *didōmi* power of God that helps us to overcome our timidity and fears in the face of men and devils, and to share boldly and courageously with others the life He has given us. Through the power of the Holy Spirit we will be compelled to give to others the life we have received from God.

## V. MEGALEIOTĒS

*Megaleiotēs* is the Greek word for power that refers to the *magnificence* and *majesty* of God as seen in the transfiguration of Christ. Peter recorded for us the majesty of that event:

> *For we did not follow cleverly devised tales when we made known to you the power and coming of our Lord Jesus Christ, but we were eyewitnesses of His majesty. For when He received honor and glory from God the Father, such an utterance as this was made to Him by the Majestic Glory, "This is My beloved Son with whom I am well-pleased"— and we ourselves heard this utterance made from heaven when we were with Him on the holy mountain.* (2 Peter 1:16-18 NAS)

The majestic power of Christ cannot be fully comprehended by finite human minds. Peter said they were witnesses of His majesty and described that experience to convince those believers of the reality of the Christ's majestic power. In another instance of *megaleiotēs* power, Jesus cast out the devil that the disciples were unable to cast out. The Scriptures describe the reaction of the crowd: "And they were all amazed at the greatness [*Megaleiotēs*] of God" (Lk. 9:43a NAS). *Megaleiotēs* power is that transcending power of God that lifts humanity out of its impossible plight and transforms impossible situations. It is a beautiful word picture that describes the kind of power used to energize a freight elevator of a large industry. The freight elevator is built to hold much more weight than elevators used for transporting only people. Its cargo is too heavy for the guest elevators. Also, it is usually hidden from the eyes of the public. It is this "pulley power" of the Holy Spirit that can lift a burden that would otherwise be impossible to carry. The Holy Spirit Himself becomes our "Burden Bearer." He pulls us out of sin, out of self, out of our negative circumstances and grief, and seats us in heavenly places with Christ Jesus (Eph. 2:6).

Have you ever watched people go through severe trials with peace and near serenity? They can have peace because they have learned to know this transcending power of the Holy Spirit, the power that lifts them above their circumstances. They have learned to let Him carry the load too heavy for the human psyche. They find themselves seated in heavenly places in Christ Jesus, carried there by the power of the Holy Spirit. His power can transcend all human tragedy and lift us to a place of victorious living.

## VI. ENERGIA

*Energia* is the important Greek word for power that means a *divine energizing force that works effectually and powerfully.* The Scriptures themselves possess this kind of divine power to save our souls. James taught us to "receive with meekness the engrafted word, which is able to save your souls" (Jas. 1:21b). Paul also wrote concerning the Scriptures, "For the word of God is quick, and powerful, and sharper than any two-edged sword, piercing even to the dividing asunder of soul and spirit, and of the joints and marrow and is a discerner of the thoughts and intents of the heart" (Heb. 4:12). This verse describes the divine *energia* that cuts through the darkness of our souls as a laser beam of light cuts through flesh. The Word of God pierces our minds and emotions, revealing to us the deceptions and impure motives of our heart. Without the energizing power of the Holy Spirit coming in conviction to make the Word alive to our hearts, we could never be free from bondage to sin.

The Holy Spirit not only energizes our repentance, He also gives us divine strength to share our faith with others. Paul prayed for Philemon and his friends that they would know this power of the Holy Spirit. He prayed for them, "that the communication of thy faith may become effectual by the acknowledging of every good thing which is in you in Christ Jesus" (Philem. 6). It is this energizing power of God "which worketh in you both to will and to do of His good pleasure" (Phil. 2:13).

This *energia* power is what I felt when God so gloriously healed me, and granted me many more years to preach the Word of God. It is an exhilarating, invigorating, zealous power that rejoices in the conquering mood of the Holy Spirit as He quickens us and makes us alive to God. This divine energy causes us to live as effective lights in the darkness of this corrupt generation (Acts 2:40).

## VII. KRATOS

Our final word, *kratos*, denotes *the superior power of God, to which the final victory belongs.* In Peter's doxology, he writes, "To Him be glory and dominion for ever and ever. Amen" (1 Pet. 5:11). This dominion is the ultimate triumph that belongs only to God. Paul prayed that the Church might be "strengthened with all might, according to His glorious power, unto all patience and longsuffering with joyfulness" (Col. 1:11). Only as this divine *kratos* power of the Holy Spirit strengthens us supernaturally can we triumph ultimately over evil.

Jude declares, "To the only wise God our Saviour, be glory and majesty, dominion and power, both now and ever. Amen" (Jude 25). He acknowledges God as the eternal Victor over all the power of evil. John, the Revelator, sums up the eternal significance of this power in the sacrifice of Christ. He wrote:

*And every creature which is in heaven, and on the earth, and under the earth, and such as are in the sea, and all that are in them, heard I saying, Blessing, and honour, and glory, and power, be unto Him that sitteth upon the throne, and unto the Lamb for ever and ever.* (Revelation 5:13)

Eternal dominion belongs to God alone, who has triumphed by His great power. Our appropriation of this power ensures our ultimate victory in our individual lives and in the Church corporately.

## SUMMARY

This brief consideration of the sevenfold power of the Holy Spirit reveals an infinite, all-encompassing, eternal power that is competent to meet every conceivable need of mankind. The Holy Spirit fulfills God's purpose to redeem mankind from sin. However, eternal purpose is not just to take us to Heaven, but to make it possible for us to live victoriously here on earth. God's ultimate goal will be realized in a glorious Church without spot or wrinkle. As believers who learn to yield to the Holy Spirit and who come into right relationship with Him, we discover the omnipotent power that He offers. He changes us from the image of the fallen Adam into that of the Last Adam, Jesus Christ. He forms in us the character of God—God's own nature—as we continue to exercise our free volition and choose His life.

Why do we not see His power displayed in a greater way in the Church? I believe the answer to that inditing question is we have not made ourselves available to Him. We have not yielded completely to Him, to where His life-giving power can flow through us to meet our personal needs as well as the needs of others. Through His great power He is able, but we don't make ourselves available to Him. We depend on our own ability to face our life circumstances instead of cultivating a dependence on the power of the Holy Spirit.

God demonstrated His power when He took 12 men, filled them with the Holy Ghost, and used them to turn the world upside down—without the help of the media or any modern evangelistic method. The power of the Holy Spirit consumed these men and filled them with His purpose to win the world for Christ. They yielded to the supernatural power of the Holy Spirit as a prerequisite for living a supernatural life in Christ. So as we come into right relationship with the Holy Spirit, the same zeal that motivated those first apostles will consume us as well. Then we can truly experience the love of the God whose great desire to save mankind caused Him to give His life for them. Signs and wonders will again follow those who believe, as we expect to receive the supernatural power of the Holy Spirit for all of life's situations. Then we will also turn our world upside down to the glory of Christ and the building of His Kingdom.

### Notes

1. *International Standard Bible Encyclopedia*, pp. 1406-1417. James Orr, Ed., (Grand Rapids, Michigan: Wm. B. Eerdman's, 1976) Vol. 3, E.Y. Mullins, Author.

2. Ibid.

# Chapter 8

# *Seven Moods of the Holy Spirit*

## *Part I: Divine Purposes Expressed*

If we think of the term *mood* in a common human sense, we may misunderstand the entire concept of the moods of the Holy Spirit. We speak of people having good moods and bad moods. We often characterize people's behavior by saying they are moody. That is not a very positive way to describe people. It usually means they are immature and temperamental, given to depression. However, this negative connotation of moodiness is not inherent to the word's definition. A mood can be defined simply as *a conscious state of mind* or *predominant emotion*. We can expect the Holy

Spirit, as a divine Person, to function in a conscious state of mind and to express emotion in righteousness. It is only our unredeemed human psyches that create "bad" moods that are sinful.

When we discuss the *moods* of the Holy Spirit, we are describing a frame of mind He uses to express Himself to reveal His divine purpose for a particular situation. The Holy Spirit responds differently to different kinds of situations, though in each situation His ultimate purpose is to reveal Jesus and to fulfill the Father's eternal plan for mankind. For example, at times He will come in a convicting mood to convince men of sin. He expresses a compassionate mood when He comes as the Comforter to someone who is suffering grief.

As we describe the work of the Holy Spirit, we want to keep in mind that His moods often are expressed through human vessels. We are temples of the Holy Spirit (2 Cor. 3:16), forming the Body of Christ in the earth. The Holy Spirit does much of His work through us. So it is important for us to recognize the different moods of the Holy Spirit. Only then can we understand what He is doing and why He is expressing Himself through us in those ways. Only then can we cooperate with Him in fulfilling His purposes for His Church. Yet no matter what mood He is revealing through a human vessel at a given time, His purpose never is to exalt or call attention to that person. Exalting our fleshly nature does not promote His ultimate goal of revealing Jesus.

Unfortunately, many things that have been done in the name of the Holy Spirit have resulted in exalting a personality. The Holy Spirit's work is to exalt Jesus, not people. When human personality prevails in a situation above the exaltation of Jesus, it is out of order.

The Scriptures teach that Jesus made Himself of no reputation (Phil. 2:7). The Holy Spirit also reflects this same self-effacing spirit of humility that reveals His beautiful consecration and love for the Father. He humbled Himself in Jesus so the Father might be glorified. The Holy Spirit does not make a reputation for Himself or for our flesh. Everything we receive from the Holy Spirit should result in others seeing Jesus in us. If we receive healing for our bodies or revelation from the Word, we should not allow ourselves to rejoice as much in those gifts as we do in the Giver of those gifts. As humility characterizes the Godhead, so every mood of the Holy Spirit expresses that humility, even through human vessels. As we walk with the Holy Spirit as a Person, we will become sensitive to His moods as He expresses the humility of Christ in our lives.

## CONVICTING MOOD

*Conviction* may be defined as *an act of pleading, beseeching, or reproving.* The Holy Spirit comes to us in this frame of mind to make us God-conscious and aware of our sinful nature and sinful acts. Jesus told His disciples that He would send the Counselor to them. He said, "When He comes, He will convict the world of guilt in regard to sin and righteousness and judgment" (Jn. 16:8 NIV). Jesus was describing the convicting mood of the Holy Spirit.

Billy Graham has stated that one key to his ministry is the careful attention he gives to the altar calls. The ministry team allows no moving or leaving during that time, for that is the time the Holy Spirit comes in conviction to hearts that have heard the preached Word of God. In those moments, if people respond to the pleading of the Holy Spirit, they can come to true salvation of their souls and be born again to an eternal relationship with God. The Holy Spirit comes gently but irresistibly in His love, to show people their guilt before a holy God, and to point them to the Savior who can deliver them from their sin.

## *Conviction or Condemnation?*

Conviction from the Holy Spirit must not be confused with thoughts and feelings of condemnation. Conviction is constructive and full of hope. The Holy Spirit comes in convicting power to make us sorry for our sin and to bring us to repentance. When the Holy Spirit convicts us, He shows us exactly what sin we need to repent of. When we acknowledge our sin, we find relief in repenting of it and experience joy in accepting forgiveness. The voice of condemnation, on the contrary, is an accusing voice that speaks of failure and defeat. If we receive a mental suggestion of vague accusation that takes us into depression and despair, we have listened to the condemning voice of the enemy. These tormenting thoughts tell us such things as "You are no good and you will never be any different. You're so bad God is mad at you. He cannot or will not forgive you." Those accusations are the enemy's work of condemnation.

God never intended for us to feel condemnation. Jesus declared, "For God sent not His son into the world to condemn the world; but that the world through Him might be saved" (Jn. 3:17). The Holy Spirit came as a Helper, a Paraclete, a Counselor, and a Teacher. His convicting work will result in our coming closer to Christ, not in our wallowing in despair. Without the convicting power of the Holy Spirit we would be helplessly lost in our sin. He is faithful to shine His light on areas of darkness in our lives so we can be cleansed from all unrighteousness.

Our correct response to conviction will produce true repentance in our lives. True repentance is not just an expression of sorrow for what we have done; it is a complete turning away from the revealed sin. Repentance should become a way of life for us, not a one-time expression of confessed guilt before receiving salvation. As we behold the holiness of God and see ourselves as God sees us, each new revelation brings fresh conviction that produces repentance. Our joy becomes more full each time we are set free from an area of bondage to sin. Although the revelation of our sin may bring pain, the deliverance from its power results in the Kingdom of God coming to us in righteousness, peace, and joy in the Holy Ghost (Rom. 14:17). We are made whole as we learn to yield to the convicting mood of the Holy Spirit.

## COUNSELING MOOD

The counseling mood of the Holy Spirit reveals the *divine Teacher*. I believe that the greatest work of the Holy Spirit is teaching, for without the teaching mood He could not do any of His other work. Every new revelation and realm of light we discover in God results from the work of the Holy Spirit, who came to teach us and guide us into all truth (Jn. 14:26; 16:13). Whatever mood the Holy Spirit is manifesting, His objective is to teach us the will of God. He teaches about sin and convicts us. He teaches us how to pray. He teaches us about eternity. He comes to reveal Jesus to us. He opens dimensions of life to us so we can see who we are in the sight of God, what we need at the moment, and where we are going in the future.

The best teacher is the one who gets involved with the student in the subject he is teaching. A true teacher doesn't talk down to students, but takes a posture alongside them. Nicodemus and others called Jesus "a teacher come from God" (Jn. 3:2). The two disciples walking on the road to Emmaus exclaimed, "Did not our heart burn within us, while He talked with us by the way, and while He opened to us the scriptures?"

(Lk. 24:32) Jesus taught them while they were on the way. In this same manner, the Holy Spirit has come to be our Teacher to reveal Jesus to us so we can walk in a personal relationship with God and then share that relationship with others. The Holy Spirit is the ultimate Teacher who gets involved with us and helps us learn by walking beside us in our life situations.

However, because of the fall of man, sin has blinded us to eternal truths. We cannot receive truth from God unless the Holy Spirit reveals it to us. God desires so much for us to know Him that He uses all kinds of language techniques in the Scriptures to give us a picture of Himself. He wrote to us in types, shadows, allegories, metaphors, parables, parabolic expressions, similes, and sometimes hyperbole to reach us with His heavenly message. Then the Holy Spirit takes the written Word and makes it alive inside us. John wrote, "And the Word was made flesh, and dwelt among us…" (Jn. 1:14). He understood that God's Word is not law, but a Person. The Holy Spirit unveils the Person of Jesus within our lives, and the Word is made flesh within us as God forms His character and nature in us. That is why I think the greatest role of the Holy Spirit is as a Teacher who reveals Jesus to us so He might be unveiled in us.

Adam and his wife were forbidden to eat of the tree of the knowledge of good and evil lest they die (Gen. 2:17). When they chose to eat of that tree, they died to their relationship with God. Their disobedience produced in them a carnal mind that is hostile to God (Rom. 8 AMP). The world's philosophies of humanism, atheism, skepticism, communism, New Age, and any other self-centered rationale, have their roots in this first disobedience. Humanistic philosophy reflects this alienation from God by placing man at the center of his personal universe, independent from God. That independence, which is the root of all sin, resulted in God's removing man from the garden so he would not have access to the tree of life, which was there as well. If they had eaten of the tree of life in their sinful state, they would have lived forever in that condition, dead to God.

When man refused to be dependent upon God, he lost the mind of God, which is the source of all truth. That is when the "veil of flesh" first divided the inner chamber of man, separating the soul of man from his spirit. Man's spirit was intended to be "the way" to the Father's house. When Jesus came declaring, "I am the way, the truth, and the life" (Jn. 14:6), He gave hope to all mankind for their reconciliation to God. Man could have relationship with God through this new and living way, through the blood of Jesus (Heb. 10:19-20). Everyone who receives Christ can experience truth and life as God intended it. Unless the Spirit of Truth reveals the "Tree of Life" to us and replants it in the garden of our hearts through the new birth, we will not have the abundant life God ordained.

The Holy Spirit came to teach us so we would not be ignorant of life. Paul spoke of this ignorance when writing to the Ephesian church. He explained how the carnal mind works and then contrasted it with the mind that is taught of Christ:

*This I say therefore, and testify in the Lord, that ye henceforth walk not as other Gentiles walk, in the vanity of their mind, having the under-standing darkened, being alienated from the life of God through the ignorance that is in them, be-cause of the blindness of their heart: who being past feeling have given themselves over unto las-civiousness, to work all uncleanness with greedi-ness. But ye have not so learned Christ; if so be that ye have heard Him, and have been taught by Him, as the truth is in Jesus: that ye put off con-cerning the former conversation the old man, which is corrupt according to the deceitful lusts; and be renewed in the spirit of your mind; and that ye put on the new man, which after God is created in righteousness and true holiness.* (Ephesians 4:17-24)

Paul expected the believers to be different from Gentiles, from people without Christ, in their thinking and in their speech. The Holy Spirit comes as a Teacher to give us divine counsel and to restore truth to our minds so we can know the abundant life that Jesus promised us. As we cooperate with Him and put off our former ungodly thinking and conversation, allowing our carnal minds to be transformed, we begin to think the thoughts God intended us to think. Thus our divine Counselor teaches us to live a life of righteousness and true holiness.

## COMPASSION

*Oh that my head were waters, and mine eyes a fountain of tears, that I might weep day and night for the slain of the daughter of my people!* (Jeremiah 9:1)

This cry of Jeremiah reflects the compassionate mood of the Holy Spirit that can be called the *weeping* or *tearful mood.* It expresses God's tender caring for mankind. Natural man cannot feel godly compassion. He may feel pity or sympathetic concern, but human emotions without God do not express true compassion.

True compassion is revealed only in the nature of God. It is suffering with another, commiserating with his distress and desiring to show mercy to him. It is revealed in human hearts through a work of the Holy Spirit, when He gives us that godly ability to weep with those who weep (Rom. 12:15). Compassion is a mixed passion, one compounded of love and sorrow. Being compassionate means having a heart that is tender and easily moved by the distresses, sufferings, wants, and infirmities of others.[1] Jesus wept over the city of Jerusalem because the Jews missed the day of their visitation (Lk. 19:41-44). He was not offended that the Jews did not receive Him, but grieved. He had compassion on their ignorance and hardness of heart that kept them in darkness. He felt deeply their distress and desired to alleviate it.

When the Holy Spirit within us causes us to feel His compassion for a person, we weep with His brokenness and love. Paul instructed the Ephesians, "And be ye kind one to another, tenderhearted, forgiving one another, even as God for Christ's sake hath forgiven you" (Eph. 4:32). The more we walk in the Spirit, the more tenderhearted we will be. We will feel the same burdens operating in and through us that Christ feels when He looks on a sinful world. We will suffer the pain of love that is true compassion for lost people bound by sin. When we do, we experience the love and compassion of Christ flowing through us to help others who are in distress.

## CLEANSING MOOD

When Jesus cleansed the temple in Jerusalem, He made a whip of small cords and drove out the money changers. "And His disciples remembered that it was written, The zeal of Thine house hath eaten me up" (Jn. 2:17). This zeal of our Lord was divine indignation at the defilement of the temple that God had intended to be a house of prayer, of power, of purpose, and of purity. When the Holy Spirit comes to cleanse our own temples, His zeal against sin causes Him deep distress. Paul declared, "Know ye not that ye are the temple of God, and that the Spirit of God dwelleth in you?" (1 Cor. 3:16) The Spirit of God, who is the essence of the holiness of God, comes to our hearts to cleanse us of all unholiness so He may dwell in peace in our temples. That does not mean He would not come to us in our imperfect, sinful state. But after He comes, He patiently shines His light on one area of unrighteousness after another until He has fulfilled His divine purpose of cleansing our temples and making us holy.

This cleansing mood is the censoring, holy cry of the inner man. It is the Spirit of God and the spirit of man crying out in union against what is immoral, sinful, unjust and destructive to God's Kingdom and to the body, soul, and spirit of man. When the Holy Spirit comes to cleanse His temples, He may seem angry and harsh to us. We may feel the scourge of cords driving out the wicked thing that is defiling our lives. Yet, if we understand correctly, we will be grateful that divine love is walking in our temples to deliver us from sin, for His purposes. His anger is against the sin that threatens to destroy us. As we agree with Him, and "confess our sins, He is faithful and just to forgive us our sins, and to cleanse us from all unrighteousness" (1 John 1:9). We need to yield to the cleansing mood of the Holy Spirit so we can be changed into the image of Christ.

## COMMANDING MOOD

When Jesus rebuked the waves and winds and demanded that they be calm when the storm threatened the disciples' lives, He revealed the *commanding mood* of the Holy Spirit. He stood in that small boat and cried, "Peace, be still" (Mk. 4:39). Using the vernacular of today, He might have said, "Lie down, devil, and shut up!" Then the winds obeyed Jesus, to the disciples' astonishment. They did not yet understand the supernatural power of the Holy Spirit working through Him.

Paul, who was only a prisoner on a ship going to Italy, became commander of that ship by the power of the Holy Spirit during a crisis. When a violent storm at sea threatened the ship and the lives of all on board, and when the crew was ready to jump overboard, Paul began to command the situation by the authority of the Holy Spirit. He declared to those ungodly men that there would be no loss of life, although they would lose the ship. He said, "for this very night an angel of the God to whom I belong and whom I serve stood before me" (Acts 27:23 NAS). From that angel Paul received not only divine instructions for the situation, but also the power to carry them out. Thus his life and the lives of all those on the ship were spared as they obeyed God's servant. It was the supernatural power of the Holy Spirit that commanded that situation. Paul was simply the human vessel used to do the will of God in that moment.

We seem to enjoy the commanding mood of the Holy Spirit more than the others and desire to see it manifested among us. We love to say to the enemy, "We command you to... ." There are occasions when that is the proper response to the moving of the Holy Spirit. However, we need to remember that, as with all the moods of the Holy Spirit, His commanding mood is motivated by love. Because of man's inherent desire to rule, we need to be careful not to confuse natural "boldness" with the commanding mood of the Holy Spirit. Bossiness is not motivated by love. A person with a proud, commanding spirit is usually a person who is very insecure and desires to control others. Anyone who does not display a broken spirit and who is not teachable may simply be displaying a carnal desire to rule when commanding a situation. We can be thankful for the true commanding mood of the Holy Spirit that has authority and power to change any situation for God's glory.

## *CONQUERING MOOD*

When the Holy Spirit expresses Himself in the conquering mood, He is *joyful, triumphant,* and *victorious.* "For this purpose the Son of God was manifested, that He might destroy the works of the devil" (1 John 3:8). The original meaning of the Greek word used here for destroy is *loū.* It means that Jesus came to outdo, undo, and overdo *everything* the devil ever did. Truly understanding Jesus' ultimate triumph over evil makes us shout "Hallelujah!" When a person or a church realizes that kind of victory, the Holy Spirit is ready to rejoice as the conquering armies in Bible history did when they returned home with the spoils. In those days the whole city would turn out and line the streets to praise the soldiers as they marched home in triumph over their enemies.

After the Holy Spirit convicts us of sin and cleanses our temples through our repentance, we sense this triumph and joy of God's presence in our lives. In those times we cannot help but rejoice, praise, and shout about the goodness of God. He has conquered the sin that was trying to destroy us, and we are free to enjoy His blessings in our lives. When a person has sought for God and found Him, the divine Conqueror comes to bring rejoicing and to express His triumph over the devil's attempt to destroy that life. Exalting Jesus in praise expresses the conquering mood of the Holy Spirit. In this place of rejoicing, dancing, and shouting, we are aware that principalities and powers previously standing against us in the heavenlies have been brought down.

When David came against Goliath, he declared "…but I come to thee in the name of the Lord of hosts…" (1 Sam. 17:44). His confidence was in the Lord, who was the conqueror of this giant and all the others who dared to defy God. I like to describe this conquering, joyful and triumphant mood as the jubilation we feel when, through the power of the Holy Spirit, we have conquered every demon in sight! We have cut off Goliath's head and are standing on the top of the highest hill, rattling our other four smooth stones (1 Sam. 17:40), looking around to see if there are any more giants to be conquered. Someone has suggested that the other four rocks were for Goliath's four brothers. Surely the Lord has equipped us with five stones to fight the enemy. He has given us His name, His Word, His blood, His Spirit, and His faith. These stones, when exercised in the "sling" of praise, make us more than conquerors.

This same kind of jubilation accompanied the victory in another Old Testament crisis—when Haman as well as his ten sons were hung on the scaffold erected for Mordecai (Ester 9:25). In still another battle, when King Jehoshaphat faced a formidable enemy, he sent the singers and praisers ahead of the army, "that they should praise the beauty of holiness" (2 Chron. 20:21). Then God sent ambushments against the enemies, and these enemies proceeded to destroy themselves. Jehoshaphat's army didn't have to fight at all. They simply went and collected the spoils from the slain armies. Likewise the Holy Spirit is the mighty conqueror of the enemies who are too strong for us, and He will cause us to rejoice in triumphant victory when we see them defeated.

## SUMMARY

We have described six of the seven moods through which the Holy Spirit expresses His purposes. As we walk in the Spirit, we learn to recognize His various moods when He expresses them in our individual lives and in the corporate expression of the Church. We must learn to yield to the Spirit of God within us, to agree with His purpose for the moment, and allow Him to weep or rejoice through us. We must accept His cleansing and listen to His commands. As we do, He will reveal Jesus to us, and lead and guide us into all truth. He will bring us into deep communion with the Father as we allow our personal relationship with God to become more intimate by cultivating a life of prayer.

The seventh mood of the Holy Spirit, which is the subject of the last chapter, is His communion mood. Communion between God and man has always been the ultimate goal of God's love. Yet we can scarcely begin to comprehend the love of God until we have first learned to commune with Him. The epitome of our relationship with the Holy Spirit is realized in learning to yield to His communion mood.

### Notes

1. Noah Webster, *American Dictionary of the English Language*, 1828.

# Chapter 9

# *Seven Moods of the Holy Spirit*

## *Part II: Communion: God's Desire for Man Realized*

God's ultimate desire for mankind is to commune with Him, so He can reveal His great love for him and communicate His will to him. He is able to do that through the communion mood of the Holy Spirit. The Holy Spirit expresses His communion mood through the multifaceted realms of prayer. We learned in an earlier chapter that the Holy Spirit comes to establish communion between our spirits and God, who is Spirit, as He works through the office of supplication.

Although the prayer *mood* of the Holy Spirit is integrally related with His *office* of prayer, we would miss much revelation of God's deep desire to commune with man if we did not study them separately. We can expect these two truths, the office of prayer and the mood of prayer, to overlap and intertwine, yet the revelation of each needs to be grasped in its singularity. Then comparing the Holy Spirit's work in the office of supplication with His communion mood will give us a more complete perspective of this many-faceted diamond of prayer.

Too often we think of prayer as simply our talking with God. We don't realize that God the Father, God the Son, and God the Holy Spirit want to talk to us in prayer. True prayer is two-way communication with God. In the broader meaning of the word, communion encompasses seven different aspects of prayer which the Holy Spirit uses to teach us to communicate with God. When we look at communion in its deepest meaning, however, we will understand that it is the most intimate of all realms of prayer. It is that relationship ordained of God to completely satisfy our hearts as well as His own. Every form of prayer has its necessary function and must be properly cultivated in the life of the believer; thus we need to understand the Holy Spirit's desire for each aspect of prayer.

**Petition.** We are all so familiar with the prayer of *petition* that we do not need to discuss it in detail. This is the kind of prayer that asks for what we and others need. The Scriptures are clear that we are to ask God for what we need. Paul taught us to make our requests known unto God with thanksgiving (Phil. 4:6). James wrote that we have not because we ask not, or we ask amiss (Jas. 4:2-3). Jesus taught us to ask in His name and the Father would give us what we asked (Jn. 16:23-24). Although the Scriptures clearly teach that we must bring our requests for things we need to God, we must be careful to watch our motivation for asking. It is easy to be selfish when we petition God, since the conversation in this kind of prayer is usually one-sided and self-centered. We need to be sure we are in agreement with the Holy Spirit in what we are asking, and that our requests are promoting the Kingdom of God and His will and purpose for our lives or for the lives of those people whom we are petitioning God for.

**Thanksgiving.** "It is a good thing to give thanks unto the Lord" (Ps. 92:1a). The prayer of *thanksgiving* means to offer thanks to God from a grateful heart for what He has done. The psalmist taught us that thanksgiving is the proper way to enter the presence of God: "Enter into His gates with thanksgiving, and into His courts with praise: be thankful unto Him, and bless His name" (Ps. 100:4). Our thanksgiving is to be a genuine thankfulness to the Lord for what He has done for us; for His mercy, His grace, His longsuffering, and His goodness to us. Listen to Paul's instructions: "In everything give thanks; for this is God's will for you in

Christ Jesus" (1 Thess. 5:18 NAS). This command immediately follows his instruction to "pray without ceasing" (v. 17). Clearly, our attitude in prayer is to be one of thanksgiving.

If we have a thankful spirit, we will be thankful to other people and will express our gratitude freely. It is impossible to yield our minds to a critical spirit while we are enjoying a thankful heart. That should be reason enough for us to cultivate the attitude of thankfulness. According to the Scriptures, unthankfulness (ingratitude) will be a characteristic of people who live in the last days (2 Tim. 3:1-2). Paul taught the Ephesians that Christians should be "always giving thanks for all things in the name of our Lord Jesus Christ to God, even the Father" (Eph. 5:20 NAS). We need to cultivate expressing a spirit of gratitude as a way of life and offer prayers of thanksgiving continually to our God.

**Supplication.** As an aspect of the communion mood of the Holy Spirit, *supplication* applies specifically to the humble and earnest cry that comes from the deep desire of the spirit and soul. David cried out to the Lord, "Hear the voice of my supplications, when I cry unto Thee" (Ps. 28:2a). The Holy Spirit gives us these deep cries and yearnings for the will of God to be fulfilled in our lives and in the lives of others.

This was the testimony of the early church in the Book of Acts: "These all continued with one accord in prayer and supplication..." (Acts 1:14). A study of the early church reveals the impact that earnest prayer had upon impossible situations; it brought supernatural intervention. Peter was delivered from prison by an angel on one occasion as the Church prayed (Acts 12). On another occasion the whole place where they were praying was shaken and they were empowered to speak boldly amid the threatenings against them (Acts 4:31). God answered their fervent cries in their time of need.

To Timothy, Paul wrote, "I exhort therefore, that, first of all, supplications, prayers, intercessions, and giving of thanks be made for all men; for kings, and for all that are in authority; that we may lead a quiet and peaceable life in all godliness and honesty" (1 Tim. 2:1-2). This command to pray for our leaders means more than a perfunctory "God bless you" that we might pray when we celebrate our national Independence Day. The Holy Spirit energizes us with heartfelt desires for the will of God to be done in the earth. God hears the cry of our supplications as we follow the scriptural admonition to pray earnestly. As individual believers who together form the Church, we need to evaluate the intensity of our prayer life. If we sense a lack of desire, we can ask the Holy Spirit to come and fill us with His deep cries of supplication.

**Intercession.** This is the prayer of standing in the gap for someone else. We notice that all three members of the Godhead intercede for and through us to fulfill the eternal plan and purpose of God for our lives, which is to be transformed into His image. Jesus ever lives to make intercession for us (Heb. 7:25), and the Holy Spirit makes intercession for the saints according to the will of the Father (Rom. 8:26-27). Intercession is not a special ministry for only a few. Everyone who walks with the Holy Spirit knows intercession as He burdens their hearts for the needs of others. Many lives and churches have been snatched from the burning fire by the prayers of faithful intercessors.

Moses, the great intercessor, pleaded more than once for God to not destroy the rebellious nation of Israel as they wandered in the wilderness, murmuring and complaining. In that same way, God gives us burdens to pray for those around us. He trusts us to carry a burden of intercession for a life that would otherwise be destroyed. As we learn to yield to the Holy Spirit in intercession, we begin to pray until we see His wonderful answer in that life or situation.

**Praise.** We will look at praise and worship as two different ways of expressing our love to God. In *praise* we turn our eyes to God and away from ourselves. If we enter His gates with thanksgiving, we can go on into His courts with praise when we magnify Him for His greatness and His goodness (Ps. 100:4). In this context, praise means to make a show in raving about Him, to the point of being clamorously foolish. We praise Him for who He is and for His mighty acts toward the sons of men. We exalt Him as we recognize His love and power. Through praise we honor and give credit and homage to our Lord.

**Worship.** We do not define *worship* as a general term for coming to church or for singing praises. True worship occurs when our spirits have experienced a divine encounter with the living God. The Hebrew word for worship, *shachah,* can be translated as "bow down, crouch, do reverence, prostrate, and beseech humbly." The Greek word for worship most used in the New Testament is *proskuneō.* It means "to kiss toward." In worship the believer expresses the affection and deep devotion of his heart in the presence of God. The comprehensive meaning of worship, then, is to respect, esteem, love, admire, and reverence God. In its deepest sense, *worship is a heart's response to the manifest presence of God.*

### Praise and Worship Contrasted

What is the difference between praise and worship? Although these terms are used interchangeably by some, we can see from our definitions that there is a significant difference we need to understand. The purpose of praise is to bring us into God's presence. Worship is our heart response to Him when we come into a conscious realization of His presence. Praise and thanksgiving exalt God for what He has done. Worship is our love response to who He is; it is an inevitable response of the loving heart in the presence of God. When, for example, the curtain of Heaven is drawn back and we get a glimpse of what is happening in the presence of God, we read, "...And the four and twenty elders fell down and worshipped..." (Rev. 5:14). God's manifest presence evokes such awe and reverence that often we cannot speak, but must prostrate ourselves before Him in worship. So we express our deepest love and adoration to the Lord in the place of worship.

God is seeking a people who will worship Him "in spirit and in truth" (Jn. 4:23). When Isaiah was in the presence of God, he saw the truth about himself and cried, "Woe is me" (Is. 6:5). In the place of worship we not only see God, but also our sinfulness in comparison to a holy God. Then we worship Him by repenting and pouring out our wills and desires at His feet in prayer, asking for His will to be done. In return, we receive His life-giving, eternal purposes for us. In worship we have a vital key to personal change. True worship presupposes a life of submission to the Lordship of Christ. It expresses our comprehensive devotion to God out of love for Him and out of all-consuming passion to please Him in all.

### Profitable Values of Praise and Worship

Many of us learned to praise and worship before we knew the implications of where God was leading us. Have you ever asked the question, "What does worship do for me?" Worshiping Him is ordained by God as the highest purpose for mankind. As we learn to walk in that purpose, however, what we can expect as the results in our lives?

**The presence of God is manifested.** First we can expect praise and worship to bring the manifest presence of God into our midst. As we saw earlier, the Bible teaches the omnipresence of God (meaning God is everywhere). It teaches the abiding presence of God for believers (Jn. 15). It reveals God's manifest presence every time He moves supernaturally in behalf of His people. God desires to manifest His presence to our lives and in our churches. True worship brings His manifest presence to His people.

**Right relationship is achieved.** Worship brings us into right relationship with Christ. "One thing I have desired of the Lord, that will I seek after; that I may dwell in the house of the Lord all the days of my life, to behold the beauty of the Lord, and to inquire in His temple" (Ps. 27:4). Why do you suppose God said through Samuel to Saul, "The Lord hath sought him a man after His own heart" (1 Sam. 13:14)? David had learned that the greatest satisfaction man can experience is to worship God.

That is why we were created in the beginning: to have fellowship with our heavenly Father. Fellowship is that free communication of loving hearts one to another. David did not ask for either material or temporal things; his desire was for fellowship and communion with the Lord. Fellowship is established through our prayer life. What is our own fellowship (prayer life) like? David prayed, "Let my prayer be set forth before thee as incense; and the lifting up of my hands as the evening sacrifice" (Ps. 141:2). In God's plan, prayer-fellowship is the link to a higher realm of worship.

**Divine love is received.** When we experience God's manifest presence of divine Love, He gives us divine ability to love one another genuinely. Jesus said, "A new commandment I give unto you, That ye love one another" (Jn. 13:34a). If we are honest with God and with ourselves, we will admit that this command has been extremely difficult to obey. The natural man does not love the unlovely. We love those who are loving, who are attentive to us, and perhaps those who serve us. But what is our reaction to even a Christian brother who is irritating, insulting, or in some way obnoxious?

At our conversion we received a measure of divine love for one another, and that love deepens when we receive baptism of the Holy Spirit. Yet often our own prejudices, opinions, and natural feelings hinder the expression of His love through us to others. If our ideas are challenged, for example, or our opinions crossed, or our plan is not honored, how do we react? Are we tolerant and understanding of others' views?

Or are we like the disciples whom Jesus rebuked when He said, "Ye know not what manner of spirit ye are of" (Lk. 9:55b)? That is where guile and pretense have their entrance. We know that love is the scriptural pattern and requirement, so we strive to act in a loving way. But many times we only play the part without experiencing the reality of love in our hearts.

**Worship changes the picture.** As we worship God with extravagant love and complete submission, He changes our perspective! We perceive the "Christ" in each other. Although faults and imperfections are still there, love forgives and overlooks them. When our vision is horizontally (earthly) inclined, we see only trouble and heartache. But if we lift our eyes vertically, looking to Jesus, we see people as God sees them. Then we can love them as He does. Worship gives us God's perspective of life.

**A Throne is in our midst.** The Scriptures teach that God is enthroned on our praises (Ps. 22:3). We enthrone Him as we worship at His footstool. As we worship corporately around His throne, He unites our hearts and establishes His harmony in the Church. In a prophetic vision the prophet Joel described that unity: "...and they shall march every one on his ways, and they shall not break their ranks: neither shall one thrust another; they shall walk every one in his path..." (Joel 2:7-8). Joel was describing the unity the Church would know as a military force marching in formation. He saw prophetically the beauty of a great host of people in total harmony. To be a part of that army requires daily discipline and training, both individually and corporately. Each soldier must commit himself unreservedly to the one who gives the commands. The life of the whole depends on the total cooperation of each individual. The Church today is vigorously striving for unity but often finding none. True unity will come only when the Church experiences spiritual worship.

The apostle Paul gave us a picture of unity when he described the Church as a body: "Now ye are the body of Christ, and members in particular" (1 Cor. 12:27). Each member surrenders his privilege of individual recognition and decisions to become a living, vital "supply joint" that provides increase and mobility to the Body of Christ, the Church. We know there is power in unity and we want to walk in it. But it seems that when we get one member in his place, another will break rank. Jealously, envy, bitterness, and strife infiltrate the ranks no matter how valiantly we labor. The wisdom of the hour is to find out which way God is moving and to get into step with Him. Worship in the presence of God melts our hearts and brings us to repentance for wrong attitudes that cause disunity.

**Worship places us on the offensive.** One outward form of praise involves the lifting up the hands. The psalmist cried, "Lift up your hands in the sanctuary, and bless the Lord" (Ps. 134:2). Raising our hands can be a sign of surrender and can testify to the resurrection power of Christ. It can represent an aspect of warfare as well. The psalmist acknowledged that the Lord was with his hands in battle when he wrote, "Blessed be the Lord my strength, which teacheth my hands to war, and my fingers to fight" (Ps. 144:1). Warfare is a part of life for every Christian who expects to be victorious over his enemies.

David understood that praise was an effective weapon against his enemies. He wrote, "Out of the mouth of babes and sucklings hast Thou ordained strength because of Thine enemies" (Ps. 8:2a). When Jesus quoted the psalmist, He substituted the word "praise" for the word "strength": "Out of the mouths of babes and sucklings Thou hast perfected praise" (Mt. 21:16). Praise is a spiritual strength against our enemies when we learn to truly worship the Lord in spirit and truth. What does this praise do? It stills the avenger and puts the enemy to flight. That is the reason satan hates worship; it puts him to flight. David instructed the saints to be joyful and to "Let the high praises of God be in their mouth, and a two-edged sword in their hand" (Ps. 149:6). In this way we are to defeat all our enemies. We assume our offensive position through worship, and actually make war in high places.

Paul understood this when he wrote:

*For the weapons of our warfare are not carnal,
but mighty through God to the pulling down of
strong holds; casting down imaginations, and
every high thing that exalteth itself against the
knowledge of God, and bringing into captivity
every thought to the obedience of Christ.*
(2 Corinthians 10:4-5)

One of satan's most effective maneuvers is to attack
our thought life and cause us to imagine all sorts of un-
realities. How often have you been tormented by feelings of unworthiness, guilt, or just vague uneasiness
concerning your relationship with God? It would be
wonderful to just "take our minds out of gear" so nothing could affect us. Since that is impossible, we either
fill our minds with godly thoughts or the enemy in-
vades us with lying vanities. Praising God establishes
a proper perspective and becomes a spiritual weapon
that pulls down imaginations and brings into captivity
every thought to the obedience of Christ. It is impossible to worship the Lord and remain discouraged.

**Worship represents the voice of the Lord in our
midst.** In the Book of Hebrews these words are ascribed to Jesus: "I will declare Thy name unto My brethren in the midst of the church will I sing praise unto
Thee" (Heb. 2:12). In an actual worship service where
the Body of Christ shares in prophecy, spiritual songs,
and exhortation, who is speaking? Paul tells us here
that it is Jesus speaking. Each believer is contributing,

bringing to one another the full message of Christ. If we fail to receive from our brothers and sisters in a corporate expression of worship, we will miss much of what God is speaking to the Church.

**Worship enables us to rightly divide the Word of truth.** The Old Testament pattern of God's provision for His people to receive the Word serves as an example for the Church today. The prophet Ezekiel described the order of the priestly ministry, which is a perfect prototype of God's purpose for His ministry today:

> *But the priests the Levites...they shall come near to Me to minister unto Me...And they shall teach My people the difference between the holy and profane, and cause them to discern between the unclean and the clean.* (Ezekiel 44:15,23)

The order of worship established here is first faithfulness, then worship, then teaching. In faithfulness these Old Testament ministers were to draw near to the Lord. So we must have a daily communion and fellowship with Him, becoming intimately acquainted with the Lord. Then they were to worship; "They shall minister unto Me." Finally, they were to teach the people and cause them to discern between good and evil. So who is qualified to minister and rightly divide the Word of truth? Is it the one who draws from natural ability and good training, or the one who has been in the presence of the Lord? It is in the presence of the Lord that we receive revelation of the Word. Since that is true, should we not make certain that our contact with God is fresh and living, in order that the spirit of wisdom and revelation in the knowledge of Him is our portion (Eph. 1:17)? As we are obedient to God, we become enraptured with the Person of the Lord Jesus Christ. Our needs become secondary, and pleasing the Father takes precedence in our lives over everything else.

Praise and worship, both privately and corporately, need to become priorities with the people of God. We should cry with the psalmist, "I will bless the Lord at all times: His praise shall continually be in my mouth" (Ps. 34:1). Only then can we expect to enjoy the benefits God intended for His people. As we focus on the goodness of God, our hearts will be filled with gratitude and our automatic response will be to praise Him.

## Communion

We have studied communion in a broad sense as the expression of prayer that applies to all of communication between God and man. The eternal plan of God, which included sending the Third Person of the Holy Spirit to the earth, is ultimately realized when that relationship of communion is established in the hearts of men and women who accept salvation through the blood of Christ. In its purest essence, however, *true communion* with God is the result of a deeply personal love relationship with Him. Jesus said, "Behold, I stand at the door, and knock: if any man hear My voice, and open the door, I will come in to him, and will sup with him and he with Me" (Rev. 3:20). As we come into the place of worship in the presence of God and experience the joy of relationship with Him, we can commune with Him in a very intimate way. He desires to have this personal fellowship with us so He can speak quietly to our spirits and we can hear His voice of love speaking to us.

Intimacy in relationship involves two persons who want to share their love with each other. God, who is Love, desires to share that love personally to every heart that will invite the Holy Spirit to reveal Jesus to it. God wants to share His love with us in a way that impregnates us with the living Word. As He lifes us by His Spirit, we can take that divine life to others by sharing His living Word. As we learn to give our love to Him in worship, we begin to know His loving response to us in the intimacy of communion. Paul prayed for the Corinthians, "The grace of the Lord Jesus Christ, and the love of God, and the communion of the Holy Ghost, be with you all. Amen" (2 Cor. 13:14). Through this intimate relationship of communion with God we experience the reality of His love and Person in such a way that He can never again be just a creed or an influence in our thinking. He becomes a Person to be loved and obeyed, a Person who is more real than any other on earth.

God's purpose for creating mankind was to commune with him and share His love with him. Redemption involves the entire Godhead working together to bring man back into that love relationship. Our initial salvation experience does not complete the work of redemption; it only starts that process. As we cultivate a life of prayer, we continually come into a more intimate relationship with God that satisfies not only our hearts, but His as well.

## *SUMMARY*

Learning to commune with the Holy Spirit makes us more sensitive to His other moods. We then learn to know Him as a Person and can cooperate with His purposes as He executes them through His offices and expresses them through His moods. The Holy Spirit can then anoint our eyes to see and our ears to hear the will of God for every moment of our lives. At last our hearts will be satisfied as we, in turn, satisfy the heart of the Father in this most intimate of prayer relationships: communion with God.

The Holy Spirit is clearly revealed as a divine Person throughout the Scriptures. We can know this wonderful Third Person of the Godhead in all the beautiful facets of His personality as we seek Him in prayer and in the Word. In the next volume we will learn more explicitly how to enter into a personal relationship with Him through the baptism of the Holy Spirit. In it we will study the purposes of the gifts He brought to the Church, and learn how to be led by Him as children of God. Paul taught, "for all who are being led by the Spirit of God, these are the sons of God" (Rom. 8:14 NAS). We can safely conclude, then, that we must learn to be led by the Spirit of God to come to maturity and be called sons of God. In this book we have learned that adoption as sons of God happens at maturity and signifies that we are true sons of God with knowledge. As we come to maturity, we can defeat the enemies pursuing us. The Spirit of God leads us into personal victory and teaches us how to win in spiritual warfare, pulling down strongholds that would try to defeat us. He will enable us to be a part of His living organism, the Church that He is building in the earth. And He will teach us how to receive our inheritance in Christ. It is our responsibility to cultivate this divine relationship so we can "reign in life through the One, Jesus Christ" (Rom. 5:17 NAS).

# Volume 2:
# Walking in the Spirit

# Contents
# Volume 2: Walking in the Spirit

# Foreword

I have been a friend of Dr. Fuchsia Pickett's for more than 20 years. I've invited her to my church as a teaching evangelist on repeated occasions when I was a pastor in Oregon. Later I taught with her in her Bible school in Plano, Texas, and over the past ten years we've repeatedly shared the platform as speakers in conferences and conventions. I can verify that she is an anointed woman filled and thrilled with God's Word.

I doubt if I have ever met a person who spoke more of, depended more on, or enjoyed the Holy Spirit more than Dr. Pickett. The Spirit of God is not a theme to her; He is a Person of the Godhead who lives in her. She has studied His message, methods, and ministries with the keen eye of a research professor and with the emotions of a student deeply in love with the instructor.

Her inquiry has taken her beyond the common concepts of the gifts and fruit of the Spirit. What she offers us here in Volume 2 of her life study on the Person and work of the Holy Spirit is a fresh insight on the infilling of the Spirit, and the subsequent outworking of that indwelling.

I am a contributor to this book, so I may speak with some bias, but I am convinced that much of what is written in this book is unknown by the great body of believers who have been baptized in the Holy Spirit in the past 30 years. Much emphasis has been placed on the unction of the Spirit, but little attention has been given to the function of God's Spirit.

Although this book contains some wonderful personal experiences, it is not a testimonial book. It is a theological treatise on the baptism of the Holy Spirit and how it should affect the daily life of believers. It is "must" reading for anyone serious about the ongoing work of the Spirit in his or her life and ministry.

Judson Cornwall
Phoenix, Arizona

# Chapter 1

# *When He Is Come*

## *Divine Mission*

*And when He is come, He will reprove the world of sin, and of righteousness, and of judgment* (John 16:8).

Jesus declared to His disciples that it was expedient that He go away. He promised them that if He went away, He would send them a divine Comforter, the Holy Spirit (Jn. 16:7). Although they grieved at the thought of His leaving, He continued to talk to them about the work of the Holy Spirit who would come to comfort them. He told them that the Holy Spirit would reprove the world of sin, of righteousness, and of judgment.

I wonder if it seemed strange to the disciples to relate the idea of comfort and reproof so closely. The

1

Greek word for *reprove* can be translated also to mean *convince, convict, expose,* and *rebuke.* Jesus taught that part of the Holy Spirit's work is to reprove or convince men of sin, of righteousness, and of judgment. Someone has wisely observed: "These three things are the most difficult to impress on any man, for he can always attempt to justify himself by asserting an inexcusable motive for evil actions, or by pleading a relative scale of ethical standards in the place of absolute righteousness, thereby assuming that judgment is indefinitely deferred so that it is no real threat."[1] Such is the lost state of mankind for whom the Holy Spirit came to do His divine work. He must convict men of their lostness and blindness in these three areas of moral failure: sin, righteousness, and judgment.

*"Of sin, because they believe not on Me"* (Jn. 16:9). It is impossible for a person to produce conviction in the heart of another person. Only the Holy Spirit can reveal the deceitfulness of our hearts and make us realize the greatness of our iniquity in the eyes of a holy God. The particular sin to which Jesus is referring, the one of which the Holy Spirit will convict, is not what we have labeled "gross sins," those such as adultery, murder, stealing, or drunkenness. No, it is the sin of *unbelief*—that failure to believe in Christ as the Savior who alone can forgive us of our sins. Unbelief in Jesus Christ results in the rejection of God's only means of forgiveness and brings all the condemnation of other sins upon the one who fails to appropriate

Christ's salvation through faith. The sin of unbelief negates the efficacious, vicarious, substitutionary, mediatorial work of Calvary. This tragic fact makes unbelief the greatest sin.

As George Smeaton has so aptly stated it:

The sin of unbelief is here described, with all the erroneous guilt attached to it, as a rejection of the proposal of reconciliation, as the chief and supreme sin, because a sin against the remedy,— as sinful in itself, and as preventing the remission of all other sins...original and actual, with all their guilt, that are remissable through faith in Christ. But this sin involves the rejection of the graciously provided remedy; and final unbelief has nothing to interpose between the sinner and righteous condemnation...The sin of unbelief is here described as if it were the only sin, because, according to the happy remark of Augustine, while it continues, all other sins are retained, and when it departs, all other sins are remitted.[2]

Only the convicting work of the Holy Spirit can bring us to a realization of our sinfulness, causing us to turn to Christ and cry for mercy. We can be thankful for His convicting power that turns us from darkness to light and convinces us that we need a Savior. That reality brings true comfort to a lost, sin-sick soul in its misery.

*"Of righteousness, because I go to My Father..."* (Jn. 16:10). The righteousness of which the Holy Spirit convinces mankind is not human righteousness, but Christ's righteousness. The resurrection and ascension of Christ into the presence of the Father attest to His righteousness. Had Jesus been an imposter, as the religious world insisted He was when they crucified Him, the Father would not have received Him. The fact that the Father did exalt Him to His right hand vindicated Him of the charges, the accusations, and railings the religious leaders and the multitude heaped upon Him when they crucified Him. It also proves that Jesus paid the full price for the sins of the whole world, which had been laid upon Him. Smeaton describes Jesus' sacrifice in this way:

> To convince the world of righteousness must mean that the Spirit gives convincing evidence, not merely that His cause was good, or that He is innocent, but that in Him is the righteousness that the world needs, the imputed righteousness that He graciously provided for us and becomes ours by faith.[3]

Jesus' return to the Father gave evidence that He had fully completed the task He had been sent into the world to do. He had provided righteousness for those who would believe on Him. Although we have to admit, with the prophet, that our righteousnesses are as filthy rags (Is. 64:6), if we believe in Christ, He will justify us before the Father. Then we can live "just-as-if-I'd never sinned."

**"Of judgment, because the prince of this world is judged"** (Jn. 16:11). Aren't you glad that verse reads "*is* judged"? It means the devil has already been judged and is now judged. Jesus said on another occasion, "Now is the judgment of this world: now shall the prince of this world be cast out" (Jn. 12:31). Since Christ has judged the prince of this world, all who follow the devil will be judged as well. Because of that judgment, the world stands guilty of refusing to believe in Christ. Its condemnation is proclaimed by the righteousness that Christ exhibited in His going to the Father. Therefore, nothing but judgment awaits the world. The greatest demonstration of that judgment is that the prince of this world is judged.

The Holy Spirit has come, then, according to Jesus, to convict men of sin, of righteousness, and of judgment. Unfortunately, even some Christians don't understand the nature of this reproving and convicting work of the Holy Spirit. The Holy Spirit does not function in the physical environment or atmosphere, apart from human vessels. He convicts men through the power of the written Word as it is read, and through the preached Word as it is heard. He does His convicting work, as well, *through* Spirit-filled believers who live godly lives as a testimony for righteousness before others who do not know Christ.

On the Day of Pentecost, when the disciples were filled with the Holy Spirit, Peter stood up to preach to several thousand people who experienced the convicting power of the Holy Spirit through his message and so repented of their sins and were baptized. Because the Holy Spirit works through believers, it is imperative that each believer live a Spirit-filled life, walking in the Spirit. The Holy Spirit will be faithful to convict believers continually, as well, of the presence of sin in their lives and to help them cry out to be forgiven and delivered from its power.

## PROGRESSIVE REVELATION OF GOD

We can hope to have insight concerning God only according to the ways God has chosen to reveal Himself to us. The Scriptures declare:

> *God, who at sundry times and in divers manners spake in time past unto the fathers by the prophets, hath in these last days spoken unto us by His Son, whom He hath appointed heir of all things, by whom also He made the worlds* (Hebrews 1:1-2).

This passage teaches us that God's way of revealing Himself to mankind, after the time of the prophets, was through His Son, Jesus. Jesus Christ perfectly revealed God the Father. That same passage in Hebrews declares that Jesus is "the brightness of His glory, and the express image of His person..." (Heb. 1:3). Jesus reinforced this truth when He said to His questioning disciples, "He that hath seen Me hath seen the Father" (Jn. 14:9b).

Do you see the progression here in the revelation of God to man? The Father is revealed to us by the Son, and the Son is revealed to us by the Holy Spirit. G. Campbell Morgan states this truth in an interesting way; he refers to Jesus as the revelation of the Father and calls the Holy Spirit the "interpretation of the revelation."[4] Although the Godhead is one Triune God, each member has His particular place and function regarding redemption as revealed in the Scriptures. Jesus said of the Holy Spirit:

> *Howbeit when He, the Spirit of truth, is come, He will guide you into all truth: for He shall not speak of Himself; but whatsoever He shall hear, that shall He speak: and He will show you things to come. He shall glorify Me: for He shall receive of Mine, and shall show it unto you. All things that the Father hath are Mine: therefore said I, that He shall take of Mine, and shall show it unto you* (John 16:13-15).

According to this passage, the Holy Spirit did not come to minister only to the sin question. Jesus continued to declare to His disciples the work of the Holy Spirit, describing Him as the Spirit of truth. Note the five things that Jesus said the Holy Spirit would do: (a) He will guide you into all truth; (b) He will not speak on His own initiative (meaning out of His own resources), but whatever He hears, He will speak; (c) He will show to you what is yet to come; (d) He shall glorify Jesus, for He shall take of Jesus'; and (e) shall show it to you (Jn. 16:13-15). These are emphatic statements concerning what the Holy Spirit *will do—not maybe so, not might or perhaps*—but *that He will do*. When the Holy Spirit comes to our individual hearts and to our churches, we can expect Him to work in these wonderful ways to reveal Jesus to us.

## THE WORK OF THE HOLY SPIRIT IN CHRIST

Before we relate the coming of the Holy Spirit to our own lives, it will be profitable for us to understand the integral relationship of the Holy Spirit to the Person and ministry of our Lord Jesus. This relationship is especially significant as it pertains to the humanity of Jesus. The Holy Spirit has little to do with the deity of our Lord, for Jesus was God Himself. As John so clearly declares, "In the beginning was the Word, and the Word was with God, and the Word was God" (Jn. 1:1). But the Holy Spirit does have *much* to do with Christ's human nature as Christ humbled Himself to take upon Him the form of a servant in order to bring the plan of redemption to mankind (Phil. 2:7-8).

### In His Birth

Of course, we understand that Christ did not have His beginning in the manger in Bethlehem. He existed from all eternity and before eternity, back in the eons of the ages before time began. He who always existed was sent by the Spirit into the world (Is. 48:16). It was the Holy Spirit who facilitated His coming, for Jesus was conceived by the Holy Spirit. When the angel of the Lord appeared to Mary, he declared: "The Holy Ghost shall come upon thee, and the power of the Highest shall overshadow thee: therefore also that holy thing which shall be born of thee shall be called the Son of God" (Lk. 1:35). Then the angel of the Lord appeared to Joseph, her husband-to-be, saying, "Joseph, thou son of David, fear not to take unto thee Mary thy wife: for that which is conceived in her is of the Holy Ghost" (Mt. 1:20b).

The divine conception of the Lord Jesus did not involve calling a new being into life as when other human beings are born. This divine One who had existed eternally, through His conception, was now entering into relationship with mankind as a human being with human nature. He was not conceived in sin, for His conception was holy, wrought by the Holy Spirit. Paul explains clearly that Christ, who was as God and equal with Him, emptied Himself and "took upon Him the form of a servant, and was made in the likeness of men" (Phil. 2:7).

This Greek word for *emptied* means *parked or set aside*. Christ's conception involved His willingly laying aside His deity and taking on a human nature. He set aside His deity when He became man, completely yielding Himself to the Holy Spirit and being empowered by Him. Jesus was fully God and fully Man, but He lived by the power of the Holy Spirit while on earth, having emptied Himself of His divine powers. Although He was still Christ, the Creator of the universe, He lived on earth as Jesus, the Man, empowered by the Holy Spirit. He said of Himself, "I can of Mine own self do nothing..." (Jn. 5:30). It is important that Christians understand this reality, that we not look at Jesus' victorious life and say, "Yes, but He was God." In living His life as a man, Jesus taught us that the source of victory is being filled with, empowered by, and obedient to the Holy Spirit at every moment.

Without the Holy Spirit, even the incarnation of Jesus through conception would not have been possible. Likewise in our regeneration, our new birth is impossible without the Holy Spirit creating the life of God in us.

## *His Presentation at the Temple*

Mary and Joseph took Jesus to Jerusalem to present Him at the temple, fulfilling the law by offering the sacrifice required for a firstborn male (Lk. 2:23). There was an old priest there named Simeon who had served God devoutly. He prayed that he not die until he see the salvation of God. "And it was revealed unto him by the Holy Ghost, that he should not see death, before he had seen the Lord's Christ" (Lk. 2:26). The Scriptures say that Simeon went into the temple "by the Spirit" on the day that Mary and Joseph took Jesus to present Him according to the law.

The Holy Spirit revealed to Simeon that this baby was indeed the Christ for whom he had been waiting. This godly priest began to prophesy over Jesus, to the amazement of His parents. Then Simeon declared that he was ready to die, for he had seen the salvation of God. The Holy Spirit also included Anna, the prophetess, in this revelation of Jesus' coming. She had served God night and day with fastings and prayers, and He revealed to her that this babe was the long-awaited Savior. She began to give thanks to God and to tell everyone who was looking for redemption that Jesus, the Christ, had indeed come (Lk. 2:36-38). Perhaps the revelation of Jesus to these two is more striking because of its contrast to all those who did not recognize His coming. Only those who knew God by the Spirit enjoyed this initial revelation.

## His Growth to Maturity

Jesus was not created as an adult like the first Adam was. He grew and developed as any other child grows, except that He did not possess any of the detriments of a sinful nature. Luke tells us, "And the child grew, and waxed strong in spirit, filled with wisdom: and the grace of God was upon Him" (Lk. 2:40). Jesus grew into a beautiful young man filled with such wisdom that He astonished the temple rabbis of Jerusalem when He was only 12 years old. He was hearing them and asking them questions, and "all that heard Him were astonished at His understanding and answers" (Lk. 2:47). Jesus' understanding of the Scriptures was not just a result of childhood studies common to Jewish boys, but was the result of the work of the Holy Spirit in Him. Isaiah's prophecy hundreds of years earlier was beginning to be fulfilled when the boy Jesus was in the temple that day, though it would be realized in its fullest sense after His baptism. Isaiah prophesied:

> *And there shall come forth a rod out of the stem of Jesse, and a Branch shall grow out of his roots: and the spirit of the Lord shall rest upon Him, the spirit of wisdom and understanding, the spirit of counsel and might, the spirit of knowledge and of the fear of the Lord; and shall make Him of quick understanding in the fear of the Lord...* (Isaiah 11:1-3).

Christ's divinity could not grow or develop in any way; it was perfect and complete. But His humanity did develop and increase in its abilities by the power of the Holy Spirit.

## His Baptism

John the Baptist was baptizing people in the Jordan when he looked up and saw Jesus coming to him to be baptized. Although John did not feel worthy to baptize the Lamb of God, Jesus said to him, "Suffer it to be so now: for thus it becometh us to fulfil all righteousness..." (Mt. 3:15). When John baptized Jesus, the Spirit of God descended like a dove and lighted upon Him. A voice from Heaven confirmed that Jesus was His beloved Son in whom He was well pleased (Mt. 3:16-17). The Holy Spirit was equipping Jesus, in His baptism, for His earthly ministry that was to follow. But first, He led Him into the wilderness to be tempted by the devil.

## His Temptation

The Scriptures clearly indicate that the Holy Spirit not only led Christ into the wilderness (Mt. 4:1), but that all the time Christ was there the Holy Spirit was with Him, enabling Him to overcome the severe temptations of the evil one. Luke tells us that Jesus was full of the Holy Ghost when He was led by the Spirit into the wilderness (Lk. 4:1). By the power of the Holy Spirit, Jesus' human nature was given the strength to withstand the enemy and to overcome the severe temptations placed before Him. His victory was not because of qualities of His divine nature infused into His human nature, for then He would no longer have been a man. Being a complete man, He relied only on the indwelling Holy Spirit for His ability to resist the temptations of the evil one. When He had conquered temptations of the devil by declaring, "It is written,"

Luke tells us He "returned in the power of the Spirit into Galilee" (Lk. 4:14a).

We know that Jesus was not cornered by the devil. He was led out, or as Mark said, *driven* by the Spirit into the wilderness to meet the enemy (Mk. 1:12). This can be very instructive for believers who find themselves in a place of testing or temptation. The Christian who is subject to temptation or personal testing is not necessarily out of the will of God. There are times in life that we must face the tempter, as Jesus did, with a clear response: "It is written." As we allow ourselves to be filled with the Holy Spirit, we have the same possibility of victory as Jesus, who conquered the devil through the power of the Holy Spirit.

## His Ministry

The Holy Spirit anointed Jesus with power for His earthly ministry as well. Jesus, Himself, attributed His works to the divine anointing of the Holy Spirit who worked through Him when He stood in the temple and declared:

*The Spirit of the Lord is upon Me, because He hath anointed Me to preach the gospel to the poor; He hath sent Me to heal the broken-hearted, to preach deliverance to the captives, and recovering of sight to the blind, to set at liberty them that are bruised, to preach the acceptable year of the Lord* (Luke 4:18-19).

Peter also preached this truth to the house of Cornelius, telling them that "God anointed Jesus of Nazareth with the Holy Ghost and with power: who went about doing good, and healing all that were oppressed of the devil; for God was with Him" (Acts 10:38). It was through the divine power of the Holy Spirit that Jesus could do miracles. The Pharisees had accused Jesus of casting out demons by the power of Beelzebub, the prince of demons. But Jesus showed them the foolishness of thinking that satan would cast out himself. Then He instructed them that if He "cast out devils by the Spirit of God, then the kingdom of God is come unto you" (Mt. 12:28). His ministry was performed by the power of the Holy Spirit who is also resident within us today as Spirit-filled believers.

## His Transfiguration

*...Jesus taketh Peter, James, and John his brother, and bringeth them up into an high mountain apart, and was transfigured before them: and His face did shine as the sun, and His raiment was white as the light* (Matthew 17:1-2).

When Jesus was transfigured before His disciples, the unveiling of the glory of God that was in Him was seen in His human vessel. That unveiling was done by the blessed Holy Spirit. How awesome that the manifested presence of the glory of the infinite God was seen for a few moments by the disciples! Is it any wonder that Peter wanted to build three tabernacles?

## His Death

It was not enough that Jesus suffer and die for our sins; He had to do so in the proper manner. Abraham Kuyper expresses this fact so clearly:

> Christ did not redeem us by His suffering alone, being spit upon, scourged, crowned with thorns, crucified, slain. This passion was made effectual to our redemption by His love and voluntary obedience. Hence there was in Christ's suffering much more than mere passive penal satisfaction. Nobody compelled Christ. He who partook of the divine nature could not be compelled but offered Himself voluntarily. "Lo I come to do thy will, Oh God, in the volume of the Book it is written of Me."[5]

Jesus was empowered and enabled by the Holy Spirit to offer this acceptable sacrifice for the sins of the whole world. The Scriptures, comparing Jesus' sacrifice to that of the blood of bulls and goats, declare: "How much more shall the blood of Christ, who through the eternal Spirit offered Himself without spot to God, purge your conscience from dead works to serve the living God?" (Heb. 9:14) The perfection of Christ's sacrifice in His obedient, loving attitude was made possible by the eternal Spirit of God. Without the enabling of the Holy Spirit, the Man, Jesus, could not have offered Himself as a perfect sacrifice to God.

## His Resurrection

Sometimes the resurrection of Jesus is attributed to the Father (Acts 2:24). Other times it is said to be the work of the Son Himself (Jn. 10:17-18). But the resurrection is also in a special way the work of the Holy Spirit. Our intent is not to separate the Godhead in our thinking, but to show the inter-relatedness of Their working together to accomplish the redemption of mankind. Paul writes, "But if the Spirit of Him that raised up Jesus from the dead dwell in you, He that raised up Christ from the dead shall also quicken your mortal bodies by His Spirit that dwelleth in you" (Rom. 8:11). The Spirit of God working with the Father gave resurrection life to Jesus. He still offers that same resurrection life to every believer who will receive from His hand the things of Jesus.

## Birthing the Church

In Volume 1, *Presenting the Holy Spirit: Who Is He?* we outlined the seven offices of the Holy Spirit and how He executes them. We observed the Holy Spirit's work in salvation, understanding that the believer is born again by the power of the Holy Spirit. Jesus stated clearly that if a man is not born of water and of the Spirit, he cannot see the Kingdom of God (Jn. 3:5). Natural life is given by natural birth. Spiritual life can only be given by being born again from above by the Spirit of God.

Adam lost his spiritual life when he sinned. Many believe it was the indwelling presence of the Holy Spirit that he lost. God had warned that death would follow disobedience to His word. Because of his sin, Adam was left in spiritual darkness and was spiritually dead. Myer Pearlman describes the terrible results of this loss of the Holy Spirit in unregenerate man since the fall:

> In relation to understanding, the unconverted cannot know the things of the Spirit of God (I Cor. 2:14). In relation to the will, he cannot be subject to the law of God (Rom. 8:7). In relation to worship, he cannot call Jesus Lord (I Cor. 12:3). As regards practice, he cannot please God (Rom. 8:8). In regard to character he cannot bear spiritual fruit (Jn. 15:4). In regard to faith he cannot receive the spirit of truth (Jn. 14:17). This new spiritual life is imparted to the believer through the indwelling Holy Spirit which is the mark of a New Testament Christian. "But ye are not in the flesh but in the Spirit if so be the Spirit of God dwelleth in you..." (Rom. 8:9.) One of the most comprehensive definitions of a Christian is that he is a man in whom the Holy Spirit dwells. His body is the temple of the Holy Ghost in virtue of which experience he is sanctified as the tabernacle was consecrated by Jehovah's indwelling (I Cor. 6:19). This is not to be confused with the baptism of the Holy Spirit

which is an outpouring of the Spirit *after* salvation. It is not the impartation of spiritual life but rather power for spiritual service.[6] (Emphasis added.)

Jesus' death and resurrection made it possible for all the effects of the fall of man to be reversed. We have only to believe on Him and be born again from above by the Spirit of God to begin living a life that God ordained for us from the beginning. Today, His Church on the earth is intended to be the Body of Christ demonstrating to the world the supernatural life that is received through the Holy Spirit.

## Commissioning the Disciples

During the 40 days He remained on earth after His resurrection, Christ also gave commandments to His disciples by the power of the Holy Spirit. Luke declares, "Until the day in which He was taken up, after that He through the Holy Ghost had given commandments unto the apostles whom He had chosen" (Acts 1:2). It was "through the Holy Ghost" that the Lord Jesus gave the commandments to the disciples, commissioning them and sending them forth. This teaches us how vital the power of the Holy Ghost is today to the ministry of the servants of the Lord.

As the Holy Spirit guides each Christian who is serving God, it is wonderful to realize that it is the voice of Jesus speaking to them as He did when He commissioned His first disciples. It is the same Jesus who commanded those first disciples who is today guiding, commanding, commissioning, and directing His servants by the same blessed Holy Spirit. We are not dependent upon the physical presence of the Lord to be led by Him. Our guidance comes, as it did then, by the work of the Holy Spirit in our lives.

## Baptizing the Church

Perhaps the most important thing that Jesus has done for His followers, after having purchased their redemption by His death and resurrection, is to baptize them with the Holy Spirit. John the Baptist declared to his followers that when the Lamb of God comes, "He shall baptize you with the Holy Ghost, and with fire" (Mt. 3:11c). As necessary as the Holy Spirit's presence was in all the ministry of our Savior, it is no wonder He was so intent that those who carry on His work would also be empowered by the same mighty Holy Spirit.

It is indeed wonderful that believers today have this same Spirit, this same empowering, and this same anointing. How else could His work be accomplished? Jesus said, "...He that believeth on Me, the works that I do shall he do also; and greater works than these shall he do; because I go unto My Father" (Jn. 14:12). He made provision for believers to be empowered by the Holy Spirit in the same way He was, and to do greater works than He did. I personally cannot do a greater miracle than Jesus. By "greater works" is meant that through many people, the Church, more miracles will be accomplished. The corporate Body of Christ can minister to multitudes that Jesus, as one Man, could not reach. As the Head of His Body, the Church, Jesus knew that greater works would be accomplished through God's eternal plan for a glorious Church on earth when He returned to His Father.

## Progressive Sanctification

The Holy Spirit's work is to first bring light to the darkness of unbelievers, lovingly wooing them to accept the sacrifice of Jesus. In Volume 1, we described how the Holy Spirit baptizes the believer into the Body of Christ. We also saw that the Holy Spirit bears witness to the believer who has been born again and is now a child of God. All this takes place in regard to our salvation when we are born again. Then, subsequent to regeneration, the Holy Spirit begins to do a specific work that is different from that of the new birth. He begins to sanctify the believer, making him holy in thought, motive, and deed. This is a beautiful process that takes place as He changes us "from glory to glory" and imparts to us the character of our Lord Jesus Christ, bringing us to maturity. In order to accomplish this work, the Holy Spirit enables us to mortify the deeds of the flesh.

The Scriptures teach clearly that if we live after the flesh we will die, but if we through the Spirit do mortify the deeds of the body, we shall live (Rom. 8:5-13).

The word *carnal* in the Scriptures describes that which is fleshly, pertaining to the old man, our Adamic nature. That is the nature the Christian must endure until the Holy Spirit comes to enable him to mortify his flesh and live victoriously in the Spirit. The Holy Spirit's work is to restore us into the image of God, producing His character in us as we continually yield ourselves to Him.

## THREEFOLD REVELATION

The Holy Spirit has come to reveal the life of our precious Lord Jesus (a) *to* us, (b) *in* us, and (c)*through* us. As He does this precious threefold work, Christ will be able to live His life in us and through us. In the first aspect of this threefold revelation of Jesus Christ, the Holy Spirit reveals Jesus *to* the believer, which results in regeneration, as we have discussed. Then He comes to produce the fruit of the Spirit *in* the believer so that the life of our Lord Jesus becomes our life. The fruit of the Spirit is a description of the character of Christ (Gal. 5:22-23). In order to produce the character of Christ in us, He enables us to exchange our self-life for the Christ-life, thereby sanctifying us. As this fruit abounds in the life of the believer, he is growing unto the measure of the stature of the fullness of Christ (Eph. 4:13).

Then the Holy Spirit works *through* believers in the ministry of service to the Body of Christ and to the world. Through His baptism, He equips us to minister to others by giving us revelation of the Word of God and by helping us to pray according to the will of God. He gives spiritual gifts for this purpose and anoints us for the fulfilling of His purposes. We must remember, however, that the Holy Spirit never magnifies Himself or any human vessel through whom He operates. He came to magnify and glorify, extol and honor the Person and ministry of our Lord Jesus Christ. Whenever the Holy Spirit is truly having His way, Christ alone is exalted.

On the Day of Pentecost, Peter declared, "Therefore let all the house of Israel know assuredly, that God hath made that same Jesus, whom ye have crucified, both Lord and Christ" (Acts 2:36). Jesus has been exalted to the right hand of the Father, and the Holy Spirit has come to magnify Him. In Old Testament times, God was magnified through the law and the prophets. Then when Jesus came in the flesh, He was the manifestation of God to the world. Now God manifests Himself to the world through the Holy Spirit's revelation of Christ through human vessels, believers who allow the character of Christ to be developed in their lives.

*When He is come!* What a precious reality awaits every heart and church that gives the Holy Spirit His rightful place. There is no other way to know God except the Spirit of God reveal Him to our hearts. As we prepare to seek Him, we can be assured that He *will* come, for it is His will to reveal Jesus to every seeking heart. The Holy Spirit calls every person to come to God and receive full redemption as Christ provided it. Our positive response to Him will assure us of a divine relationship with God that He intended for us to enjoy.

## Notes

1. Author unknown.

2. George Smeaton, *The Doctrine of the Holy Spirit*, (London: Banner of Truth Trust, 1958), p. 178.

3. Ibid.

4. G. Campbell Morgan, *The Gospel According to John*, (New York: Fleming H. Revell Co., 1943).

5. Abraham Kuyper, *The Work of the Holy Spirit*, (Grand Rapids, Michigan: Wm. Eerdmans Publication Co.).

6. Myer Pearlman, *Knowing the Doctrine of the Bible*, (Springfield, Missouri: Gospel Publishing House, 1937), p. 306-307.

# Chapter 2

# *The Baptism of the Holy Spirit*

## *Divine Enduement With Power*

*For John truly baptized with water; but ye shall be baptized with the Holy Ghost not many days hence* (Acts 1:5).

The word *baptism* comes from the Greek word *baptizo*, which means "to be put into or buried into, made a participant or partaker." It does not mean being poured upon, as some have interpreted it to mean. Baptism involves three distinct elements. First there is a baptizer; second, a candidate; and third, an element into which the candidate is baptized. Baptism cannot occur with only one person present; there must be a candidate and a baptizer. Several different baptisms are taught in the Scriptures where these three elements are present to effect true baptism.

## DOCTRINE OF BAPTISMS

The Scriptures refer to the doctrine of baptisms in the plural form of the word. They teach us that baptisms are among the foundation stones of our faith. For example, we are admonished to leave the doctrine of baptisms and other foundational teachings to go on to maturity (Heb. 6:1-2). It follows, then, that if we are not settled in these basic doctrines, we cannot mature properly. Is a person's spiritual foundation solid, who has not been a participant in all the baptisms? No. To become mature Christians, we must first embrace these foundational doctrines. God intends for our lives to become strong "spiritual buildings" for the purpose of Christ inhabiting them.

If a foundation stone is missing, or if it does not fit properly, that building will be shaky. There is nothing wrong with going to God and saying, "My foundation is not secure. If I need a stone changed or put in, please do it. I don't want to be shaken when the winds come." In times of testing, the house that is not secure on its foundation will fall.

If the foundation stone of repentance is not laid correctly in our lives, for example, we won't be stable in our walk with God. Without the assurance that we are born again and at peace with God, we will realize one day that we have been trying to live a life style we don't have the power to live. Nothing can substitute for repentance as the basis for peace with God. How are we going to *walk* in the Spirit, be *led* by the Spirit, *abide* in the Spirit, and *cooperate* with the Spirit if we are not first born again?

Some have never identified themselves with Christ's death by participating in water baptism. That foundation stone is lacking in their lives. Others need to be endued with power from on high—baptized in the Holy Spirit. And all must take up their cross daily and follow Christ even into the baptism of suffering, yielding to the Holy Spirit in their trials and learning to exchange their lives for Christ's. Only as these foundation stones are properly laid can believers expect to mature in Christ.

As we observe briefly these biblical baptisms, we are not discussing them in order as we experience them. For example, some people receive the baptism in the Holy Spirit before participating in water baptism; others receive water baptism first. The Scriptures cite instances of these baptisms happening in both orders.[1] Yet each of these baptisms needs to be a part of our personal experience if we expect to fulfill God's purposes for our lives.

*Baptism of Repentance*

Jesus referred to the baptism that John preached as the *baptism of repentance.*[2] There were believers in the New Testament who were asked with what baptism they were baptized, and they replied, "with the baptism of John" (see Acts 18:25). John the Baptist came to "prepare the way of the Lord and make His paths straight" (see Mt. 3:3). Closer study shows that he preached a fivefold message. First, he preached *repentance*, crying out, "Repent ye: for the kingdom of heaven is at hand" (Mt. 3:2). Second, he preached *remission of sins*, baptizing those in water who confessed their sins (Mt. 3:6). Third, he preached *restitution* for wrongdoing (Lk. 3:11-14); and fourth, he preached the *receiving of the Holy Spirit* when Jesus came. John the Baptist declared, "I indeed baptize you with water; but one mightier than I cometh, the latchet of whose shoes I am not worthy to unloose: He shall baptize you with the Holy Ghost and with fire" (Lk. 3:16). Fifth, he preached *righteousness*, crying, "Make straight the way of the Lord, as said the prophet Esaias [Isaiah]" (Jn. 1:23b). The baptism of John is the first baptism every person must experience to become a born-again Christian. Repentance is the requirement for coming to Jesus.

The Scriptures teach that through repentance, not only are we born again, but we also are baptized into the Body of Christ, the family of God. The apostle Paul wrote to the Corinthians, "For by one Spirit are we all baptized into one body..." (1 Cor. 12:13). What does that mean? Being placed into the family of God is a real happening. It places us into the Church, a living organism of which Christ is the Head. The Word, the seed of God, is placed into our dead spirits and we are quickened and made alive, born of His Spirit. In that supernatural quickening, we become a part of His Body, baptized into the Body of Christ.

We can easily define the three elements of baptism in this experience. The Holy Spirit is the baptizer, and we are the candidates for baptism. What is the element into which the Holy Spirit baptizes us? The Body of Christ, the Church. We are dependent upon the work of the Holy Spirit for the very initiation of our life in God as well as for every aspect of its development. Thank God for this convicting power of the Holy Spirit that shows us our sin and cleanses us when we confess it. Through the gift of repentance, the Holy Spirit is able to baptize us into the Body of Christ.

## Baptism in Water

The second baptism we see in the Scriptures is *baptism in water*. This baptism follows our baptism into the Body of Christ; it is a public demonstration that we are following Jesus' example in baptism.[3] In water baptism, of course, the baptizer is the minister, the candidate is the believer, and water is the element into which we are baptized. Although these three elements all pertain to the natural realm as opposed to the spiritual, we must not think that this baptism is merely a physical ceremony.

Water baptism is a spiritual reality. It is an experience of our being identified with Christ. It is our testimony of declaring that our old man is identified with Christ in His death, burial, and resurrection. We miss the significance of our identification with Christ if we believe that water baptism is only an external ceremony. Our participation in water baptism makes us a partaker of this identification with Christ in His death.

God doesn't ever ask us to play-act. Because water baptism is a spiritual experience, when we are baptized in water we should expect a change to take place in our lives that will declare to the world that salvation is working in us. It is a time of appropriating the greater aspect of the redemptive work of Christ: an identification with the death of our self-nature. In this act we declare that our natural self-life is dead, and we become a partaker of His death for our death. The circumcision of our hearts begins with this obedience to follow Christ in water baptism. God begins cutting away the sinful and destructive self-life as we raise a tombstone in that watery grave and declare, with John, "He must increase, but I must decrease" (Jn. 3:30).

### Baptism Into the Holy Spirit

Third, there is the *baptism into the Holy Spirit*, which we want to study in more depth in this chapter.

To properly define this baptism, we must address the erroneous teaching of some who believe that baptism into the Holy Spirit is the same as our baptism into the Body of Christ. Understanding the three elements involved in baptism helps to clarify this confusion.

Of course, the candidates who are believers in Christ are the same for both the baptism into the Body of Christ and the baptism of the Holy Spirit. It is the baptizer who is different. As we have seen, the Holy Spirit baptized us into the Body of Christ. According to the Scriptures, however, it is Jesus who baptizes us into the Holy Spirit. John declared, "I indeed baptize you with water; but one mightier than I cometh, the latchet of whose shoes I am not worthy to unloose: He shall baptize you with the Holy Ghost and with fire" (Lk. 3:16). In this baptism, the Holy Spirit becomes the divine element into whom we are baptized. After the Holy Spirit baptizes us into the Body of Christ, it is Christ who baptizes us into the Holy Spirit, filling us to overflowing with the Third Person of the Godhead.

So we see the three members of the Godhead working in the redemption of a soul. Jesus taught, "If a man love Me, he will keep My words: and My Father will love him, and We will come unto him, and make Our abode with him" (Jn. 14:23). He also said that the Holy Spirit "dwelleth with you, and shall be in you" (Jn. 14:17b). The Father, the Son, and the Holy Spirit, the entire Godhead, dwell in the believer. They are in us and we are in Them—part of the family of God.

## Baptism of Suffering

A final baptism that we must mention as taught in the Scriptures is the *baptism of suffering*. Jesus said, "But I have a baptism to undergo, and how distressed I am until it is accomplished!" (Lk. 12:50 NAS) He was, of course, referring to His death on the cross. Jesus knew He would have to endure a baptism of suffering because that was the purpose for which He came. He not only endured the physical agony of death by crucifixion, but also the emotional and mental anguish of becoming the sin offering, bearing the sins of the whole world. It was the Father who baptized Jesus into this suffering. Jesus referred to it as the cup His Father had given Him. In Jesus' agony in Gethsemane, we hear Him pray to His Father, "Nevertheless not My will, but Thine, be done" (Lk. 22:42b). It was the cross of Calvary that was the element used to effect this baptism of suffering as a vicarious, propitiary sacrifice for the salvation of mankind.

Jesus did not exempt His disciples from a similar fiery baptism. When the mother of James and John took her sons to ask Jesus to let them sit, one on the right hand and the other on the left in His Kingdom, Jesus said to them, "Ye know not what ye ask. Are ye able to drink of the cup that I shall drink of, and to be baptized with the baptism that I am baptized with?..." (Mt. 20:22). When they assured Him they were able, He replied that they would know His baptism, but it was not His to say who would sit with Him in glory. And He taught His disciples, "If anyone wishes to come after Me, let him deny himself, and take up his cross, and follow Me" (Mt. 16:24 NAS). A cross is for crucifixion, and that means suffering.

As we surrender to the Christ-life, we find that where the will of God contradicts our wills, there a cross is laid upon our self-lives that causes suffering and death. When our thoughts and desires do not agree with God's, we must choose to deny them. In that denial we find the cross upon which they must die. What should be our attitude in this suffering? We should not become morbid in it. Instead, we should respond as Jesus did, "who for the joy that was set before Him endured the cross" (Heb. 12:2b). Although there is death on one side of the cross, there is life on the other, for out of death comes life. Resurrection power awaits us on the other side of the cross. Paul declared this:

*For if we have become united with Him in the likeness of His death, certainly we shall be also in the likeness of His resurrection, knowing this, that our old self was crucified with Him, that our body of sin might be done away with, that we should no longer be slaves to sin* (Romans 6:5-6 NAS).

Our suffering brings death to our sin nature, which we exchange for the nature of Christ in resurrection life. All suffering is not caused by our personal sin. Whatever cross the Father ordains for us, however, in our personal baptism of suffering, we must be willing to yield to submissively. It is a matter of consecration, the giving up of our will, our way, our walk, our words, our works, our worship, and our warfare in exchange for His. In this way we will enter into the fellowship of His sufferings and be transformed into the image of Christ.

## UNDERSTANDING THE BAPTISM OF THE HOLY SPIRIT

Having seen the scriptural pattern of baptisms, we can focus now on the significance of what it means to be baptized into the Holy Spirit.[4] We must always keep in mind that we cannot receive anything from God without the work of the Holy Spirit. As we have seen, it is the Holy Spirit who convicts us of sin, washing it away in the blood of the Lamb when we repent. So He is working in our lives before we are saved to draw us to God and cause us to recognize our need of Him. It is He who bears witness in our spirits that we are born-again children of God.

Then, after we are born again, there is an "enduement with power" that Jesus promised to His disciples. Just before He ascended into the clouds, Jesus specifically instructed His disciples to wait for the enduement of power they would receive when the Holy Spirit came. To understand this baptism more fully, it will help us to study the disciples' experience of new birth and their subsequent enduement with power on the Day of Pentecost.

*Resurrection Morning*

The morning that Jesus rose from the dead, Mary Magdalene had gone to His tomb. When she found the tomb empty and had announced her findings to the disciples, they ran to investigate what had happened. After they left, Mary was standing outside the tomb crying, when she saw a man there whom she thought must be the gardener. How sweet must have been her joy when Jesus called her name and she recognized her lovely Savior! As she fell to worship Him, He asked her not to touch Him, saying, "I have not yet ascended to the Father..." (Jn. 20:17 NAS). He couldn't let her touch Him because, as our High Priest, He had to present Himself to the Father as the spotless Lamb slain for our sins.

Jesus came to earth to fulfill all the law of God. According to that law, the high priest took the blood of the slain lamb into the holiest of holies in the tabernacle. From the time they were cleansed until they went into the holy place, the Old Testament priests were not allowed to be defiled by man. The law said that if the priest was clean when he went into the presence of God with the blood sacrifice, he would live. Otherwise, he would die in the presence of God. When the priest came out of the tabernacle, he declared to the people that their sins were covered for another year. The blood of the lamb had atoned for their sins.

Jesus had prayed His priestly prayer, died, and had risen from the dead. But when He saw Mary that morning, He had not yet gone into the heavenly tabernacle as our slain Lamb, so she could not touch Him. He had been cleansed; He was alive; He became the Lamb slain that the Old Testament types had foreshadowed. Never again would there have to be a lamb slain because Jesus became the eternal paschal sacrifice for sin. We know Jesus was accepted in the Father's presence during the first part of resurrection day because He came back to appear to His disciples. Jesus carried His own blood into the presence of God and sprinkled it on the heavenly mercy seat. When He came back that day, He had fulfilled all the types and shadows regarding the atonement.

Until the day of Jesus' death on the cross, everyone had looked forward in time to the coming of the Messiah—every type and shadow pointed to the Lamb of God who would take away the sin of the world. Those who walked in obedience to the law were counted righteous. When Jesus walked on this earth, He was still under the law and He fulfilled the law by walking in obedience to His Father without sin.

Jesus' supreme sacrifice became the mediatorial, efficacious, vicarious, substitutionary work of redemption.

Each of those words explains what happened at Calvary. His dying was mediatorial; He became our mediator before the justice of God. Efficacious means it is as effective today as it was the day He died. Vicarious and substitutionary mean He died in my stead the death I deserved to die. But Jesus didn't complete the redeeming work until He went to Heaven, took His blood, and came back as a spiritual being in a glorified body.

Then He appeared on the road to Emmaus and walked with two disciples (not of the 12 disciples), causing their hearts to burn as He opened the Scriptures to them. At the end of that day, as the disciples were in an upper room with the doors locked, Jesus came and· stood among them and said, "Peace." He showed them His hands and His side. (See Luke 24.) The disciples were overjoyed! There was no doubt in their minds that this was their Lord. He could not be an imposter—He had been crucified and now He was alive!

### Divine Breath

Later Jesus *breathed* on them and said to them, "Receive the Holy Spirit" (Jn. 20:22 NAS). When He breathed on them, He breathed His life into them. Jesus was no longer *with* them; He would now be *in* them. This is what Paul described as "Christ in you, the hope of glory" (Col. 1:27). That was the day the "Jesus" who had walked with and worked through the disciples became "The Christ" of His Church through this divine impartation to His disciples. Then, as we shall see, the Church was baptized in the Holy Spirit on the Day of Pentecost.

Although some evangelicals teach that the disciples' experience of receiving Jesus' breath was the same as the baptism of the Holy Spirit, it is clear from the Scriptures that the disciples did not receive His baptism here, but His breath. The Greek word used here for breath is *pneuma*. The Greek word for baptism, as we have seen, is *baptizo*. There is a great difference between being breathed upon and being baptized. Although they did receive an impartation of Christ's life when He breathed on them, their baptism in the Holy Spirit was still to come.

### Divine Blessing

Later, just before His ascension, Jesus led His disciples out to Bethany and *blessed* them. That blessing is a reality that Jesus gives to all who are born again. In that setting He also gave them the commission to preach the gospel to the whole world.

### Divine Baptism

It was during these same days before His ascension that Jesus instructed His disciples to wait in Jerusalem, saying, "For John truly baptized with water; but ye shall be baptized with the Holy Ghost not many days hence" (Acts 1:5). This was the promise of the Father of whom Jesus had said, "He dwelleth with you, and shall be in you" (Jn. 14:17b).

Although people had not been baptized in the Holy Spirit before, He did move *upon* people in the Old Testament. I have found 17 places in the Scriptures that the Holy Spirit moved upon people. And most, if not all, of the gifts of the Holy Spirit listed in the New Testament operated through these Old Testament saints as well. People who were moved upon by the Holy Spirit prophesied, had words of wisdom, words of knowledge, power to work miracles, and power to heal. The Scriptures declare that the Holy Spirit settled upon them to empower them for these supernatural acts.

Now, in the fullness of time, the Father would send the Comforter at Jesus' request. The disciples could expect the Holy Spirit to come on a certain day because He had always fulfilled all of the feast days and oblations. The more we study the precious truths revealed through scriptural types and shadows, the better we understand that God's timing was according to divine pattern. The Holy Spirit would not come any other day but the Day of Pentecost because He *is* Pentecost.

The Day of Pentecost was the second period of the Jewish feast days. The first included the Feast of Unleavened Bread, Feast of Passover, and Feast of Firstfruits—representing the death, burial, and resurrection of our Lord. Jesus had just fulfilled this first period of feasts by His death and resurrection, providing the reality it foreshadowed. Fifty days later in the Jewish calendar, the head of every Jewish family was supposed to come to the temple on Pentecost Day to celebrate the Feast of Pentecost. Since Jesus had been with His disciples for 40 days after His resurrection, there were only 10 days left before the Feast of Pentecost would arrive.

What a thrilling account Luke gives us of the Holy Spirit's coming! He wrote:

*And when the day of Pentecost was fully come, they were all with one accord in one place. And suddenly there came a sound from heaven as of a rushing mighty wind, and it filled all the house where they were sitting. And there appeared unto them cloven tongues like as of fire, and it sat upon each of them. And they were all filled with the Holy Ghost, and began to speak with other tongues, as the Spirit gave them utterance* (Acts 2:1-4).

It was on that day when the disciples and all those in the upper room were baptized in the Holy Spirit that the world first saw the Church. The Church was baptized on the Day of Pentecost. The disciples were saved before the Day of Pentecost, filled with joy and commissioned by Jesus. Then the Church was empowered as Jesus had promised on the Day of Pentecost and displayed to the world.

## *Two Kinds of Tongues*

Many sincere Christian people have not accepted the reality of the baptism of the Holy Spirit with the initial evidence of speaking in tongues because they have not understood what happened on the Day of Pentecost. Some evangelical denominations teach that the gifts of the Spirit functioned only in the early Church and are not functioning today. According to this teaching, the disciples received the *gift* of tongues (as taught in First Corinthians 12) on the Day of Pentecost. Because some evangelicals believe that the gifts are not operating in the Church today, they teach that believers do not speak in tongues now when they receive the baptism of the Holy Spirit. Some teach that the other spiritual gifts Paul listed for the Corinthians are not necessary for the Church today either, although they concede that God could use them if He wanted to, for example, on the mission field as a sign to unbelievers.

Evangelicals also teach that God gave spiritual gifts, such as tongues, to the early Church mainly to show there was no difference between the Jews and the Gentiles. They point to passages such as Acts 10, which relates the story of Cornelius and his household of Gentiles who received the Holy Spirit. Those Jews present knew that the Holy Spirit was poured out on the Gentiles because they "heard them speak with tongues, and magnify God..." (Acts 10:46). That purpose having been accomplished, there is no need for these gifts to function today, according to those who embrace this theology.

I was trained in this evangelical theology, so I did not accept the fact of tongues as the initial evidence of receiving the baptism of the Holy Spirit. As I studied the Scriptures, however, desiring to know the truth regarding this biblical experience, I went to a Pentecostal preacher to ask him if he could define for me the tongues in the second chapter of Acts. My question was, "Did the disciples speak with a tongue of ecstasy that was the initial evidence of the baptism of the Holy Spirit, as well as the gift of tongues as taught in First Corinthians chapter 12?" If there were two kinds of tongues there, I would accept the doctrine of the baptism of the Holy Spirit that is subsequent to regeneration as the Pentecostals teach.

I knew, from studying the Word, that the gift of tongues needed to be interpreted and that it was given to edify and to convince the unbeliever. I also read in Acts that on the Day of Pentecost, men from many nations heard in their own languages the disciples speaking of the glories of God, and 3,000 souls were saved. It was obvious to me that the gift of tongues was functioning there. Yet Pentecostals teach that the tongues a person speaks when baptized in the Holy Spirit is unknown to all except God. The conflict in my understanding was I saw the gift of tongues in action on the Day of Pentecost, but did not see the unknown tongues as the initial evidence of the baptism of the Holy Spirit operating that day.

When I asked this Pentecostal minister if he could differentiate the tongues for me in Acts 2, he declared that the gift of tongues was not operating on the Day of Pentecost. I had read Acts too well to accept that. I repeated, "You mean that is not the gift of tongues as listed in First Corinthians chapter 12 that was functioning when all nations heard God glorified in their own languages?" He said, "No, the gift of tongues did not function on the Day of Pentecost." His answer discouraged me from accepting the reality of this baptism, for I knew the gift of tongues was functioning that day. Because I thought that the gifts were not for today, I felt that speaking in tongues could not be a part of the baptism of the Holy Spirit.

What I didn't understand had happened on the Day of Pentecost, took me 17 years to realize. Only then could I receive this experience as God intended it. Since receiving the baptism of the Holy Spirit with the evidence of speaking in tongues, I have been able to help scores of evangelical people receive this wonderful experience because of the light I received from my divine Teacher.

## Day of Pentecost Revisited

What happened that historical day when the Holy Spirit descended upon the disciples? When the drama opens in the second chapter of Acts, it is the Day of Pentecost. It is a feast day of the Jews for which many came to Jerusalem from every nation. These Jews are meeting in the temple. In the upper room, something else is happening. Let's open the curtain on the first scene of this drama. There are 120 people sitting in a little upstairs room. When the Day of Pentecost was fully come, or dawned, the Holy Spirit came to them. The Jewish tradition considered the time of daybreak as six o'clock in the morning. So I believe the Scriptures are specifically stating that the Holy Spirit arrived at six o'clock in the morning, at the dawning of the Day of Pentecost. This fact will become more significant as the drama unfolds.

Now, as we watch this scene unfold at daybreak, the Scriptures say, "And suddenly there came from heaven a noise like a violent, rushing wind, and it filled the whole house where they were sitting" (Acts 2:2 NAS). The Scriptures clearly state that this was the Holy Spirit coming. And when He came, "there appeared to them tongues as of fire distributing themselves, and they rested on each one of them" (Acts 2:3 NAS).

Each person was filled with the Holy Spirit and began to speak with other tongues as the Spirit was giving them utterance. The Phillips translation renders this tongue, "the tongue of ecstasy," which means "an overflow of something inside that has spilled out." When this supernatural splash took place, 120 people "overflowed." They were speaking in a language that didn't mean anything to anyone but God. No one understood this ecstatic language of the Spirit. When these 120 people exploded in an ecstatic expression of praise to God given by the Holy Spirit, it caused a stir in the city that created the next scene of this divine drama.

When the curtain opens on scene two, something has happened in the town. "Now there were Jews living in Jerusalem, devout men, from every nation under heaven" (Acts 2:5 NAS). The crowd in the temple was going through the *ritual* of Pentecost, not knowing that the *reality* of Pentecost had come in Person. When they heard the sound from the upper room, "the multitude came together, and were bewildered, because they were each one hearing them speak in his own language" (Acts 2:6 NAS). This multitude is not in the upper room, for there were too many people to have fit into that small area. The people in the upper room have gone out to see the multitude. It is at this time that these Jews from every nation hear the disciples speaking in languages that they can understand.

The tongues the multitude hears are not Heaven's language of ecstasy that the disciples received at the dawning of the day. What the multitude hears now in their own languages is called "divers tongues" in the Scriptures, which are tongues specifically given for the unbeliever to hear (1 Cor. 14). The disciples couldn't have spoken in these divers tongues if they had not received the baptism in the Holy Spirit and spoken in tongues of ecstasy, for it is He who gives the gift of tongues. They were baptized in the upper room as "tongues as of fire" sat on each of them. They have been talking to God since the dawning of the morning in tongues of ecstasy, and now God is speaking back through them to the nations in divers tongues.

To show us which nations were there and what languages they spoke, the Scriptures list the nationalities. "Parthians and Medes and Elamites, and residents of Mesopotamia, Judea and Cappadocia, Pontus and Asia, Phrygia and Pamphylia, Egypt and the districts of Libya around Cyrene, and visitors from Rome, both Jews and proselytes, Cretans and Arabs..." were all present (Acts 2:9-11 NAS). These unbelievers heard messages from God in their own languages supernaturally. God communicated His message to every nation in a matter of a few hours, without the help of television or satellites like we have today.

It is Peter who sets the time period of this scene for us as three hours after the Holy Spirit first came to the disciples in the upper room. When some mocked and said that the disciples were full of sweet wine, Peter stood up and reminded them that people did not drink that early in the day, at nine o'clock in the morning. The Holy Spirit had come when the Day of Pentecost had fully dawned, probably about six o'clock in the morning. So the disciples had spoken in tongues of ecstasy for two or three hours before the "unbelievers" from all those nations showed up. It was when the disciples came to greet the multitude that the Holy Spirit gave them divers tongues to communicate to all the nations represented the glories of God they were experiencing.

That Pentecostal preacher couldn't answer my question and I spent 17 years serving God without receiving an answer. I knew the gift of tongues was operating on the Day of Pentecost because I had read how Paul described it to the Corinthians. But I didn't understand that the tongue of ecstasy came to those disciples before the gift of tongues did until a precious saint of God, Rev. Ralph Byrd, walked by me one morning when I was praying, and asked, "What time of day did the disciples get the baptism?"

I replied smartly, "Nine o'clock." He said, "I asked you what time the *disciples* were baptized." I repeated, "Nine o'clock." He didn't accept my answer. He asked me again, a third time, the same question. I looked at him intently and said, "Daddy Byrd, I don't know much, but Peter said it was nine o'clock." He retorted, "I didn't ask you what time Peter said it was." Then he walked off and left me without explaining anything. So I got my Bible and began to study and talk to my Teacher. It was then He made me to understand the difference between the tongues of ecstasy the disciples received at the dawning of the day, and the gift of tongues that operated through them for the multitude in the second scene when Peter, defending them, said it was but nine o'clock in the morning. This understanding dispelled my confusion for I saw that the coming of the Holy Spirit included the initial baptism of the Holy Spirit with the 120 as the day dawned in that small upper room. Those who had tarried there were "all filled" and spoke ecstatically in other tongues, glorifying God. Then, later that morning, the multitudes came and God gave the disciples divers tongues to declare the works of God to all the nations, and 3,000 unbelievers were saved.

I have a deep concern for others to be able to differentiate between the initial evidence of Holy Spirit baptism, where speaking in tongues is an overflow in a language known only to God, and the tongue that is interpreted to man and understood, as Paul teaches (1 Cor. 12). We announced in a meeting recently that people should invite their denominational friends to come to a special meeting where we would teach concerning the baptism of the Holy Spirit. We believed that as we taught the clarity of this truth, they would see and understand. In that meeting, 48 people received the baptism of the Holy Spirit through our simply reading chapter 2 from the Book of Acts and dividing it into the two scenes of God's drama on Pentecost Day. When we finished reading, these sincere Christians came to the altar and received the baptism of the Holy Spirit with the evidence of speaking in tongues.

## Why Tongues?

Why do we need to speak with tongues as an evidence of receiving the baptism of the Holy Spirit? Perhaps we need to answer this question first: Why were 17 different nationalities in Jerusalem that day witnessing the phenomena of the disciples glorifying God in their languages? God, in original creation, made one language until men decided to build the tower of Babel and become as God, and so pride entered their hearts. Then God confused their languages and scattered them across the earth. From the time of the building of the tower of Babel to the Day of Pentecost, nothing brought men together in one language.

On the Day of Pentecost, as the disciples had humbled themselves to wait for the promise of the Father, God had a message for all mankind. He didn't deliver His message through confusion; every man heard it in his language. Now, for the first time since Babel, the Body of Christ can speak the same language, a heavenly one. The language of the Holy Spirit is the only language that is not a part of the curse. It is a language of the heavenly world coming from our spirits by the power of the Holy Spirit.

This tongue of ecstasy is also our heavenly prayer language that no one understands but God. That is why it is called an unknown tongue. No one has to interpret it as is required for the gift of tongues. The believer soon realizes that the world, the flesh, and the devil are his three enemies. The only time that we speak without these enemies knowing a word we say is when we speak in an unknown tongue. It becomes our private line to God that gives us direct access to Him. We pick up that heavenly "telephone" and call Heaven, and the devil doesn't know a word we are saying. The world and flesh don't know that language; that is the reason they hate it.

However, when the Holy Spirit prays to God out of our spirits in His heavenly language, He will, if we ask Him, give back through our minds the revelation of what He prayed to God about or for us. As we yield to the Holy Spirit within, out will flow worship, ecstasy, and joy. We can sing to Him, shout to Him, and pray to Him in that tongue of ecstasy that overflows. Only God the Father, Jesus, and the Holy Spirit know what we are saying as we pray in that heavenly language.

As we speak to God in the language of the Spirit, Paul said we are edified as our spirits pray. He declared that he would pray and sing in the spirit as well as with his understanding (1 Cor. 14:14-15). Although he gave specific instructions for the use of tongues in a public service, he in no way meant to deny the reality or power they exert in a believer's life. He even declared that he spoke in tongues more than all of them

(1 Cor. 14:18). In his letter to the Corinthians, he was simply correcting the problem of tongues being misused in public services in a way that was creating confusion.

After receiving the baptism of the Holy Spirit, I understood that the gifts of the Spirit were for today as well. There is nothing in the Scriptures to indicate otherwise, for these gifts are given to edify the Church. As we allow the Holy Spirit to fill us continually, we will gain greater understanding of the gifts of the Holy Spirit.

## Notes

1.  Scripture references to the order of receiving baptisms: Lk. 3:16; Acts 1:8; 10:44-46; 11:15-16.

2.  Scripture references to the baptism of repentance: Mt. 21:25; Mk. 1:4; 11:30; Lk. 3:3; 7:29; 20:4; Acts 1:22; 10:37; 13:24; 18:25; 19:3-4.

3.  Scripture references to the baptism in water: Mt. 3:11, Mk. 1:8; Lk. 3:16; Jn. 1:26,28,31,33; Acts 1:5; 1 Pet. 3:21.

4.  Scripture references to the baptism of the Holy Spirit: Mt. 3:11; Lk. 3:16; Acts 11:16.

# Chapter 3

# *Gifts of the Holy Spirit*

## *Part I: Divine Enablement to Know*

### *HONOR IN THE GODHEAD*

We discussed in our first volume, *Presenting the Holy Spirit: Who Is He?* the fact that the Holy Spirit is God. Although many Christians have referred to Him as an "it," or gifts, or tongues, and some believe He is merely an influence, He is none of these. He is a divine Person, the Third Person of the Godhead. The Scriptures are full of affirmations of this truth, giving the Holy Spirit at least 40 different titles and listing at least 27 attributes of His divine personality. (See Appendix A.) Therefore, we should attribute as much honor to

God the Holy Spirit as we do to God the Father and God the Son. In order to properly evaluate the work of the Holy Spirit, it seems very important that we should closely observe how the three members of the God-head have been at marked pains to provide for the honor of the other. We should be as careful to give each of Them that honor as They are.

How careful the Father was to guard the glory of His beloved Son when the Son laid aside the visible in-signia of His deity and took upon Himself the form of a servant. The Father's voice was then heard more than once proclaiming, "This is My beloved Son." Then how constantly did the incarnate Son revert attention from Himself and direct it to the Father who had sent Him, saying, "…The Son can do nothing of Himself, but what He seeth the Father do…" (Jn. 5:19). In like manner the Holy Spirit is not here to glorify Himself, but to exalt Jesus, whose advocate He is.

Blessed is it then to mark how jealous both the Father and the Son have been to safeguard the glory and provide for the honor due the Holy Spirit, as we shall learn from our study. Although this blessed Trinity is one God, yet the Scriptures reveal Them to us as three parts of the Triune Godhead, perfect in unity yet differing in function. Thus each one of the Persons of the Trinity is careful to provide for the honor of the others. Accepting this spiritual reality will prevent us from dishonoring the Holy Spirit by being critical of

His gifts and manifestations, and will help us to properly evaluate His divine work in the earth.

## COMING OF CHRIST AND OF THE HOLY SPIRIT PARALLELED

Many and marked are the parallels between the coming of Christ and the coming of the Holy Spirit. The coming of both Christ and the Holy Spirit were subject to Old Testament prediction. During the past century theologians have written much about Messianic prophecy. But unfortunately, the promises that God gave concerning the coming of the Holy Spirit have seemed vague to many people. Yet the prophets definitely predicted the descent of the Holy Spirit (Joel 2:28) as well as the incarnation of the Savior (Is. 7:14).

Just as Christ had John the Baptist announce His incarnation and prepare His way, so the Holy Spirit had Christ Himself to foretell His coming and to make ready the hearts of His disciples. Just as it was not until the fullness of time had come that God sent forth His Son, so it was not until the Day of Pentecost was fully come that God sent forth His Spirit. As the Son became incarnate in the holy land of Palestine, so the Spirit descended in Jerusalem.

Just as the coming of the Son of God into the world was accompanied by mighty wonders and signs, so the descent of God's Spirit was attended by dramatic displays of divine power. The advent of each was marked by supernatural phenomena. The angelic host announcing Jesus' birth found its counterpart in the "sound from heaven as of a rushing mighty wind" (Acts 2:2) announcing the coming of the Holy Spirit. As an extraordinary star marked the house where the child was, so a divine sound of rushing wind and cloven tongues of fire marked the house where the Spirit came.

Concerning the coming of Jesus, there was both a private and public aspect to it. The birth of the Savior was made known unto a few. But when Jesus was to be made manifest to Israel, He was publicly identified. At His baptism the heavens opened, the Spirit descended as a dove, and the Father spoke from Heaven. Correspondingly, the Spirit was given to the disciples privately when the risen Savior breathed His life into them and said, "Receive the Holy Spirit" (Jn. 20:22 NAS). Not until the Day of Pentecost did the Holy Spirit become public, when the disciples received His baptism. All the multitude in Jerusalem was then made aware of His descent when it was noised abroad.

The advent of the Son was for the purpose of the eternal Word becoming incarnate, made flesh to dwell among us. So too, the coming of the Spirit was for the purpose of His becoming incarnate in our flesh. Jesus declared to the disciples that the Spirit of Truth would come and dwell *in* them (Jn. 14:17). The Third Person of the Trinity came to take up His abode in man, to whom it is said, "Know ye not that ye are the temple of God, and that the Spirit of God dwelleth in you?" (1 Cor. 3:16)

When Christ was born into the world, we are told that Herod was troubled, and all Jerusalem with Him. In like manner, when the Holy Spirit was given, we read, "Now when this was noised abroad, the multitude came together, and were confounded..." (Acts 2:6). It was prophesied that when Christ should appear, He would be unrecognized and unappreciated. So it came to pass. In like manner, the Lord Jesus declared He would send the Spirit of Truth, "whom the world cannot receive, because it seeth Him not, neither knoweth Him" (Jn. 14:17a).

As the Messianic claims of Christ were called into question, so the advent of the Spirit was at once challenged. We read that on the Day of Pentecost the multitude all "continued in amazement and great perplexity, saying to one another, 'What does this mean?' " (Acts 2:12 NAS) The analogy is yet closer, for as Christ was termed a wine-bibber, so of those filled with the Spirit some of the multitude "were mocking and saying, 'They are full of sweet wine' " (Acts 2:13 NAS). Also, as the public coming of Christ was heralded by John the Baptist, so the public descent of the Spirit was interpreted by Peter.

God appointed unto Christ the execution of the all-inclusive work of redeeming us from satan's interruption of our Father's eternal plan for mankind, and reproducing His divine character in mankind. Even so the Spirit has been assigned the momentous task of effectually applying the virtues of the atonement and restoring believers to the image of God through the impartation of His character. As the Son honored the Father in the fulfillment of His eternal purpose, so the Holy Spirit glorifies the Son in the fulfillment of His divine mission. The Father paid holy deference to the Son by bidding the disciples, "Hear ye Him" (Mt. 17:5). In like manner the Son showed that respect to our Teacher when He said, "He that hath an ear, let him hear what the Spirit saith unto the churches" (Rev. 2:29). And, as Christ committed His saints to the safekeeping of the Holy Spirit, so the Spirit will yet deliver us in safety at the return of Jesus (Jn. 14:3).

These interesting parallels give insight into the comprehensive love of God for mankind, as well as show the honor and love that exists between the members of the Godhead. May our hearts be enlarged through this understanding to grasp the true significance of the work of the Holy Spirit in the earth. His is an eternal mandate to bring complete redemption to lost mankind for all who will choose to know Him. With this perspective, we can better understand the importance of spiritual gifts and how to give them their rightful place in our lives and churches.

## PURPOSE OF THE SPIRITUAL GIFTS

A complete presentation of the Holy Spirit cannot be made without a thorough discussion of spiritual gifts. There are approximately 100 New Testament references to the subject of spiritual gifts, or to the exercise of those gifts that are listed in chapter 12 of First Corinthians. (This number is exclusive of the miracles of Jesus recorded in the Gospels.)

In spite of these frequent references in Scripture to the manifestation of the gifts of the Spirit in the New Testament Church, most of our theology books seem to ignore spiritual gifts. If they include a paragraph or two, it is usually with the inference that spiritual gifts ceased to function in the Church after the apostolic age. There is not the slightest suggestion in the New Testament that any endowment of the Spirit will cease before Jesus returns. On the contrary, the Word declares that the gifts and callings of God are without repentance (Rom. 11:29), which in the Greek means *irrevocable*. With that in mind, let's consider the significance of spiritual gifts for the Church today.

## SPIRITUAL GIFTS DEFINED

Spiritual gifts are not latent human talents or trained abilities brought to heightened expression. The *pneumatic charismata* are not simply more of what is already resident in men, displayed in excellence. Neither are they enhancements of human personality. They are *the manifestation of the miraculous working of our Lord wrought by the Holy Spirit.* The Holy Spirit is the channel for the operation of these supernatural gifts, whether seemingly ordinary or seemingly extraordinary.

The nature of the spiritual gifts can be determined largely by the vocabulary used in the Scriptures to refer to them. The first clear reference to the gifts as a supernatural phenomena is found in First Corinthians 12, verses 1 through 7. These verses deal with the gifts as a class and provide a vocabulary for their description. They are called *spirituals*, translated from the Greek word *pneumatica*. Paul literally wrote, "Now concerning spirituals, brethren, I would not have you ignorant" (1 Cor. 12:1). The word *gifts* in that verse is in italics, meaning that it is not found in the original Greek manuscript. The first reference to this phenomena classifies them merely as spirituals, or "things of the spirit." The same description is used in First Corinthians 14:1. This reference is probably to the gifts, although in First Corinthians 14:28, this word *pneumaticos*, in the masculine gender, is applied to "spiritual persons." F.F. Bruce, in his commentary on the Book of First Corinthians, states that *pneumatica* is referring to the persons "endowed with spiritual gifts." So the spirituals in one sense refer to gifts, and in another refer to persons having spiritual gifts.

Spiritual gifts, *charismata*, include diversities of gifts (1 Cor. 12:4). The Greek word, *charisma*, which means "spiritual gifts," comes from the basic word *charis*, which means grace. Charisma is a divine enablement, an endowment, or grace bestowed freely by God. The text in First Corinthians refers to the gifts as spirituals because they are *capacities freely bestowed by the Holy Spirit.* They cannot be merited, bought, or earned for they are of divine origin. They operate through a Spirit-filled person, but in a real sense they are gifts to the Church, to the whole Body of Christ. The apostle Paul explains this diversity and the necessity of each member of the Body of Christ functioning properly, using the analogy of the human body (1 Cor. 12:12-27). Each manifestation of the Spirit is for the common good of the Church. So when the Holy Spirit manifests Himself through a divine gift operating through a believer, its purpose is to reveal and glorify Jesus, for the profit of the corporate Body of Christ. This includes ministry either to one person, to several, or to a whole body, as the Lord moves supernaturally to meet the needs of His people.

*Proper Motivation: Love*

When instructing the church concerning the use of spiritual gifts, Paul said, "Let all things be done unto edifying" (1 Cor. 14:26c). The words *edify* and *profit* are used eight times in Paul's first letter to the Corinthians with relation to the operation of these gifts. If a spiritual gift is exercised without the proper motivation of love, it will not edify the Body and will therefore be unprofitable. Whatever the manifestation of the Spirit, its only purpose is to build and strengthen the unique structure that is Christ's Church. Any exercise of the spiritual gifts that does not result in edifying the Body of Christ and glorifying Jesus is out of order. The

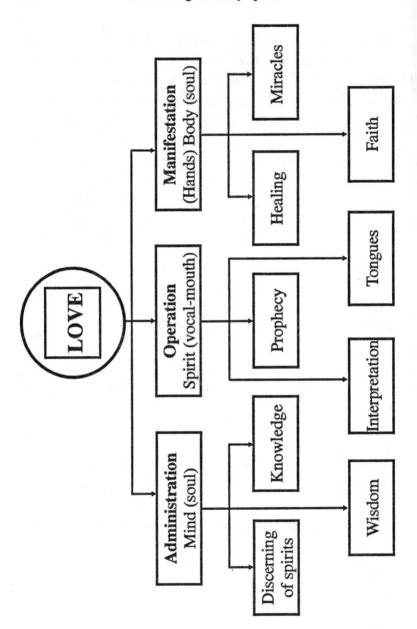

test of the validity of exercising a gift then, is the benefit it brings to the community of believers.

As part of Paul's exhortation to the Corinthians to desire the best gifts, he tells them also to follow *the way of love*. Many different kinds of gifts are named and listed throughout the letters to the Corinthians and the Romans. However, love is not listed as a gift (see diagram).[1]

Some teach erroneously that love is the greatest gift. However, love is not a gift; *it is the way by which we are to be guided and motivated.* Paul interrupted his discourse on spiritual gifts to declare with urgency that all the *charismas* must be exercised through love. He declared that the person who exercises gifts without love becomes nothing and gains nothing.

It is a tragedy that some individuals who have been blessed with spiritual gifts have become nothing in the eyes of God because they lack compassion, patience, kindness, long-suffering, and other attributes of love (1 Cor. 13). Love should always be the motivation for seeking and the way of expressing each of the spiritual gifts. If love is truly present in the church that is manifesting spiritual gifts, those gifts can have a tremendous impact, bringing God's power and presence. When the gifts of the Spirit are infused with the love of God, the Body of Christ is blessed and, in turn, becomes a blessing to others.

Because of the great value the spiritual gifts have in building the Body of Christ, believers should desire them. The apostle Paul encourages the Corinthians to eagerly desire spiritual gifts (1 Cor. 14:1 NIV). This is by no means a self-oriented desire for personal blessing. As noted before, the purpose of the gifts is to reveal Jesus and to edify the Body of Christ. For that reason the spiritual gifts are to be earnestly desired. The whole Body of believers should desire all the gifts of the Spirit to be manifested, not just a few of them. Through variety of expression, multiple needs are met. The whole fellowship of believers is built up by seeing the unveiled beauty of our Lord through the supernatural expressions of the gifts.

To be sure, the Holy Spirit distributes spiritual gifts as He wills, but this is not without regard to the desires of those members of the Body of Christ who wish to be used by the Holy Spirit. Concerning this Christ-focused ministry, each person has a distinctive role to fulfill. To each one is given the manifestation of the Spirit, and each person in the local church can be involved in that expression. Believers should not look to one person or to a few to minister in the gifts in a local church. Rather, they should look to the Lord, expecting Him to minister by His Spirit through all who are present. Of course, this calls for individual responsibility of a high order. This means that believers should closely follow the leading and prompting of the Holy Spirit, and whenever He exercises a gift it should be brought forth in harmony and proper order.

As we consider individually the spirituals listed in chapter 12 of First Corinthians, we will continue to discover the goodness of God in giving gifts to His Church. Studying these nine gifts separately, we will better understand how each can be used for the edifying and building of the Body of Christ. Also, we will learn the safeguards the Scriptures give us to maintain the valid manifestation of these powerful spiritual gifts.

## WORDS OF WISDOM AND KNOWLEDGE

*For to one is given by the Spirit the word of wisdom; to another the word of knowledge by the same Spirit* (1 Corinthians 12:8).

The Greek term in this verse translated "word" is *logos*. It is a common New Testament term that is also translated as "utterance" or "message." These two *logos* gifts, the word of wisdom and the word of knowledge, head a list of nine diverse ways in which the Spirit is manifested for the common good of the Body of Christ (1 Cor. 12:7). Traditionally, these two gifts have been understood differently by various parts of the Body of Christ.

One of the ways charismatic believers define the word of knowledge is "a supernatural insight that gives a Spirit-filled believer specific information about a person and situation, spontaneously revealed to him by the Holy Spirit." According to this popular understanding, a word of knowledge is a mental impression, a picture, or vision, through which the Holy Spirit discloses some hidden fact or circumstance concerning people, places, or things. Similarly, a word of wisdom, according to this view, is a spontaneous revelation of wise guidance or knowledge rightly applied. Although these are legitimate definitions of the function of these two spiritual gifts, they are not the only way the Scriptures define them.

The Scriptures also refer to these two kindred manifestations of the Spirit as "gifts of speaking." According to this definition, these gifts function as "spontaneous revelation of divine truth from the Word of God spoken forth." Thus, teaching and preaching under the anointing of the Holy Spirit that includes speaking forth divine revelation is also a manifestation of these revelatory gifts. It is my conviction that this is the greater manifestation of the gifts of word of wisdom and knowledge.

We would wonder why Paul began his discussion of these nine spirituals with the words of wisdom and knowledge. In all likelihood it was because wisdom (*sophia*) and knowledge (*kenosis*) were watchwords of the Corinthian church, a Greek congregation that was fascinated with human philosophy and the gift of oratory. The language Paul used here apparently referred back to the problems that he addressed in the first chapter of this book (1 Cor. 1:17–2:16), in which he denounced worldly philosophy expressed in empty human eloquence. In the early sections of his letter to the Corinthians, Paul had much to say on the subject of wisdom. (He referred to "wisdom" or "wise" 20 times in the first two chapters, and mentioned "knowledge" or "know" 16 times in the first eight chapters.) The Greek word Paul used for *knowing* referred to intimate relationship through the revelation of the mind of Christ. At issue was the Corinthians' emphasis of speaking through humanly attained wisdom and knowledge, a practice that contradicted Paul's Spirit-empowered preaching of the cross.

Rejecting the common criteria for spirituality according to the Corinthians, Paul declares that Christ sent him to preach the gospel, not with words of human wisdom, lest the cross of Christ be emptied of its power (1 Cor. 1:17). He wrote:

> *And when I came to you, brethren, I did not come with superiority of speech or of wisdom, proclaiming to you the testimony of God. For I determined to know nothing among you except Jesus Christ, and Him crucified. ... And my message and my preaching were not in persuasive words of wisdom, but in demonstration of the Spirit and of power, that your faith should not rest on the wisdom of men, but on the power of God* (1 Corinthians 2:1-2,4-5 NAS).

Paul implied that the *words*, translated from *logos*, of his message were not of human origin, or mere philosophical speculation. Instead, his message came from another source: the Holy Spirit. Not only were his words accompanied by convincing proof of God's power (undoubtedly signs and wonders), but the message itself was a powerful demonstration of the Spirit's presence (1 Cor. 2:4). Then, in discussing the spiritual gifts, Paul used the Corinthians' own special terms to begin his list (1 Cor. 12:8). In this way he reduced words of wisdom and knowledge from the Corinthians' fascination with human abilities, and the arrogance it produced, to true revelation by the Holy Spirit.

Words of wisdom and knowledge are probably best understood in Paul's explanation in the following words: "But God hath revealed them unto us by His Spirit: for the Spirit searcheth all things, yea, the deep things of God" (1 Cor. 2:10). These gifts function through a revelation of God Himself. The Holy Spirit plumbs the "deep things" of God, searches out His profound thoughts, breathes on them, and lifes them to believers' hearts through revelation. Those believers who receive such revelation will be able to proclaim that revelation to others and see them lifed by the word as well. The words of such a message, although framed by the mind of the speaker, spring from a higher source. That is what Paul meant when he wrote, "Which things also we speak, not in the words which man's wisdom teacheth, but which the Holy Ghost teacheth…" (1 Cor. 2:13). A person who so speaks will not depend on previous training, human wisdom, or eloquence, but on the power and the inspiration of the Holy Spirit.

Thus, a word of wisdom has as its source Christ Jesus, "who of God is made unto us wisdom, and righteousness, and sanctification, and redemption" (1 Cor. 1:30). Paul explained that he spoke God's wisdom "in a mystery, the hidden wisdom, which God predestined before the ages to our glory" (1 Cor. 2:7 NAS). God's wise plan of redemption was secret and mysterious in the sense that it was hidden in God from all human eyes. But it is now manifest in Christ and revealed through the Holy Spirit. Yet God's wisdom remains hidden to those who consider the message of the cross foolishness (1 Cor. 1:18; 2:14), not understanding God's eternal purpose.

The primary and authoritative revelation of God's secret wisdom and eternal purpose was given to Paul (1 Cor. 4:1) and to other apostles and prophets (Eph. 3:3-6), that now it might be made known unto the Church. According to these Scriptures, insight into divine wisdom was given as a spiritual gift and spoken forth to the entire Body of Christ through these apostles and prophets (1 Cor. 12:8). This concurs with what we have said, that a word of wisdom may be a special impartation to a particular person preaching a message given by the Holy Spirit. The Holy Spirit enables that person to declare divine truth in a way that transcends his or her natural capacity or experience. We call this "preaching by revelation." If it contains predictive revelation, we classify it as prophetic.

Paul links wisdom and knowledge when writing to the Romans (Rom. 11:33) and to the Colossians (Col. 2:3). His understanding of the manifestation of the gifts of the Spirit is sometimes difficult to determine. Yet there is some biblical evidence that suggests that the two gifts are complementary: the word of wisdom, a preaching gift expressing a message of God's plan of redemption; and the word of knowledge, a teaching gift expressing a message of particular outworking of that plan. Paul writes:

> *Now we have received, not the spirit of the world, but the Spirit who is from God, that we might know the things freely given to us by God, which things we also speak, not in words taught by human wisdom, but in those taught by the Spirit, combining spiritual thoughts with spiritual words* (1 Corinthians 2:12-13 NAS).

Here he refers to "knowing things." Perhaps this is a reference to the wide range of blessings that God has graciously bestowed on us in Christ. Out of the knowledge of these things, in words taught by the Holy Spirit, we then speak. This again suggests that a word of knowledge comes forth as teaching or in giving direction for the application of the wisdom spoken.

As we mentioned, the idea that words of wisdom and knowledge should be viewed as speaking gifts, though common among evangelical scholars, is not the popular understanding among charismatic believers. When first introduced to this view, the question is raised, "Does accepting this view make us lose the spontaneous revelatory gifts that we presently call word of wisdom and word of knowledge?" No, they would simply be redefined as prophecy.

In the Scriptures, when people reported spontaneous insight the Holy Spirit had given them, Paul called it prophecy. He wrote:

> *But if all prophesy, and there come in one that believeth not, or one unlearned, he is convinced of all, he is judged of all: and thus are the secrets of his heart made manifest; and so falling down on his face he will worship God, and report that God is in you of a truth* (1 Corinthians 14:24-25).

Although many charismatic believers would say that when secrets of the heart are manifest the words of knowledge and wisdom are functioning, Paul here includes that phenomenon in prophecy. This is true also of writers in both the Old and New Testaments who considered supernaturally revealed information through words, visions, or dreams a prophetic revelation. For example, David's sin with Bathsheba was revealed to the prophet Nathan (2 Sam. 12:1-12). The battle plans for the Assyrians were revealed to the prophet Elisha (2 Kings 6:8-12). The interpretation of King Nebuchadnezzar's dream was revealed to Daniel in a night vision (Dan. 2:19).

In the New Testament it was through the gift of prophecy that the Holy Spirit revealed that a famine would occur around the world (Acts 11:28), that Paul would be taken captive in Jerusalem (Acts 21:10-11), and that a specific spiritual gift would be given to Timothy (1 Tim. 4:14). When Jesus told a Samaritan woman some specific details about her life, she said, "Sir, I perceive that thou art a prophet" (Jn. 4:19). It was because the secrets of her life were revealed that she called Jesus a prophet. As we study the gift of prophecy in more depth in a later chapter, we will understand its purpose more clearly. We are simply contrasting it here with the revelation gifts of wisdom and knowledge to understand more clearly the definition and function of each.

The revelatory gifts of wisdom and knowledge can have tremendous impact in building the Church as they supply understanding of the will and purpose of God in various situations. They are so necessary for the impartation of present spiritual truths from the Word of God. Everyone who ministers the Word of God needs to wait on God and earnestly desire the prophetic revelation of His Word in order to be effective in his or her ministry. Only then will we keep in step with the Holy Spirit as He leads the Church.

## *Spirit of Wisdom and Knowledge*

In his letter to the Ephesians, the Holy Spirit through Paul prayed that they might receive a spirit of wisdom and revelation in the knowledge of Him (Eph. 1:17). The stated purpose for that revelation is that they may know "what is the hope of His calling, and what the riches of the glory of His inheritance in the saints" (Eph. 1:18). This was not only Paul's prayer for the church at Ephesus, but also the Holy Spirit's prayer for all "the faithful in Christ Jesus" (Eph. 1:1c). That includes the Church today.

This prayer is not for just a word of wisdom or a word of knowledge, but for the *spirit of wisdom and knowledge* to be ours as well. If we are faithful, we can be recipients of this divine spirit of wisdom and revelation in the knowledge of God and His purposes for His Church. I believe the hour has come when we will no longer have to depend only on a word of wisdom or a word of knowledge, but will receive the *spirit* of wisdom and the *spirit* of knowledge as we give the Holy Spirit His proper authority in the Church.

## *DISCERNING OF SPIRITS*

*...to another discerning of spirits...* (1 Corinthians 12:10).

The gift of discerning of spirits completes the cycle of the revelatory gifts of the Spirit. There is nothing that God knows that may not be made known to man, as the Holy Spirit wills, through the agency of one or more of these three gifts. Everything within the realm of human destiny, whether divine or evil, natural or supernatural, past, present, or future, comes within the parameters of these three revelatory gifts.

The biblical phrase, "discerning of spirits," comes from the Greek word *deakreisis*, and is defined as a verb: "to discern, to discriminate, or to distinguish." This verb form (used in Hebrews 5:14) speaks of those "who by reason of use have their senses exercised to discern both good and evil." Paul used this word when questioning whether there was anyone wise enough to judge between the brethren, as to which was right in a certain dispute (1 Cor. 6:5). He used it also to reproach the Corinthian brethren who had not discerned the Lord's body, failing to understand what communion meant (1 Cor. 11:29).

Later in that same book, when Paul was setting the gifts in order, he said that the prophets should speak two or three, and let the other judge or discern (1 Cor. 14:29). This seems to infer that someone present should be able to discern the validity of the gift of prophecy when it is manifested. All Spirit-filled believers are able to judge vocal gifts and their operations in a measure, on the basis of whether they are spiritually edifying to the Body. However, when the gift of discerning of spirits is operating, spiritual discernment will be more accurate and effective.

The discerning of spirits is not keen mental penetration or the revelation of people's character or thoughts as through a kind of mental telepathy. It is not psychological insight, nor the critical ability to discover faults in others. Neither is it a supernatural power that operates by the will of man, for all God-given spiritual gifts operate only through the will of the Holy Spirit. There are supernatural powers that operate through the will of man. Such forces as clairvoyance, hypnotism, magic, witchcraft, cultism, sorcery, and spiritualism, though real supernatural forces, are satanic in their origin and operate through the perverted will of man.

The Scriptures indicate quite clearly that the gift of discerning of spirits is the God-given ability to discern the source of a spiritual manifestation, whether it is the Holy Spirit, an evil spirit, or merely the human spirit. It is important to remember that the gift of discerning of spirits is not for the purpose of judging people, but for judging the kind of spirit behind the manifestation, to determine whether it is holy, evil, or human. The gift of discerning of spirits enables the believer to recognize the spirit that has evidenced itself in supernatural power over human bodies, minds, or organs.

Discerning of spirits does not deal exclusively with demon spirits, but allows a person to see God's angels at work as well. It can reveal God's protective angel forces as Elisha the prophet saw them (2 Kings 6:16-17). This gift enabled Stephen to see the Lord just before his martyr's death (Acts 7:55-56), and allowed John to see Him when in exile on the isle of Patmos (Rev. 1:10-16). It often enables believers to see Christ Jesus in the midst of worshipers.

Discerning of spirits enables the possessor of this gift to see through all outward appearances and know the true nature of a situation or the source of an inspired utterance. Seducing spirits or lying spirits are responsible for doctrines of devils and damnable heresy in the Church (1 Tim. 4:1-2; 2 Pet. 2:1). The gift of discerning of spirits can discover the enemy's plan of seduction and can unmask demon miracle workers (Rev. 16:14). The Scriptures admonish believers to "try the spirits whether they are of God: because many false prophets are gone out into the world" (1 John 4:1). It is vital for the health of the Church that we be able to discern correctly the spirits that are influencing believers.

### Notes

1. Dr. Fuchsia Pickett, *The Holy Spirit Manual*, from the Outline Study Series, p. 14.

# Chapter 4

# *Gifts of the Holy Spirit*

## *Part II: Divine Enablement to Do*

### *GIFT OF FAITH*

*To another faith by the same Spirit...* (1 Corinthians 12:9).

In Part I we introduced the three gifts that supernaturally enable us to *know*. Now in Part II we want to introduce the three gifts that enable us to *do* supernaturally: faith, healings, and miracles. God imparts by His Spirit not only understanding, but also ability. It is insufficient to know; we must also be empowered to do. Of the three gifts of power, faith is undoubtedly the greatest. One writer expressed the power of faith this way: "From Paradise to Patmos, faith marks the trail of the company of the blessed, the heaven-bound, happy-hearted pleasers of God."[1]

The gift of faith is *a supernatural impartation of faith by the Holy Spirit whereby that which is desired by God and spoken by man shall come to pass.* It projects into the eternal realm to bring a supernatural solution into an earthly situation. The gift of faith is given to produce heavenly miracles this side of Heaven. Although it is distinct from the working of miracles, as we shall see, it produces them nevertheless. However, receiving the gift of faith does not make it impossible for its possessor to doubt God anymore. Nor does the gift of faith fit a man for Heaven anymore than speaking with other tongues or any other spiritual gift does. It simply operates by the will of the Spirit through a yielded vessel to bring the will of God to a given situation.

The gift of faith does not include or substitute for all other faith that is taught in the Scriptures. For example, it is distinct from the saving faith that comes before salvation as a gift from God (Eph. 2:8). The gift of faith can be received only after salvation, which is true of all the other spiritual gifts as well.

Faith is the only gift of the Spirit to be included in the list of the fruit of the Spirit (Gal. 5:22-23). This fact reveals to us the necessity of every believer having a quality of faith that grows and develops in order to live fruitful lives. Though all believers may not have the gift of faith operating in their lives, we must all allow that fruit of faith to grow in our lives. The fruit of faith is for character; the gift is for power. Fruit grows, while a gift is a sudden endowment.

The gift of faith differs from other realms of faith, then, as a specific manifestation of supernatural faith given by the Holy Spirit to accomplish a specific purpose. In its operation, the element of danger is often the catalyst that triggers the gift of faith. It gave personal protection in perilous circumstances, such as when Daniel was thrown into the lion's den (Dan. 6:17-23), and to the three Hebrew children thrown into the fiery furnace (Dan. 3:16-18). It was used for supernatural sustenance in famine or fasting, as in the case of Elijah and the widow's meal barrel (1 Kings 17:12-16). It was used for supernatural victory in the fight against Amalek (Ex. 17:11), and to assist in domestic and industrial problems, as when the widow's oil was multiplied to pay her debt (2 Kings 4:1-7). The gift of faith was used to receive the astounding promises of God, as when Abraham received his son Isaac miraculously (Rom. 4:20). It was used to raise the dead and cast out evil spirits as well.

Through the gift of faith, God reveals His will and gives power to believe it in the face of impossible circumstances. The Holy Spirit may speak His will to a person through an inner voice or through a vision, and then give a sense of certainty that what has been revealed must happen. We call this knowledge a *rhema* from God—a living word. *Infusion* is a term that best describes the dynamic at work in the gift of faith. Besides revealing His immediate will through a *rhema*, a vision, or an inner voice, God also gives a divine deposit of peace, power, and confidence. This faith is an eternal knowledge imparted to a person that declares an act of God is coming to pass as the spoken words proclaim.

The beautiful chronicle of acts of faith given to us in the Book of Hebrews (chapter 11) teaches us that all divine action is an expression of faith. It was by faith that the elders obtained a good report, and by faith that we understand the worlds were framed by the word of God. By faith Abel offered unto God a more acceptable sacrifice than Cain, and by faith Enoch was translated. Noah and his household were saved by faith, and Abraham answered the call of God by faith. Although we cannot chronicle here all the heroes of faith listed for us in the Scriptures, we mention some to show that as the Scriptures teach, "without faith it is impossible to please [God]" (Heb. 11:6a). God's work will only be accomplished through acts of faith.

Although this gift is a wonderful manifestation of the power of God given to help the Church, we must include here a word of caution regarding its proper use. The whole dynamic involved in the gift of faith is significantly different from a person deciding he or she wants something to happen and therefore speaks according to that desire, claiming it as reality by the mere speaking of it. In the operation of the gift of faith, God initiates the action and our words simply acknowledge what He is revealing and doing, making His will a present reality. Presumption, based on human desire that calls on God to fulfill it, is a dangerous counterfeit to the operation of the gift of faith.

## GIFTS OF HEALING

*...to another the gifts of healing by the same Spirit* (1 Corinthians 12:9).

Sickness is definitely a result of the fall of man—of original sin. There would have been no sickness on earth had there been no sin (Gen. 2:17; Rom. 5:12). This does not mean, however, that when a person is sick, it is because he or she has sinned. Sickness is not necessarily the result of personal sin, but of sin being in the world. The good news of the gospel is that Jesus has provided healing as part of redemption, the remedy for sin.

The gifts of healing are supernatural manifestations of the Holy Spirit in the sphere of disease, given to the Church for the purpose of removing all manner of sickness and infirmities. These gifts bring supernatural healing without the use of natural means of any kind. They are the miraculous manifestation of the Spirit for the banishment of all human ills, whether organic, functional, nervous, acute, or chronic. They must not be confused with the services of the medical profession or the power of mind over matter. Whatever difficulties writers have discovered in defining other gifts of the Spirit, this particular gift seems to be understood by all.

The Scriptures teach many purposes for the gifts of healing that demonstrate the love of God for mankind. (See Appendix B.) These gifts may operate in various ways: through a word, by the laying on of hands, a shadow passing by as with Peter, and even a piece of fabric, as in Paul's ministry. The anointing with oil that James teaches, however, is not the operation of the gifts of healing (Jas. 5:14), but an obedient response to the Word.

Someone frequently used by God in the gifts of healing sees healings take place regularly, often, quickly, progressively, and sometimes dramatically. This spiritual gift is not earned, learned, or purchased. But, oh, what marvelous things happen when the Holy Spirit operates through a human vessel for healing! Temporary and terminal illnesses are healed. The afflicted, lame, and infirmed are made whole. Mental and emotional problems are cured.

As vessels through which this gift is manifest, we need to remember that healing is not a result of our ability, but of our availability. It is always God's supernatural ability working through our availability that brings healing. Often this gift is ministered by the laying on of hands as the Scriptures teach. Some people experience a sensation of the transfer of power like an electrical current or surge of warmth flowing when they minister this gift to a sick person. Sometimes the healing occurs through a Spirit-prompted word of authority or a command directed to the pressing disease. Often healing comes through a simple, specific prayer after a time of counseling.

## Plurality in Healing

The apostle Paul, when listing the spiritual gifts, literally speaks of gifts of healings (1 Cor. 12:9). This plural form suggests that different kinds of illnesses require diverse types of healing, implying there may be sub-categories of this gift. We could perhaps relate it to the idea of general practitioners and specialists in the medical profession. During the years I have been involved in ministry, I have seen that some can minister healing effectively to those with the same problems from which they have been healed, but not as effectively in other situations. For example, I have seen those who have been healed themselves from stuttering who have an effective ministry of healing to those who stutter. Some who have had limbs straightened specialize in praying for those who have crooked limbs. You might ask why this happens. I believe the Holy Spirit distributes different gifts of healing among believers to keep us humble and dependent on God and one another.

Some scholars teach that the plural listings of the gifts of healings may be used to show that this manifestation of the Holy Spirit has several divine operations. Just as there are classes of diseases, so each of the gifts of healing probably has a counteracting effect on some particular disease class. Some people are greatly used in healing cancers and tumors. Others seem to be empowered to restore sight or hearing. Also, as said before, quite frequently the person has himself been healed of the malady for which he now seems gifted to heal others. Other scholars point out that it is not a stationary gift for a person to use, which is true also for all the spiritual gifts. Therefore, since each and every healing is a gift of the Spirit, it is listed in the plural form.

*Avenues of Healing*

There are several different avenues through which we can receive healing. First, there is preventive healing, which is perhaps the best of all. As we learn to take care of our bodies—eating properly and getting the rest and exercise we need—we will live in health. A second avenue for healing is that which comes through medical science. We do not discount the wisdom that has been unlocked through medical research and study to bring healing to many.

The healing that supersedes these natural means is that which comes through the gifts of healing. Sometimes it is an instantaneous healing in which God does what doctors could not do. At other times it is a progressive healing, as suggested in the Scriptures when we read, "…as they went, they were cleansed" (Lk. 17:14). The Scriptures refer also to healing that comes through the Word alone. "He sent His word, and healed them, and delivered them from their destructions" (Ps. 107:20).

Of course, the age-old question of many is, "Why do some people get healed and others do not?" A dear saintly minister, Brother Ralph Byrd, who has spoken much wisdom into my life, said this to me early in my walk in the Spirit: "God heals enough people to let you know He can, and doesn't heal enough others to let you know that you can't." God has the right to use people as He desires in the area of healing. And, of course, we cannot deny the sovereignty of God in healing as in all other areas of life.

I believe the fact that not everyone is healed ultimately works for our good. It discourages spiritual pride and convinces us of the interdependency on members of the Body of Christ. Believers need to recognize that Jesus' healing ministry has been entrusted to the entire Body of Christ, not to a few prominent ministers with extraordinary healing gifts. Some believers are frequently used to minister healing, and may be considered to have gifts of healings (1 Cor. 12:30). Yet the Holy Spirit may choose to manifest a gift of healing to any believer who is yielded to Him to meet a specific need. We must always remember that the Healer is Jesus. Healing gifts, however they are manifested, are a direct result of our heavenly Father's enduring love, mercy, and provision for His children.

Although we may continue to grapple with the difficult question of why everyone is not healed of every sickness, we can only respond with heartfelt gratitude each time someone is made whole. No matter how often I have been used to minister healing through the years, I have always seen it as an expression of Jesus' deep compassion for the sick and suffering. Each time someone is healed, I am awed by God's choice to use men and women as His vehicle to deliver His mercy through gifts of healings.

As with the other gifts, we must never forget that what is done must be done by Jesus. We cannot do it. We are not the healer; Jesus heals. He uses human instrumentality, but it is Christ who does the healing. And we must learn to trust our heavenly Father's sovereign wisdom, His time element, and His grace. I believe we are going to see the greatest era of healing we have ever seen in the next move of God.

## GIFT OF WORKING OF MIRACLES

*To another the working of miracles...* (1 Corinthians 12:10).

"The working of miracles" is the translation of the Greek *energemata dunameon,* which literally rendered means "operations of supernatural powers." As with the gifts of healing, these terms are plural. The Scriptures seem to indicate that each miraculous manifestation of power operates along with the gift of faith (Mt. 17:20). In the New Testament, events of supernatural origin are called "signs," "wonders," and "miracles" (Acts 2:22,43; 6:8; Heb. 2:4). They refer to events of divine power that cause wonderment and at the same time reveal something about God's ways. Simply stated, *a miracle is an event or action that seemingly contradicts known scientific laws, superseding them due to a supernatural act of God.*

The miracles of our Lord always bring a revelation of the Father and are signs of His Kingdom. They are fingerprints of God's wisdom, love, and mercy. Jesus never acted out of character, so every miracle was in harmony with the revelation of God in Christ. It is noteworthy that the term *wonder* is never used by itself in the Scriptures, but is always found with the term *signs*. For example, we read this: "God also bearing them witness, both with signs and wonders, and with divers miracles, and gifts of the Holy Ghost, according to His own will" (Heb. 2:4). God does not manifest His power just to cause wonderment alone. He always signifies or teaches something with His signs and miracles that will help in building His Kingdom.

Miracles are never pointless spectacles to make people gape; they are life-changing acts of God, reflecting the mind and heart of God that desires to help people. The vast majority of New Testament miracles involved bringing wholeness to peoples' bodies and lives, restoring the blind and lame, casting out demons, and even raising the dead in a moment's time. The gift of miracles, or working of powers, operates immediately in the realm of meeting the needs of men and women.

We should note that there were some miracles in the ministry of Jesus that seem to have accompanied His ministry alone. As we read the Gospels, we see Jesus turning water into wine, stilling storms on the sea, multiplying food, and walking on water. These were performed with the "ultra" motive of revealing His Father to mankind. We do not have any records of His disciples doing these things in their ministries. Paul, for example, did many miracles of healing and deliverance, but he did not still the storms that left him shipwrecked three times.

God can and does sometimes perform miracles in the realm of nature today. However, it is His miracles to people of healing, restoration, and deliverance that are in more abundant evidence. The greatest miracle God is performing today is the redeeming and restoring of mankind in the building of His Church. All God's power is miracle power, and Christianity is a miracle movement from start to finish.

The *dunameis* power that the disciples received at Pentecost was a "potency," or latent force waiting to be drawn upon. When the need arose and they responded in faith, this *dunamos* potential exploded into energy. It can be compared to the electrical energy resident in a bulldozer's battery. Faith is like turning the key in the ignition and expecting the power in that battery to loose its electrical energy which surges into the starter and propels the engine. In the early Church, as the apostles were obedient to God's calling, many signs and wonders were done through them (Acts 2:43). Soon after Pentecost, for example, Peter and John healed a lame man at the temple gate (Acts 3:1-8). Other examples of miracles in the Scriptures include supernatural deliverance from imprisonment (Acts 5:18-20; 16:23-30); raising the dead (Acts 9:36-42); and Paul shaking off the poisonous viper (Acts 28:3-5).

Healing the sick and casting out demon spirits also may be classified as gifts of miracles when there is a great sign value, as when Paul was at Ephesus and great soul-winning resulted (Acts 19:11). The same is true of Peter when just his shadow's falling upon the sick brought healing (Acts 5:12-15). This sphere of miraculous ministry continued beyond the 12 apostles to Stephen, Philip, and Barnabas, and continued throughout the early Church. Although those who work miracles may not have asked specifically for the gift, miracle power is automatically a result of the "package deal" of the great commission and Pentecost. Those who obeyed what Jesus commanded found that Jesus would do what He promised.

God often works His miracles through the most unlikely people, such as Philip, the table-waiter. The apostles chose Philip as one of seven men assigned to distribute food to the Greek widows (Acts 6:1-5). The Bible says he was of good reputation and full of the Holy Spirit, which are wonderful qualifications for waiting tables. But Philip discovered his greater potential as he worked diligently to serve God. After the church in Jerusalem was scattered, Philip went to Samaria to preach Christ. There the Lord worked miracles through Philip and unclean spirits crying with a loud voice came out of many who were possessed (Acts 8).

I believe Philip is a good illustration of the person God uses to work miracles. He was a *faithful worker, a zealous witness, diligent and faithful over a few things*. He worked diligently to preach the good news and God empowered him through the anointing of the Holy Spirit to work miracles. Unless we obey and go where there is a work to do, the gifts of the Spirit are superfluous. We must make ourselves available to relationship with God first, then to the work of God, and the gifts will come as divine enablements to do that work. They are not for armchair Christians who are not involved in the work of God. Someone has said there is no such thing as an "anointed couch potato."

## *The Key to Miracle Power*

To experience the miracle-working power of God, we must listen to and obey by faith the voice of the Holy Spirit. This is why it has been such a cry of my heart that the Church learn to have a personal, intimate relationship with the Holy Spirit. Without that relationship, we will not be able to hear and obey Him. This principle is clearly seen in a memorable miracle of the Gospels, that of Peter walking on the water (Mt. 14:22-33). Peter was exactly where Jesus had commanded him to be: in the boat. From that place of obedience he could step out into the sea, the "miracle area" where Jesus was, but even then only when commanded by Christ. Note that he did not attempt to move until Jesus said, "Come." Peter's faith rested wholly on the word of Christ's command. Although many criticize Peter for taking his eyes off Jesus and sinking, it is only fair to acknowledge that he did walk on water at Jesus' beckoning, which none of us have done.

Again, let us conclude with a word of caution. Presumption is not faith. God is not obligated to do the miracle we ask if we are "showing off," calling attention to ourselves, or enjoying an ego trip. We must patiently wait for God's moment. As we enter the area where a miracle is needed, we should pray, "Lord, what is the key to Your power and anointing for this situation?" Of course, Jesus offers us the best example of miracle-working. He was found among the poor and beggars, the wretched, the lepers. He lavished love upon the unloved; He healed for no other reason than to reveal the Father's love and His compassion for lost mankind.

To summarize, then, the people who will receive God's gift of miracles are those who: (a) are faithful to any task to which God has called them; (b) are filled with zeal for the gospel; (c) are servants in situations where the miraculous is needed to do His work; (d) are willing to obey His leading; and (e) are filled with compassion for the hurting. God's manifold purpose for working miracles is to reveal the glory of God, to demonstrate His power and love, to minister to people who know nothing of Jesus, to destroy the works of the enemy, and to terrorize satan. When we see miracles happening that result in changed lives, deliverance, and healing, we know that Jesus is there. That was the way He ministered when He was on earth, and it is the way He ministers now by His Holy Spirit through His Church. Even as Jesus cannot change, but is the same yesterday, today, and forever (Heb. 13:8), so the gift of the working of miracles will remain in the Church until His return.

## TONGUES AND INTERPRETATION OF TONGUES

> *...to another divers kinds of tongues; to another the interpretation of tongues* (1 Corinthians 12:10).

In our study of the baptism of the Holy Spirit (Chapter 2), we defined and discussed two kinds of tongues that are given to the believer. The tongue of ecstasy accompanies our initial baptism in the Holy Spirit and gives us a wonderful prayer language through which we are personally edified (1 Cor. 14:4). It does not require interpretation, for we are speaking to God, not to men.

The second kind of tongues, described in the Scriptures as "divers kinds of tongues," is given for the edification of the church. It must be interpreted so the message can be understood by all. When Paul gives instructions for public services, he tells the Corinthians to avoid confusion by not speaking in tongues without giving interpretation. Although he acknowledges that he speaks in tongues more than all of them together, he emphasizes the importance of the gift of interpretation functioning in a public service so the church may be edified. Some might ask, "Since tongues that are interpreted are equal to prophecy, according to First Corinthians 14:5, why not be content with prophecy?" The Scriptures teach that tongues are a sign for the unbeliever (1 Cor. 14:22). God has ordained tongues to do a work in hearts, and we should give them their rightful place.

As speaking in tongues is not conceived in the mind but comes miraculously by the Spirit of God, so interpretation of tongues emanates from the Spirit rather than from the intellect of man. There is a peculiarity in the gift of tongues, in that it has no meaning without the interpretation. *Interpretation of tongues is the supernatural showing forth by the Spirit of the meaning of an utterance in other tongues.* The interpreter does not understand the tongue he is interpreting; therefore, he is not translating the unknown language. The interpreter simply looks to God in dependence on Him to show forth the meaning just as the speaker in tongues yields in dependence on God for the supernatural utterance. (Although education, temperament, nationality, and similar factors influence our speech patterns, the Lord doesn't choose His mouthpieces because of their fluency in language or even their spiritual maturity.

their fluency in language or even their spiritual maturity. Amos, the farmer, was a prophet of God as well as Isaiah and Jeremiah, who had different cultural backgrounds.) In the mind of God, the message in tongues and the interpretation of it are the exact and most blessed link. In the mind of man, the two utterances are quite independent, though equally direct from God, requiring dependence on the Holy Spirit for both manifestations.

## Purpose for Interpretation of Tongues

The gift of interpretation makes clear to the understanding of the possessor what has already been an edification of his spirit in other tongues (1 Cor. 14:13-14). Obviously, it is not necessary that everything we utter in other tongues in private be given interpretation. But in circumstances where interpretation is necessary or desirable, God will give one so our minds as well as our spirits may profit. Donald Gee, the great Pentecostal theologian, writes:

> The purpose of the gift of interpretation is to render the inspired utterances by the Spirit which have gone forth in a tongue unknown to the vast majority present available to the general understanding of all by repeating them distinctly in the ordinary language of the people assembled. The same Holy Spirit Who inspired the speaking in other tongues whereby the words expressed flow from the Spirit rather than through

the intellect is able to inspire the interpretation also. Interpretation is therefore inspirational, ecstatic, spontaneous as the utterance.[2]

Those who speak in other tongues are expressly instructed to pray for the ability to interpret (1 Cor. 14:13). The purpose of this regulation is not to silence those who speak with tongues, but to ensure that the church be edified if no other interpreter is present. It is a safeguard to the church to ensure that there will not be a tongue without an interpretation. One who speaks forth in a tongue in a public service must take the responsibility to interpret if someone else does not. It is significant that although the gift of interpretation of tongues is not distributed exclusively among those who have the gift of tongues, those who speak with tongues are by far the most common possessors of this gift.

The Greek word for *interpretation* in the Corinthian letter means to explain thoroughly, *not* to translate. This explains why sometimes an utterance in tongues is much longer or shorter than the subsequent interpretation. However, the interpretation can be a literal translation of the message in tongues if the Spirit chooses to give it in that way. Frequently someone in the audience understands the tongue that has been spoken, and God gives a literal translation for the sake of that person's faith. That is what the Holy Spirit did for me. Although I was a minister, I was an "unbeliever" regarding tongues. I heard a message in tongues given in the Hebrew language. Because I had studied some Hebrew and understood part of the interpretation, I was convinced that these gifts were truly a manifestation of the Spirit of God.

The Bible enjoins us to let one interpret. "If any of you use the gift of tongues, not more than two, or three at the most should do so—each speaking in his turn—and someone should interpret. If there is no one able to interpret what is said, they should remain silent at the meeting of the church..." (1 Cor. 14:27-28, 20th Century Translation). This does not mean that the same individual must always interpret in all meetings, nor even that the same person must interpret all messages. "Let one interpret" means that when there is speaking in tongues in a message form, someone must interpret. Moffatt's translation reads as "Let someone interpret." This word further indicates that one individual message should not receive more than one interpretation, even though a dozen worshipers might have been able to interpret it.

A principle in the operation of the gifts is this: The greater the gift, the more faith it takes to operate it. More faith is needed to interpret tongues than to give a message in tongues, since it is understood by the human mind. As we learn to yield to the Holy Spirit to allow His gifts to flow through us, our faith will become stronger. In this way the Holy Spirit can use us more effectively to bless the Body of Christ.[3]

The third spiritual gift in this group of vocal utterance gifts is, of course, prophecy. Because of the present-day significance that is being given to the restoration of prophecy to the Church, I have dedicated the next chapter to a study of prophecy. For that reason we will not define it here. However, before we proceed, we need to mention that the work of the Holy Spirit is not limited to these nine manifestations. There are more than these nine gifts listed in the Scriptures.

## VARIETIES OF GIFTS

*And God hath set some in the church, first apostles, secondarily prophets, thirdly teachers, after that miracles, then gifts of healings, helps, governments, diversities of tongues* (1 Corinthians 12:28).

Paul is mentioning gifts that were already well-known to the Corinthians who came behind in no good gift. How can we express the value of one who functions in the gift of helps when what is needed most is *help*? Yet I have heard those who have this spiritual gift demean themselves by saying, "I just have the gift of helps." We need to evaluate spiritual gifts by how they bless the Body of Christ rather than how much recognition they give a person.

To the Romans, Paul introduces other gifts that illustrate his purpose of discussion:

*Having then gifts differing according to the grace that is given to us, whether prophecy, let*

*us prophesy according to the proportion of faith;
or ministry, let us wait on our ministering: or he
that teacheth, on teaching; or he that exhorteth,
on exhortation: he that giveth, let him do it with
simplicity; he that ruleth, with diligence; he that
showeth mercy, with cheerfulness* (Romans 12:6-8).

These gifts are ministries given by God as well for the
building of the local church. How many have considered *giving* to be a spiritual gift? We need those who
exercise this gift as much as those who prophesy. And
when mercy is needed, how welcome is the kindness
that is received!

Then to the Ephesians Paul wrote concerning five
gifts given to the Church of Christ:

*And He gave some, apostles; and some,
prophets; and some, evangelists; and some, pastors and teachers; for the perfecting of the
saints, for the work of the ministry, for the edifying of the body of Christ* (Ephesians 4:11-12).

These gifts given to the Church by Christ are different
from the gifts given to the Church by the Holy Spirit.
The spiritual gifts given by the Holy Spirit are resident
in the local church, to be manifest by the will of the
Spirit. The Holy Spirit operates these gifts through
believers to edify that local church. In contrast, the
gifts Christ gave the Church can transcend the local
church, becoming a blessing to the whole Body of

Christ. We call these gifts the five apostolic gifts or the fivefold ministry. These gifts are people, given to the Body of Christ and anointed to minister in certain spiritual offices to believers, to equip them for the work of the ministry. When God sets apart a person for a spiritual office, He bestows upon him a divine enablement that corresponds to that office, equipping him to do the ministry He has ordained.

Some theologians have limited the number of spiritual gifts to nine, to correspond to the nine fruit of the Spirit listed in Galatians 5. But a careful searching of the Scriptures reveals other fruit of the Spirit besides the nine that are listed there. For example, Peter admonishes Christians:

> *...giving all diligence, add to your faith virtue; and to virtue knowledge; and to knowledge temperance; and to temperance patience; and to patience godliness; and to godliness brotherly kindness; and to brotherly kindness charity* (2 Peter 1:5-7).

Paul also mentions 17 works of the flesh and ends the list with the phrase "and such like." Surely if the flesh can produce more than 17 evil works, the Holy Spirit can produce a greater number of virtues that reveal an aspect of divine love. Failing to recognize all the gifts that God has given to the Church will only limit our capacity for receiving the blessings that He intends for us to enjoy.

*Summary*

The Holy Spirit stood with Peter and filled him, not only on the Day of Pentecost, but also when he stood before the Sanhedrin and testified boldly that there was no other name under heaven whereby men could be saved (Acts 4:8-12). In the Book of Acts (which could be called the Acts of the Holy Spirit), the Holy Spirit dominated the scene. Through Peter and John, Stephen, Philip, Paul, Barnabas, Silas, Agabus, and others, the Holy Spirit was the invisible, divine Comforter who had taken Christ's place as Teacher and Leader among His disciples. At the Council in Jerusalem, at the church in Antioch, and all similar deliberations, He administered the affairs of the Church. Through the gifts of government, from the original visitation in the parent church at Jerusalem to similar visitations in the churches at Samaria, Cesarea, Antioch, Pisidia, Galatia, Ephesus, and Corinth, the Holy Spirit personally filled the believers. What Christ could not do when He walked on earth as a man, the Holy Spirit did by indwelling the lives of these yielded believers and working through them the mighty works and words of power like those that were wrought in Jesus' ministry.

This very real Commander in Chief led His infant Church on to victory. That was the secret of the phenomenal success of the early Church. They were unlearned men, without silver or gold. Their church machinery was very simple, made up of prophets, evangelists, pastors, teachers, elders, and deacons. They were men and women who were bound together chiefly by ties of love and a common purpose. They had no prestige. Paul declared that the apostles were made as the filth of the world, an offscouring of all things (1 Cor. 4:13). They were the sect that was everywhere spoken against, yet they turned the world upside down. The gospel was preached to every creature under heaven, and churches were established. The only explanation for this phenomenal success was the fact that the apostles and their converts were filled with the Holy Spirit. The Holy Spirit was honored and given proper authority and control over their lives. He indwelt believers with power, investing them with His gifts. He went with them to prison, to the martyr's stake, to the whipping post. They went with Him and He with them. Together, the Holy Spirit and His body, the Body of Christ, marched on to amazing victory, through the apostolic days.

May we be admonished that this is the need of the Church today. The prophet declared:

*And it shall come to pass afterward, that I will pour out My spirit upon all flesh; and your sons and your daughters shall prophesy, your old men shall dream dreams, your young men shall see visions: and also upon the servants and upon the handmaids in those days will I pour out My spirit* (Joel 2:28-29).

Truly, the need of the Church in this hour is for the Holy Spirit to be given His rightful place of authority and honor so the gifts of the Spirit can flow in purity and power. Paul exhorted the Thessalonians to "quench not the Spirit" (1 Thess. 5:19). May we not be guilty of quenching the Spirit in our assemblies today, but follow Paul's exhortation to give the Holy Spirit His liberty to move among us. Only in that way can He reveal to us the things of Jesus and be allowed to build His Church effectively in the earth.

### Notes

1. Author unknown.

2. Source unknown.

3. The study of these gifts was compiled from notes written by Dr. Judson Cornwall for home fellowship group studies when he was associate pastor at Fountaingate Ministries in Dallas, Texas.

# Chapter 5

# Gifts of the Holy Spirit

## Part III: Divine Voice—Prophecy

*...the testimony of Jesus is the spirit of prophecy* (Revelation 19:10).

Because of the impact that prophecy is making on the Church today, both negatively and positively, I feel there is a need to understand clearly what the Scriptures teach concerning prophecy, the prophet, the gift of prophecy, and the spirit of prophecy. The present emphasis on the prophetic ministry in the Church has brought great blessing where it has been properly understood. It has also brought devastation to individual lives and churches when scriptural guidelines have not been followed for its operation. God's Word clearly teaches the parameters of true prophecy in all its dimensions. Only as we apply ourselves diligently to obey these principles will we benefit from God-given prophecy and be protected from what is false.

There is a desire in all of us to know the future—economically, politically, and especially spiritually. I continually receive mail and telephone calls from people telling me what they believe will happen in the future or inquiring what I feel will happen in the future. I heard recently that the psychics' telephone number announced on television is the most-called number ever made available on television. Although we condemn psychic power because of its ungodly source, we mention it to show how badly people want someone to tell them what is going to happen.

To have a prophetic anointing from the Holy Spirit to declare truth is not the same as giving an educated prediction. It is more than divine inspiration, or even revelation at times. Prophecy is more than one of the nine gifts listed in First Corinthians. True prophecy is *a divine ability to accurately perceive and proclaim present spiritual realities and to predict and prepare for the future.* One writer has referred to prophecy as the early winds of the coming season blowing across the earth. It is the dawn of tomorrow coming through the night of a dying day.

When the Church truly functions as God intended, it functions *prophetically.* Because the Scriptures declare that the testimony of Jesus is the spirit of prophecy, we understand that if our Lord's voice is being heard in the Church speaking through Spirit-filled believers, we are hearing a voice of prophecy. He will speak through such vehicles as (a) prophetic preaching; (b) the office of the prophet; (c) the gift of prophecy; (d) musical prophecies; (e) the song of the Lord and of the Bride to the Bridegroom; (f) prophetic prayers; and even (g) the prophetic reading of the Scriptures.

## Prophecy Demonstrated in the Scriptures

As we have stated, true prophecy is the divine ability to perceive, predict, proclaim, and prepare for the future. Prophecy in the Old Testament is depicted as both human activity and divine activity. God is the source of the prophetic message and human vessels become the channel for relating that message to the people concerned. Two Old Testament Hebrew words depict these divine and human aspects of prophecy. The Hebrew word *nataf* means "to fall as drops of rain." This word pictures the divine activity of prophecy as the prophetic message proceeds from God, falling from Heaven like raindrops. *Naba* is the Hebrew word for prophecy that means "to bubble up or gush forth." This word shows the human activity involved in prophecy, our human response to the prophetic anointing of God. The prophetic message pours forth from the prophet as water bubbling and gushing from a fountain.

A prophetic utterance is also described in Scripture as "the word of the Lord," from the Hebrew word *dabar*. The etymological meaning of this word is "to drive forward that which is behind." Thus the prophetic word has a creative force that drives forward to accomplish its message. This concept of a prophetic word having a dynamic creative force is also described by Paul in the New Testament. He requested the church in Thessalonica to pray for them that the word of the Lord would have free course (2 Thess. 3:1). The Greek word *trecho*, which is translated to "have free course," literally means "to run." This word is descriptive of a Greek runner who is running a course on which there are no barriers or hindrances to impede his progress. Thus Paul is asking for prayer that there will be nothing to impede the creative force of the Word of the Lord from running—driving forward to its accomplishment.

In the New Testament, prophecy is further defined by the Greek word *propheteuo*, a declaration from God that could include prediction of the future as well as proclamation of divine realities. Prophecy has a fore-telling, predictive aspect as a human vessel speaks for God concerning a future situation of the people. It may also be simply forthtelling in a proclamative aspect as a human vessel becomes God's mouthpiece to speak to the present situation of the people.

In summary, we can say that prophecy is a supernatural utterance by which God communicates to people His mind and purpose, using a Spirit-filled individual as His mouthpiece. Prophecy as *foretelling* involves prediction. In this realm, the prophet speaks for God, communicating what he perceives to be God's mind for the future. Past and present can be used to deal with the future. The purpose of prophetic prediction is to produce present godliness and edification in light of the future. Prophecy as *forthtelling* is proclamation, often involving anointed preaching. Sometimes the prophet will use the past to explain the present. This realm includes exhortation, reproof, warning, comfort, and edification. The prophet is a "preacher" and "proclaimer" of the Word of the Lord. True prophecy, then, will contain one or both of these messages: prediction of future events and present instruction concerning God's will.

## Purpose of Prophecy

Since the Scriptures teach that "the testimony of Jesus is the spirit of prophecy" (Rev. 19:10), we understand that the purpose of prophecy is first of all the exaltation of Jesus. The Holy Spirit came to glorify Jesus (Jn. 16:14), and the Father has highly exalted Him above every name in Heaven and earth (Phil. 2:9). As the Head of the Church, Christ must receive honor in every manifestation of the Spirit of God. Therefore, prophecy that exalts a person or group of people is immediately suspect because the primary purpose for the coming of the Holy Spirit is to reveal Jesus.

Second, prophecy is a means of receiving verbal communication from God in our known languages. Paul said that one who speaks in tongues speaks mysteries unto God; no one understands him. But the one who prophesies speaks unto men (1 Cor. 14:2-3). In that sense, prophecy gives vocal expression to other spiritual gifts as well. For example, gifts of knowledge need the prophetic anointing for their expression to the Body of Christ. Even gifts of power often need the gift of prophecy for articulation of their manifestations.

Third, prophecy is meant to bring edification to the Church (1 Cor. 14:4). Prophecy should build up, not tear down; it should comfort, not condemn; it should instruct, not injure. God has given us the prophetic voice in all of its manifestations to exalt Jesus and to bless and build the Church. What a wonder it is that God would speak to mankind through a human vessel! How careful we should be to guard the integrity of His voice.

It is an awesome responsibility to minister under a prophetic anointing given by the Holy Spirit. For a prophet to rightly predict a future event or trend gives him or her great authority with people. For this reason, care must be taken not to use the true prophetic anointing to manipulate people to follow a person's ministry. If a person has to wear a badge or make an announcement declaring that he or she is a prophet, that one is not a prophet.

At times the Holy Spirit will speak a word of correction to a church through the prophetic word. It is important to note, however, that the ministry of *corrective prophecy* belongs only to the leader of the flock or to another minister properly submitted to that pastoral leadership. A lay person should never attempt to correct, condemn, or chastise a congregation or an individual through the use of the gift of prophecy. According to the Scriptures, the simple gift of prophecy that operates apart from the office of a prophet is to be used for edification, comfort, and exhortation (1 Cor. 14:3). Correction of a church or believer corresponds to the office of the prophet, to one who is walking in a place of responsibility and accountability before God for a particular group of people. The purpose of prophecy, then, is first to exalt Jesus and then to build the Body of Christ.

## Prophets and Apostles

To understand the restoration of the prophetic ministry to the Church, we must examine the biblical relationship between apostles and prophets. According to the Scriptures, the revelation of the great mystery of the Church was given to the apostles and prophets (Eph. 3:5). Paul teaches that the Church is built on the foundation laid by the apostles and prophets (1 Cor. 3:9-15; Eph. 2:19-22). All other ministries are to be built upon this foundation. In divine order, though all are equal in value as persons before the Lord, God has set some in the Church to be apostles, prophets, evangelists, teachers, and pastors, for the equipping of the saints (Eph. 4:11). These are different and unique gifts that in the wisdom of God are sent to the Body of Christ.

The Scriptures teach, by example, that the apostle and prophet are called to work together, to act as checks and balances for one another. I think it is dangerous for an apostle or a prophet to work alone, at least without conferring with one another and sharing their ministry together. We need to hear as a unit what the Spirit is saying to the Church. It is also clear from the Scriptures that apostles function in a governmental capacity in the church, while prophets function in a revelatory capacity. Although we would not rule out the possibility of one person functioning under both anointings, we recognize the safety of having both apostles and prophets working together in the church. We must beware lest we exalt one over the other. As we begin to understand the need for prophecy in the building of the Church, we realize how important it is for the apostles and the prophets to work together in a proper relationship.

Prophets are given by Christ, the Head of His Body, to perfect that Body through revelation. They are viewed as messengers, seers, communicators, and encouragers of the Church. Their mission is to communicate what the Holy Spirit has confirmed to the apostolic leadership, and to edify the local churches. Prophets are not intended to set up personal dynasties and to make the other giftings inferior to the office of prophecy.

New Testament examples of prophets such as Silas and Judas (Acts 15:32) and Agabus (Acts 21:10) were men who were recognized "trans-locally" as those whose prophetic ministry strengthened the local churches. It was Agabus, a prophet gifted as a seer of future events, who prophesied the apostle Paul's imprisonment (Acts 21:11). Before his conversion, Paul was a dedicated Pharisee who desperately resisted the emerging Church. But after his conversion, he was given prophetic insight into the coming season of the Church. Jesus appeared to him and he saw a light brighter than the midday sun, brighter than Phariseeism, Judaism, and all other lights. That new light that began to illumine his life brought revelation of Christ and His Kingdom.

Not only was the apostle Paul personally transformed, but the eternal plan of God for the Church that was revealed through him changed the world. He saw the startling mystery that had been hidden in God since before the foundation of the world until that time. He saw that God was going to bring all people together in Christ according to His eternal plan. He saw that the old boundaries were obliterated at the cross. He realized that this revelation was contrary to all he had believed before. And when he saw it, he moved from merely being religious to becoming prophetic, as well as apostolic. Paul not only proclaimed the change he saw, but as an apostle born out of due season, he also helped to make it happen by establishing churches through the power of the Holy Spirit.

Today, prophets and prophetesses are divinely-given ministries to help build strong churches during this transitional period. The churches that are moving on the cutting edge of what God is doing today, hearing what God by His Spirit is saying, are those that are allowing the prophetic ministry to be restored to them. We have seen this restoration of the true prophetic ministry throughout the last several decades by the correct emphasis being placed on prophetic insight in the Church.

As with each movement of the Holy Spirit, however, there have been extremes, as well as overemphases of the truth. It is said that he who walks the razor edge of truth also walks the razor edge of heresy. This has seemed particularly true concerning the prophetic ministry. Although this God-ordained ministry has been abused, misused, and mis-taught, it is still the ministry Jesus set in the Church; it has not passed away. There will always be those who respond to truth in faith, and others who will respond in fear through unbelief. We need to place our faith in God and accept the ministry of the prophetic in the fear of God as it is properly restored to the Church.

For the restoration of the prophetic ministry to be effective in the Church, it is important to understand the nature of prophecy as well as some biblical parameters given for the proper discerning of the prophetic voice. This will keep us from erroneous teaching regarding prophecy and will prevent us from making everyone a "prophet." Man-made prophets are not set in the Church by Christ. In order for the Church to prosper, we need the true ministry of the prophet to function as Christ intended.

## THE CHAIN OF PROPHECY

*The Prophecy of Scripture*

> *We have also a more sure word of prophecy... For the prophecy came not in old time by the will of man: but holy men of God spake as they were moved by the Holy Ghost* (2 Peter 1:19,21).

Because the Scriptures are the inspired, infallible words of God, the prophecy of Scripture is regarded as infallible revelation (2 Tim. 3:16). This kind of prophecy is not being spoken today because the 66 books of the Bible, the canon of Scripture, are complete.

According to the Scriptures, nothing is to be added or taken away from the Word of God (Rev. 22:18-19). Prophecy of Scripture refers to all the Scriptures generally, and more specifically to the prophetic books of the Old Testament. This is the highest level of prophecy, deserving our complete confidence and requiring the most careful and systematic interpretation.

Of course, this level of prophecy is not subject to judging; it is infallible and is the basis for judging all other realms of prophecy. Although we do not judge the utterance of the Scriptures, the Scriptures do judge our utterances, whatever they are. There is no present truth of greater authority than the Word of God, and no one whose prophecy is above being judged for its validity by the Word of God.

## *The Office of the Prophet*

> *God, who at sundry times and in divers manners spake in time past unto the fathers by the prophets* (Hebrews 1:1).

In Old Testament times a prophet was a person given to the distinctive ministry of representing God before mankind through a prophetic mantle that came upon him. The prophet was God's mouthpiece, God's spokesman, through whom the Word of God flowed, whether in forthtelling or foretelling. God established the office of the prophet for the people of Israel, who asked not to hear the voice of the Lord for themselves

(Deut. 18:15-19). Such men as Samuel, Elijah, and Amos filled the office of prophet. Women such as Deborah (Judg. 4:4), Huldah (2 Chron. 34:22), and Anna (Lk. 2:36-38), were prophetesses. A true prophet or prophetess becomes a representative of God to the people. We have already mentioned New Testament prophets who were gifts to the Church to build it through revelation received from God.

## The Gift of Prophecy

> *Having then gifts differing according to the grace that is given to us, whether prophecy, let us prophesy according to the proportion of faith* (Romans 12:6).

The gift of prophecy as listed with the other nine gifts of the Spirit (1 Cor. 12:8-10), is defined as the God-given ability to speak forth supernaturally in a known language as the Holy Spirit gives utterance. The meanings of the Hebrew and Greek words describing this gift involve ecstatic vision, burden, and inspired utterances, and can be translated as, "to break forth under sudden impulse in lofty discourse on praise or the divine counsels." This is an operation of the Holy Spirit as seen in the New Testament Church that must be exercised within divine guidelines. It is not infallible.

As we have stated, the gift of prophecy functions in three areas: edification, which means *building up*; exhortation, which is *stirring up*; and comfort, which could be called *cheering up*. Paul taught, "But he that prophesieth speaketh unto men to edification, and exhortation, and comfort" (1 Cor. 14:3). These are safe guidelines that everyone who prophesies can follow.

It is important that we approach each of the gifts in an attitude of humility. If someone gives an utterance that is not received by those who are discerning and judging by the Spirit, the one giving the utterance should not be offended. In a teachable spirit, that person should receive the correction given and pray to become more sensitive to the Holy Spirit. As believers, we should not become discouraged with the imperfectness in prophetic utterances. Rather, we need to heed the admonition of Paul when he says, "Quench not the Spirit. Despise not prophesyings. Prove all things; hold fast that which is good" (1 Thess. 5:19-21). Heeding this scriptural teaching on spiritual gifts will prevent immature and misguided manifestations that become a temptation to some to quench the moving of the Spirit.

## THE OFFICE AND GIFT CONTRASTED

Having defined the office of the prophet and the gift of prophecy, perhaps a further contrasting of their functions will give greater clarity to their uniqueness. The office and the gift are distinct for two reasons:

1. According to the Scriptures, the office of the prophet is inseparable from the person: "And He

gave some as apostles, and some as prophets..."
(Eph. 4:11 NAS). The prophet is one of the
fivefold ministries Christ gave to the Church. The
person who functions in the office of a prophet has
a prophetic mantle continually resting upon him
or her. The gift of prophecy, on the contrary, is one
of the nine gifts Paul lists (1 Cor. 12:8-10), for
which the Holy Spirit can use anyone in the
church who is yielded to Him when He chooses to
speak prophetically at a certain time.

2. Far greater gifts than this simple gift of prophecy
   are needed to make a man a prophet. For example,
   revelation of hidden things of the past, present, or
   future are necessary for the prophetic office.
   Nathan the prophet, who exposed King David's
   sin with Bathsheba, is an example (2 Sam. 12).
   This type of revelation is not included in the realm
   of the gift of prophecy.

Exercising the gift of prophecy, then, does not
necessarily result in a person becoming a prophet.
Paul's exhortation to seek to prophesy does not relate
to the office of the prophet, but to the gift of prophecy
(1 Cor. 14:1). So it is possible to operate the gift of
prophecy and not be fulfilling the office of a prophet.
It is not possible, however, to be a prophet without
having the gift of prophecy. Simply stated, *all prophets
will prophesy, but all who prophesy are not prophets.*
The gift of prophecy comes well down the list in order

of importance among the gifts, but the prophetic office is second among the offices (Eph. 4:11).

We would use these words to describe the office of prophet: representative of God, permanent office, life style, greater authority. In contrast, we would describe the gift of prophecy as follows: present expression of God's mind, temporary anointing. The gift of prophecy and the office of the prophet are similar, however, in that they are both subject to judgment by the saints on the basis of the Word, the Spirit, and the blood.

## Manifestation of the Gift of Prophecy

The gift of prophecy will be manifested, first of all, in vocal utterances in public worship services. Peter exhorted:

*If any man speak, let him speak as the oracles of God* (1 Peter 4:11a).

The Greek word for *oracle* is *logion*, which means a short utterance or short word. It can be a part of a longer utterance that includes exhorting and confirming teaching.

Second, the gift of prophecy can bring forth a message to an individual. God will sometimes encourage and edify a person with a word of prophecy. I would hasten to caution those who give or receive a personal word of prophecy, however, for it must be judged like any other prophetic word. The person receiving the prophetic word should submit it to his or her pastoral leadership that is responsible to give an account before God for the souls under their care (Heb. 13:17). I personally have seen many lives hurt and churches split through the improper use of this gift. There is safety in following scriptural guidelines in the function of spiritual gifts.

## The Spirit of Prophecy

*And I fell at his feet to worship him. And he said unto me, See thou do it not: I am thy fellowservant, and of thy brethren that have the testimony of Jesus: worship God: for the testimony of Jesus is the spirit of prophecy* (Revelation 19:10).

The spirit of prophecy is an all-inclusive term that refers to the Holy Spirit energizing men and women, causing them to speak forth inspired utterances in a known language. Since Jesus is the testimony of prophecy, when He is genuinely speaking through the members He has set in the Body, the spirit of prophecy is present. When the spirit of prophecy moves upon a church, it seems that everyone can prophesy because of the anointing of the Holy Spirit flowing at that time. On such an occasion, according to the Scriptures, all may prophesy, though it doesn't mean that all have to or should. Paul gave instructions concerning the orderly use of the gifts in the church: "For ye may all prophesy one by one, that all may learn, and all may be comforted" (1 Cor. 14:31). During these refreshing times when the spirit of prophecy is flowing in the church, it is easy for people to prophesy who would not otherwise operate freely in that gift.

The Old Testament Scriptures are full of examples of the spirit of prophecy coming upon godly men. For example, Adam prophesied concerning his bride and the marriage estate (Gen. 2:20-25). Enoch prophesied of the second coming of Christ (Jude 14-15). Noah was the preacher of righteousness because the spirit of Christ was upon Him (2 Pet. 2:5). Abraham was spoken of as a prophet (Gen. 20:7). Isaac and Jacob had the spirit of prophecy upon them as they blessed their sons (Gen. 27, 48, 49). Joseph prophesied of the exodus from Egypt (Gen. 50:24). At times the spirit of prophecy even came upon groups of people. The Lord took the same spirit that was upon Moses and placed it upon the 70 elders of Israel and they prophesied (Num. 11:24-30). During the reign of Saul, the spirit of prophecy fell upon several groups of messengers as well as upon King Saul (1 Sam. 19:23-24).

In the New Testament, as we have seen, Paul instructed the churches that tongues are for a sign to the unbeliever and that prophecy serves those who believe. He said that if an unbeliever came in and heard the church prophesying, he would be convinced of all: "And thus are the secrets of his heart made manifest; and so falling down on his face he will worship God, and report that God is in you of a truth" (1 Cor. 14:25). The testimony of Jesus in the Church will draw men unto Himself.

Under the influence of the spirit of prophecy, some-times exhortations are received and *written* before the saints gather together. They can then be shared with the saints when they gather. Writing it down preserves its simplicity, its authenticity, and unction. Also, the spirit of prophecy will break forth in times of *prayer* while we are praying publicly. I personally ex-perienced that at the beginning of my walk in the Spirit. I was praying for a person and heard the Holy Spirit changing my prayer and prophesying through it. I didn't know I was prophesying, but others told me what was happening. Then I began to experience the anointing of the prophetic mantle also when I preached the Word.

It is not uncommon for the Holy Spirit to inter-sperse the operation of the gift of prophecy with the ministry of teaching. It does not come as an interrup-tion of a "thus saith the Lord," but flows into the anointed teaching. Even *reading the Scriptures aloud* can be done under a prophetic anointing. Although satan quotes the Scriptures like a parrot, the Holy Spirit proclaims them like a prophet. We need to live in such a way as to experience the spirit of prophecy in our assemblies, that the testimony of Jesus may be given His proper place in the Church.

*The Prophetic in Music*

How beautifully the Scriptures describe the pro-phetic anointing in music and worship! The psalmist,

David, who provided so many prophetic songs for us, declared that God Himself inhabits our praises (Ps. 22:3). Paul taught the New Testament Church to "let the word of Christ dwell in you richly in all wisdom; teaching and admonishing one another in psalms and hymns and spiritual songs, singing with grace in your hearts to the Lord" (Col. 3:16). He declared that he would sing with the spirit as well as with the understanding (1 Cor. 14:15). What we refer to today as the "song of the Lord" was established under the reign of Hezekiah as he restored worship to Israel (2 Chron. 29:25-28). When Jeremiah prophesied of the restoration of Israel, he declared:

> *...Again there shall be heard in this place...the voice of joy, and the voice of gladness, the voice of the bridegroom, and the voice of the bride, the voice of them that shall say, Praise the Lord of hosts: for the Lord is good; for His mercy endureth for ever: and of them that shall bring the sacrifice of praise into the house of the Lord...* (Jeremiah 33:10-11).

We see another example of the prophetic song when Miriam sang of the great deliverance God had given (Ex. 15:20-21). The song of Moses sung by the saints is prophetic (Rev. 15:3-4). And is not the Song of Solomon the prophetic song of the bridegroom to the bride, as well as her response to her bridegroom? In light of these biblical teachings, we should expect the prophetic flow of the Holy Spirit to be a part of our corporate worship in our churches today. For the restoration of the prophetic to the church, we need to allow Him to move in our midst, refreshing us and instructing us through prophetic song and instrumental music.

## GUIDELINES FOR DISCERNING PROPHECY

### Limitations to Prophecy

Although the source of prophecy is divine, the human element is never set aside as the prophecy is communicated to man. For that reason the flow of prophecy through us will have certain limitations. According to Paul, one of the main causes of these limitations is our limited knowledge. He declared that "we know in part, and we prophesy in part" (1 Cor. 13:9). Paul also instructed us to "prophesy according to the proportion of faith" (Rom. 12:6). Our faith level is another limitation for the prophetic flow through us and usually determines its effectiveness as well. If we do not believe it is God speaking through us, no one else is going to believe it. If the message is given in fear, that fear will be transmitted through the message, diluting its impact. Because these human elements will always be present to some degree, the Scriptures give clear guidelines concerning the proper way to discern and judge the prophetic ministry.

### Biblical Testings

It is important to subject all prophecy to biblical tests, not only because of human limitations, but also because satan will stir up false prophets to deceive people. God has given us descriptions of and warnings against false prophets, as well as proofs of a real prophet and genuine prophetic gifts. The tests given in the Word of God help us determine the validity of prophetic utterances.

**Test of Humility** (1 Cor. 8:1). The first test to apply to all prophets and prophetic utterances is the test of humility. First Corinthians 8:1 teaches that knowledge puffs up, but charity edifies. Even though supernatural knowledge is present in the prophetic flow, the result should be the edifying of the church or individual through love. We should answer these questions to be sure humility is working in the prophetic ministry: Does the prophetic voice produce pride in our hearts? Does it exalt a person or Christ? Any personal exaltation of the one prophesying or of those to whom the prophecy is directed must be suspect. True prophecy will work in love through humility.

**Test of Spirit** (1 John 4:1-3). Is it the Holy Spirit, the human spirit, or an evil spirit that is responsible for the utterance? All three of these spirits can enter into the realm of prophecy and each must be discerned by spiritual people.

**Test of Worship** (Deut. 13:1-5). Does the prophetic word lead us to worship God, or lead us away from the true God?

**Test of Covetousness** (Mic. 3:11; 2 Pet. 2:1-3). Are these prophets making merchandise of the people of God? Often one of the characteristics of a false prophet is covetousness.

**Test of Fulfillment** (Deut. 18:22). Does the prophetic word come to pass or not? Time is the great prover of prophecies. We must also remember, however, that fulfillment of a prophetic word is not always immediate.

**Test of Doctrine** (Is. 8:19-20; Jn. 14:1-6; 1 Tim. 4:1-3;). Do the prophets speak in harmony with the major doctrines of redemption? Do they speak according to sound doctrine based on God's Word?

**Test of Fruit** (Mt. 7:15-23). What is the fruit of the prophet's life style? The Scriptures teach that by their fruits, not their gifts, we shall know them. Holiness of life will characterize a true prophet.

**Test of Ministry to People** (Jer. 23:18-23). Do these prophets turn the people from their sinful life styles to God? Building the Church through prophecy will result in a holy people that love God.

**Test of Value** (1 Tim. 1:18). We are to fight the good fight of faith by the prophecies that go before us. Do we value the infallible Word of God above personal prophetic words? Prophetic words instruct on a personal basis what the inspired and infallible Word of God has already told us to do on a general basis. They must never be allowed higher value in our thinking than the Word of God.

**Test of Confirmation** (Col. 3:15). Is the prophetic utterance confirmation to our spirits? Does it agree with the already revealed will of God? Does it agree with the rule of peace in our hearts? If not, we must seek the counsel of proven ministry.

**Test of Accountability** (Mt. 12:34-37). To whom is this prophet accountable? Does the prophet have an apostolic covering? Is the prophet willing to take responsibility for his or her prophecy? All New Testament prophets belonged to and were under the authority of a local church. To the first-century Church, Paul wrote that two or three prophets should speak, and the others should weigh carefully what was said (1 Cor. 14:29).

**Test of Control** (2 Pet. 2:1-3). According to the Scriptures, false prophets will exploit people out of greed, introducing heresies and leading people astray through their sensuality. Prophets are not to use their gifts to manipulate, intimidate, or control through fear the people to whom they minister out of selfish motives. Do they attempt to exercise control over believers' lives? Do their utterances manipulate or intimidate? If so, they are not true prophets.

**Test of Love** (1 Cor. 14:3; Jas. 3:17). Prophetic messages should be given in a spirit of love. Even a word of correction is to be given in a spirit of love. Information about any visions that may be negative or embarrassing should never be spoken publicly without first confronting the individual in private.

## God's Call to the Prophetic

We should not neglect to evaluate the prophetic flow in these biblical ways so we can keep from being misguided by the human element or deceived by the work of satan. These principles are God's safeguards for exercising the prophetic ministry in the Body of Christ today. Having considered them, though, we would be careful again to say, with Paul, that we should not despise prophesyings. It is our responsibility to prove all things and hold fast to that which is good so the Church can be built effectively.

God is calling the Church to the prophetic; He is restoring the ministry of prophecy to the Church. He has trusted us with divine abilities in the realm of prophecy, and we need to prove ourselves trustworthy vessels of His power. We must allow the Holy Spirit to use prophecy correctly for the building of the Church. Let's not miss it by "throwing out the baby with the bath water" just because some abuse it. As we yield our lives to the Holy Spirit to obey in all things, we will become vessels of honor for the fulfillment of His purposes.

# Chapter 6

## *The Fruit of the Spirit*

### *Part I: Divine Character Defined*

*But the fruit of the Spirit is love, joy, peace, longsuffering, gentleness, goodness, faith [faithfulness], meekness, temperance: against such there is no law* (Galatians 5:22-23).

*(For the fruit of the Spirit is in all goodness and righteousness and truth)* (Ephesians 5:9).

*But now being made free from sin, and become servants to God, ye have your fruit unto holiness, and the end everlasting life* (Romans 6:22).

It is no accident that the Word calls the Third Person of the Godhead the *Holy Spirit*. Holiness characterizes His divine nature. One of the supreme mandates of the Holy Spirit is to impart the holiness of God to us, to change us from glory to glory, giving us His divine nature and His character. As He works in each believer, He develops within us His character, which is identified by the fruit of the Spirit. God's purpose in redeeming us is that we become "a mature man, to the measure of the stature which belongs to the fulness of Christ" (Eph. 4:13 NAS).

I used to think the fruit of the Spirit was produced just like the gifts are, by the Holy Spirit. But then I began to realize that it is not the Spirit Himself who bears the fruit, but the Christ-life within us that produces the fruit of godly character in us. The Holy Spirit produces the Christ-life in us as we obey Him, causing the holiness and divine nature of our Lord Jesus to be manifest through us. The fruit of the Spirit, then, is the true character of the Christian life that replaces the self-life, or old man, as the Scriptures label our sin nature. It is the fruit of the Tree of Life, Christ, who lives in the garden of our spirits. Perry Brewster makes this observation regarding fruit-bearing Christians:

> In some ways the term "Christlikeness" is inadequate. Since the Christian is called not really to resemble Christ but to share His very life. With

deference to a great Christian classic, the life of the believer is more than the "Imitation of Christ." It is becoming a partaker of the divine nature (II Pet. 1:4). One might be bold enough to suggest that "Christness" would be nearer the mark, since the believer is more than a copy of Christ. He is part and parcel of His very being. "Bone of His bone, flesh of His flesh," as Paul daringly puts it (Eph. 5:30). Our likeness to Christ is definitely not something applied from without, as a cosmetic transformation produced by a formula of some religious make-up department. It is a genuine likeness produced by an intimate relationship with Him. Christ's own analogy of the vine and the branches upholds this (Jn. 15:1). The branches are not merely vine-like; they are a part of the vine. Likewise the fruit does not merely resemble grapes, but possesses their inherent structure and taste.[1]

Fruitfulness is the principal purpose for the existence of a tree. Jesus taught His disciples that fruitfulness was His purpose for them as well. He told them, "Ye have not chosen Me, but I have chosen you, and ordained you, that ye should go and bring forth fruit, and that your fruit should remain..." (Jn. 15:16). In this great teaching, Jesus called Himself the true vine, and His Father the husbandman. He called the disciples branches and told them to abide in Him so they could bring forth fruit. He warned them, "Every branch in Me that does not bear fruit, He [the Father] takes away; and every branch that bears fruit, He prunes it, that it may bear more fruit" (Jn. 15:2 NAS).

Jesus cursed the fig tree because it did not bring forth fruit, and in the morning the disciples found the tree had died (Mt. 21:18-19). Does He not have the right to expect to find fruit on His tree of life in His garden? Even the Old Testament carries this beautiful analogy of the bride being a fruitful garden that the bridegroom can enjoy. In the most poetic book of all we read this:

*A garden inclosed is my sister, my spouse; a spring shut up, a fountain sealed. ... A fountain of gardens, a well of living waters, and streams from Lebanon. Awake, O north wind; and come, thou south; blow upon my garden, that the spices thereof may flow out. Let my beloved come into his garden, and eat his pleasant fruits. I am come into my garden, my sister, my spouse: I have gathered my myrrh with my spice; I have eaten my honeycomb with my honey; I have drunk my wine with my milk: eat, O friends; drink, yea, drink abundantly, O beloved* (Song of Solomon 4:12,15-16; 5:1).

Thus fruitfulness is a result of a relationship that is carefully cultivated. Jesus taught His disciples they could only be fruitful by learning to abide in Him.

## PRINCIPLE OF ABIDING

The principle of abiding must be clearly understood so we avoid trying to bear fruit in our own strength. The Scriptures teach that these true Christian virtues are the fruit of the Spirit, not the fruit of human effort. Many people today are attempting to produce the fruit of the Spirit through natural efforts and character-building. They exercise their wills to produce character through philosophy, education, ethics, anthropology, mental sciences, or controlled environment. The results achieved from this human effort, though they may involve temporal good, are not the eternal fruitfulness that is produced by the work of the Holy Spirit.

### Fruit Is Character

We have stated that the fruit of the Spirit is the *character* of Christ produced by the Spirit of Christ in the believer's life. The more completely one is filled with the Holy Spirit, the greater will be the manifestation of the fruit of the Spirit in his life and work. Only when a believer is full of the Holy Spirit, continually yielding to Him, can he exhibit the full fruition of Christian virtues. When Christ is formed in the believer through the indwelling of the Holy Spirit, true Christlike character will be as natural a result as pears growing on a pear tree. It follows then that if one who professes to be a Christian is devoid of fruit, he obviously does not have the Spirit of Christ. The fruit of the Spirit is produced automatically when we are yielded to the Holy Spirit and are walking in obedience to Him.

When Paul describes the fruit of the Spirit in writing to the Galatians, he is restating the Sermon on the Mount. This description is the ideal Christian life presented in concentrated expression. Paul's love chapter to the Corinthians (1 Cor. 13) is the summary of his list of the fruit of the Spirit. He is teaching the very same principle of Christian life when he writes to the Philippians: "...whatever is true, whatever is honorable, whatever is right, whatever is pure, whatever is lovely, whatever is of good repute, if there is any excellence and if anything worthy of praise, let your mind dwell on these things" (Phil. 4:8 NAS). Any concept of Christianity that does not have as its basis the character of the fruit of the Spirit is a false teaching of Christianity.

The Scriptures clearly teach that natural man cannot hope to develop godly character without the work of the Holy Spirit in his life. Paul describes the striking contrast between the works of the flesh and the fruit of the Spirit:

*Now the deeds of the flesh are evident, which are: immorality, impurity, sensuality, idolatry, sorcery, enmities, strife, jealousy, outbursts of anger, disputes, dissensions, factions, envying, drunkenness, carousing, and things like these, of which I forewarn you just as I have forewarned you that those who practice such things shall not inherit the kingdom of God* (Galatians 5:19-21 NAS).

Spirit-filled men and women can be distinguished by their fruit in the same way that a carnal person can be identified by fleshly works. If we are abiding in Christ, the fruit of the Spirit will be manifest in our lives; it cannot be hidden. So, also, are the works of the flesh manifest in one who is not abiding in Christ. A carnal person is one who is not governed by the indwelling Spirit of God. This egocentric, self-centered life manifests the works of the flesh, while a Christ-centered life will manifest the fruit of the Spirit.

The great struggle within each believer is the struggle between self and Christ. If self wins, it becomes the central force of life, causing a person to be completely self-centered. Every descriptive characteristic of a self-centered person starts with the word *self*: selfish, self-pitying, self-glorying, perhaps even self-hating. The list of "self" words seems unending. If Christ wins this battle against our self-life, He becomes the center of our personalities, and we become Christ-centered. The happy consequence of a Christ-centered life is the manifestation of the fruit of the Spirit.

## The Nature of Fruitfulness

The principle of fruit-bearing is a "life-principle." Life develops from a life-source; it cannot be manufactured. Fruit is not made; it grows as the requirements of the life-principle are met. In contrast, the works of the flesh as described in the Scriptures are a negative result of human effort without the Holy Spirit. Samuel Chadwick, referring to Galatians 5:19-21, observed:

> The most striking feature of this contrast is its emphatic change from works to fruit. Work belongs to the workshop; fruit belongs to the garden. One comes from the ingenuity of the factory; the other is the silent growth of an abounding life. The factory operates with dead stuff; the garden cultivates a living force to their appointed end. Works are always in the realm of dead things. Every building is built out of dead material. A tree must die before it can be used by the builder. There is no life in stones and brick and steel joints and iron girders. They are all dead and in the process of disintegration. No earthly material lasts. Man's best works fail and fade and crumble and pass away. Fruit does not come of man's labor. It requires his diligence, but it is neither his invention nor his product. He does not make the flowers. No skill of his brings the golden harvest of the fields or the lush fruit of the trees. When man has done all he can do, then God begins and life proceeds. Fruit is God's work. The phrase "fruit of the Spirit" assigns the graces of the Christian character to their proper source. They are not of man's producing.[2]

The Scriptures clearly teach the life-principle involved in bearing fruit. The flesh can produce nothing but evil works, while the Holy Spirit produces Christ-life fruit. The former requires self-effort and results in death; the latter requires obedience to the Holy Spirit and produces life and peace.

## The Source of Fruitfulness

How does the Holy Spirit work in our lives to produce the fruit of a Christ-life character? The psalmist described the "blessed man" as a tree planted by the river of water that yields its fruit in its season (Ps. 1:3). He declares of this fruitful life that "his delight is in the law of the Lord, and in His law he meditates day and night" (Ps. 1:2 NAS). The place that we give the Word of God in our lives will determine our degree of fruitfulness.

**Meditation.** David doesn't say that this blessed man simply reads the Word. He *meditates* on it as well. We find the admonition to stop and meditate given throughout the Book of Psalms. The word *selah* found in many of the psalms means to meditate, to stop and think about what has been said. A word picture of *selah* is the cow chewing her cud after eating to assimilate all she has swallowed. As we read and meditate on the Scriptures, the Holy Spirit can convince us of sin that needs to be purged and can direct us to God's standard of holiness and righteousness for our lives. Apart from applying the Word of God there can be no lasting spiritual growth and no fruit-bearing in our lives.

**Spiritual Disciplines.** We have discussed the abiding principle that Jesus taught the disciples as a prerequisite for bearing fruit (Jn. 15). Truly abiding in the vine will result in an intimate relationship with Christ, allowing nothing to separate us from Him. We need to give ourselves to disciplines in our lives that will help cultivate this abiding relationship. These disciplines include not only giving ourselves to searching the Word of God, but also *hearing* the Word that is lifed by anointed preaching, as well as spending much time in *prayer* and *worship* in the Spirit. These help us feed our inner man on His life and help grace us in our relationship with Him. *Fellowship* with other believers is also an important spiritual discipline because it allows us to commune with Christ and to participate in His life indirectly, through each other. Jesus was emphatic that we can only bear spiritual fruit if we abide in Him. The life of Christ, as the life-giving sap in the vine, is essential to spiritual growth and fruit-bearing.

**Obedience.** The secret to abiding in Christ is to (a) *believe* in our spirits; (b) *obey* in our souls; and (c) *yield* our flesh to the power of the Holy Spirit. This abiding obedience involves every aspect of our person. *Obedience* is a word we sometimes don't like to hear. It seems almost an obsolete word in Christendom. We hear much about faith, but so little about obedience.

But Jesus said, "If you keep My commandments, you will abide in My love" (Jn. 15:10a NAS). Obedience brings maturity and develops the fruit of the Spirit in our lives. We cannot display the fruit of the Spirit when sin or neglect has interrupted our fellowship with Christ.

I knew a woman who was a faithful reader of the Word, and her life evidenced it by the fruit she was bearing. But for some reason she neglected her study of the Word for three or four days, and she began to be irritable and impatient. Her little four-year-old daughter observed her mother's reactions for a day, and then said to her, "Mother, why don't you get into the Word?" That four-year-old child understood Jesus' command better than most of us. As we learn to abide in the true vine, His life flows into us, producing the fruit of the Spirit to the Father's glory and to the blessing of others.

Some things about our relationship with Christ we may not fully understand. Suppose we were to ask a branch on a grapevine, "How do you grow luscious fruit?" If the branch could talk, it probably would say, "I don't know. I don't grow any of it; I just bear it. If you cut me away from this vine, I will just wither away and become useless." Just as without the vine the branch can produce nothing, so it is in our Christian lives. If we strain to work to produce the fruit of the

Spirit ourselves, we will find ourselves fruitless and frustrated.

But if we abide in Christ, maintaining a close, obedient, dependent relationship with Him, God the Holy Spirit can work in us, creating and producing the fruit of the Spirit. The manifestation of that fruit in our lives, as we have seen, is the life of the Lord Jesus in His godly character of holiness. This doesn't mean that we instantly become mature, bearing all the fruit of the Spirit fully and immediately. Even after fruit appears on the tree, it takes time—time during which the elements of wind and rain and even storms bring the fruit to maturity. This desired maturity is impossible without our continually abiding in the vine.

We should understand also that receiving the baptism of the Holy Spirit does not automatically result in the fruit of the Spirit being formed in our lives. One who has yielded his life more fully to the Holy Spirit in receiving the baptism of the Holy Spirit will obviously have the divine enabling to develop *more* fruit, *much* fruit, and fruit that *remains*. However, every believer who has accepted Christ as Savior has the Holy Spirit abiding in him. As he continues to abide in Christ he will experience the fruit of the Spirit in his life.

Because fruit-bearing is a direct result of abiding in Christ, there are deeply spiritual and fruitful Christians who have never had evidence of having received the Pentecostal experience of Holy Spirit baptism. On the other hand, it is sadly true that there are Spirit-baptized Christians who have not developed the fruit of the Spirit to any degree in their lives through consciously abiding in Christ. Both cases prove the reality that fruitfulness is not a result of receiving the baptism of the Holy Spirit, but is a result of abiding in Christ. It remains, then, that the key to the quantity and quality of fruitfulness in our lives is abiding in Christ, the Vine, in obedience to His commands.

The apostle Paul addressed the Galatians and the Corinthians concerning these issues, for many of them had received the baptism of the Holy Spirit but were still void of Christ's love. Some of these early Christians placed their priorities on the gifts of the Spirit operating through them. I have known some Pentecostal Christians who suppose that the baptism in the Holy Spirit as a single experience is the crowning attainment of the Christian life. That is not true. The real crowning attainment for any Christian is to live a Spirit-filled and Spirit-led life daily, abounding in the fruit of the Spirit. If the Holy Spirit who abides in us is hindered, grieved, and quenched while we sow to the flesh instead of yielding to the Spirit, we can expect to live a fruitless life. It is an immutable divine law that whatever we sow, we will also reap (Gal. 6:7).

We cannot overestimate the importance of abiding in the vine. Jesus taught His disciples the consequences for living otherwise: "Every branch in Me that beareth not fruit He taketh away" (Jn. 15:2a). What does He do with it? "If anyone does not abide in Me, he is thrown away as a branch, and dries up; and they gather them, and cast them into the fire, and they are burned" (Jn. 15:6 NAS). It is not the vine that is rejected, but the fruitless branch. If the branches are removed and cast into the fire, it is because they bear no fruit.

This judgment applies to born-again Christians, not mere professing believers. The expression "every branch in Me" clearly shows that some who are taken away for failing to produce fruit had once been true branches in the vine. Even though they were branches, having received life from the vine, they did not continue to abide in the vine and failed to produce fruit. It is my earnest conviction that what God requires He provides, and I believe what He provides He requires. As applied here, that means that God provides the life, the sap, and the elements necessary to the branch, and therefore He has a right to expect fruitfulness of the believer.

### Pruning Process

If one does not abide in Christ, he cannot bear fruit and, according to Jesus' teaching, will be cast away. If a branch does bear fruit, the requirement made of the fruitful branch is that it endure purging. Listen to Jesus' words: "And every branch that beareth fruit, He purgeth it, that it may bring forth more fruit" (Jn. 15:2b). This suggests the process of pruning or cutting away some areas in our lives that were once fruitful.

The primary purpose of pruning a vine is to remove the wood that produced fruit last season to force the vine to grow new wood that will produce fruit. God does not perpetuate the old; He prunes to force new growth. If we have experienced some pruning in our lives, it is not because God is mad at us, or that there is necessarily sin in our lives. It is that the Father is pleased we are bearing fruit and He knows that to increase the quality and quantity of that fruit, we need to be pruned. Pruning to the Christian is never pleasant; it suggests chastening. Sometimes the enemy whispers his suggestions to us that it is punishment. However, there is a vast difference between correction or chastening, and punishment. The former belongs to the family of God and works redemption in us; the latter belongs to satan and his angels.

The Scriptures teach that although "no chastening for the present seemeth to be joyous, but grievous: nevertheless afterward it yieldeth the peaceable fruit of righteousness..." (Heb. 12:11). God's goal in our lives is to produce fruit. He knows that at times the pruning knife is necessary to cut away the excess of "flesh" and strengthen the root so more fruit can be produced. Leaves and foliage can be very beautiful. In the spring season, I can look out in the yard, and the trees are verdant, luscious, and lively. However, there is no fruit yet. Sometimes when the Master comes He doesn't even find fruit when it is past the time that fruit should have been produced. So He must cut away the leaves of self-indulgence from our lives so we can bear His fruit.

Jesus continued, "Herein is My Father glorified, that ye bear much fruit..." (Jn. 15:8). Lest we should tend to draw back from this painful pruning process, He admonishes us to remember that our Father is the Husbandman (Jn. 15:1). He is the one who holds the knife, not man. We can safely trust ourselves to His loving care. If we had to submit to someone who didn't understand the vine, didn't know how to prune it, and caused it to bleed and die, we might have a reason to be uneasy. However, our heavenly Father is the Master Husbandman, and He holds the pruning instrument in His hand. We may ask what He uses for a knife. It is His Word, which is "sharper than any two-edged sword, piercing even to the dividing asunder of soul and spirit...and is a discerner of the thoughts and intents of the heart" (Heb. 4:12).

It is comforting in our seasons of pruning to remember how close the Father must be as He does His meticulous purging work. He will never ask other people to use the pruning shears on His vines. Sometimes I feel that some ministers try to prune the branches in their churches; but that is not God's way. Ministers are to water and care for the branches. The pruning is not left to man; it is God's work. So every branch that abides in Christ and is an integral part of the vine must never be severed from that vine. If it is, it will die. We must never allow anything to come between our source of life and ourselves.

There is no better way for our lives to be pruned than through studying the Word and applying it to our hearts, walking in obedience and yielding to what the Holy Spirit reveals to us. In that way pruning becomes a natural result of abiding in the vine as we described earlier. When Jesus spoke of pruning, He said, "You are already clean because of the word which I have spoken to you" (Jn. 15:3 NAS). The Greek root word used here for *clean* can be translated *pruned*. One version translates this verse, "Now you have already been pruned by My words" (Jn. 15:3 Phillips). If we abide in His Word, the Holy Spirit can correct us and tell us where we have fallen short and gone astray.

The Holy Spirit doesn't discourage us or condemn us; He convicts us. That means He uses the Word to point out our problem with a desire to correct it. He always has the solution. If abiding is the primary condition God sets before us to bear the fruit of the Spirit, then why do we seek to be fruitful in other ways? Why is it that the simplicity of God's way is always the way that seems so difficult for the flesh? It is, according to the Scriptures, because our spirits and our flesh are at war. Our flesh opposes the desire of the Holy Spirit to make us holy because it does not want to die. If there is sin in our lives, if there is a lack of discipline, or a broken relationship with our Lord or others, in order to abide in Christ we need to confess our sin or shortcoming and forgive others. In whatever way the works of flesh are controlling us, causing us to live in unrighteousness, we need to bring it to Christ in confession and repentance as the Holy Spirit convicts us. He will forgive us, purge us, and enable us to live the Christ-life, bearing the fruit of His character by the "lifing" of the Holy Spirit.

As we cultivate a fruitful relationship in Christ by spending time reading and meditating on God's Word and in prayer, the Holy Spirit continually reveals truth to us. Then, as we walk in obedience to that truth instead of obeying our fleshly desires, the Holy Spirit transforms us, and we begin to bring forth His fruit by the power of the Spirit. Every believer must have an unbroken relationship with Christ sustained by obedience. In unwavering faith in what Christ has done, we must acknowledge Him as the Vine and His Father as the Husbandman, the divine Pruner.

Our obedience will cause us also to be continually rejoicing in our Lord as we realize that we are redeemed and justified and are children of God. We are heirs of God, and He has preordained, foreordained, and predestined that we bear fruit. This conscious fellowship with our Lord will cause us to be fruit-bearing trees. There ought to be an ever-increasing diligence to yield to the Holy Spirit, to obey His commands, and to walk in His will so we may be fruitful. That is why Paul taught that we must live in the Spirit, be led by the Spirit, and walk in the Spirit (Gal. 5).

## THE GIFTS AND FRUIT CONTRASTED

We hear much about the gifts of the Spirit these days. Many people are enamored with the supernatural power that can flow through a Spirit-filled believer. For that reason it is important to remember that spiritual gifts are only supernatural capabilities given by the Holy Spirit, while the fruit of the Spirit is godly character. The gifts of the Spirit equip one with abilities for service in the Kingdom of God; the fruit of the Spirit reveals who one *is* in the Kingdom of God. It may be possible for us to function in the gifts of the Spirit even when we are not abiding in Christ as we should.

The Scriptures teach that fruit-bearing, rather than functioning in the gifts of the Spirit, is an indication of maturity and spirituality. Although there is a tendency among us to look with awe on someone who has many gifts of the Spirit, Paul clearly teaches that the gifts are not an indication of the depth of one's spiritual life. He wrote to the Corinthians whom, he said, "come behind in no gift" (1 Cor. 1:7), and corrected them for being carnal, unspiritual people. The gifts are given instantaneously because of our yielding in obedience to the

Holy Spirit. Fruit is not produced instantaneously; it is the result of our abiding in Christ and develops gradually. In fruit-bearing, developing traits of godly character requires *time, testings*, and *trials*.

In the Old Testament, supernatural gifts did not suggest spirituality either. King Saul was noted for his possession of the gift of prophecy. The people asked the question, "Is Saul also among the prophets?" (1 Sam. 10:11) They had heard him prophesy with other prophets. Later, during his reign as king, he dishonored the Lord, disobeyed His Word, and God no longer heard his prayers. The Spirit of the Lord even departed from him. It is obvious from this example and others that the development of godly character, not the operation of spiritual gifts, is the real indication of relationship with God.

Another way we might consider the difference between the fruit of the Spirit and the gifts of the Spirit is that gifts are plural, but fruit is not. As we have seen, there are varieties of spiritual gifts given by the Spirit for the edifying of the Church. All my Christian life I have heard people use the plural form of the word *fruit*, referring to the "nine fruits" of the Spirit. However, Paul used a singular verb, *is*, to describe the fruit of the Spirit. For example, *love* is the single channel through which the fruit of the Spirit flows. Paul then describes the other eight characteristics or facets of divine love, the fruit of the Spirit, as evidenced in the Christian's life by the power of the Holy Spirit. Paul taught that "the love of God is shed abroad in our hearts by the Holy Ghost..." (Rom. 5:5b). So the fruit of love works in our lives and manifests its beauty in eight different ways. D.L. Moody described the fruit of the Spirit this way:

> Joy is love exulting; peace is love reposing; longsuffering is love untiring; gentleness is love enduring; goodness is love in action; faith is love on the battlefield; meekness is love under discipline; temperance is love in training.[3]

We know that we are continually being filled with the Holy Spirit if we are manifesting the love of God in its many facets in our lives.

The apostle Paul teaches clearly that the gifts of the Spirit, administered without love, profit nothing to the one administering them. Amazingly, he went as far as to say that those who function in spiritual gifts are nothing without love. He begins the "love chapter" by declaring, "Though I speak with the tongues of men and of angels, and have not charity, I am become as sounding brass, or a tinkling cymbal" (1 Cor. 13:1). He continued to list the spiritual gifts we hold in awe, and declared that if he had them all but did not have love, he was nothing. Although Paul was not inferring that the gifts were useless when administered through a loveless channel, he did say, "it profiteth me nothing"

(1 Cor. 13:3). The one administering the gifts without love is the loser, not the Church.

Unfortunately, many Christians today, in their pursuit of charisma, anointing, power, and the gifts of the Spirit, have forsaken the building of character in their lives. Because of a lack of character in Christians' lives, there has been a diminishing of power in the Body of Christ. Why? The love of God is the channel through which His power flows. Ministered in love through a fruitful, spiritual life, the gifts of the Spirit are of great usefulness and great power in building the Kingdom of our Lord. We must conclude that the Holy Spirit is as much interested in character as He is in power.

What would happen if a pastor gave an altar call and asked all who wanted holiness and the character of God to come forward and stand on the left side of the altar? If he then asked all who wanted the gifts of power of the Holy Spirit to come forward and stand on the right side, I believe the larger portion of his church would be on the right side. Those desiring power would be the majority, with maybe a handful seeking character. People want power. There is something in every one of us that wants to be in control. But every Spirit-baptized servant of the Lord needs to realize the importance of godly character, especially as it relates to the gifts of the Spirit. It is most important that the life of our Lord Jesus is recognized in us as the vine that produces fruit in our lives.

## THE FRUITS AND GIFTS COMPARED

Having contrasted the spiritual gifts and fruit, let's not fail to realize, however, the vital relationship they share in common. It is not by chance nor a departure from true canonicity for the Holy Spirit to place the "love chapter" (1 Cor. 13) between the chapters dealing with the proper use of the gifts of the Spirit (1 Cor. 12; 14). My dear friend, Dr. Judson Cornwall, has keenly observed that even though the contrasts between the gifts of the Spirit and the fruit of the Spirit are great, there are at least two comparisons. First, both flow from the Holy Spirit into and through the lives of persons in whom the Spirit dwells. There is a common divine Source, even though there is an uncommon result. A second similarity is that both the gifts of the Spirit and the fruit of the Spirit are listed for us in the Bible in groups of three. In our study of the nine gifts of the Spirit listed in First Corinthians 12, we saw three gifts that supernaturally enable us to know, three that supernaturally enable us to do, and three that supernaturally enable us to speak. We have noted that the fruit of the Spirit, in essence, is love. However, the aspects of love, relating to their effect on our relationships, logically divide into three clusters as well. The first cluster—love, joy, peace—ripens toward God. The second cluster ripens toward others—longsuffering, gentleness, goodness. The third cluster, those aspects of love that grow in the shade of the vine, ripen toward ourselves—meekness, faithfulness, temperance. As the fruit of love develops in these three dimensions in our lives, we will bear the character of Christ.

As we begin to study the fruit of love with its eight characteristic facets, we might consider whether our priority has been to have the gifts of the Spirit or to develop godly character. If we recognize a lack in our lives of the love of God, though we are functioning in the gifts of the Spirit, we need to acknowledge that lack. As we learn to abide in Christ, we will become effective in building the Kingdom of God. Then we will avoid the terrible prospect of becoming a clanging cymbal, or worse, a branch that must be taken away and burned. Should we not desire to dwell continually in the love of God where we are not only safe from our enemies, but fruitful as well?

## Notes

1. Perry Brewster, *Pentecostal Doctrine*, (Cheltham, England: Reed Hearst Publishers, 1976).

2. Samuel Chadwick, *The Way To Pentecost*, (New York: Fleming H. Revell Co., 1937).

3. D.L. Moody, *Notes From My Bible, From Genesis To Revelation*, (New York: Fleming H. Revell Co., 1895).

# Chapter 7

# *The Fruit of the Spirit*

## *Part II: Divine Love, Joy, Peace, Longsuffering, and Gentleness*

### *LOVE*

*But the fruit of the Spirit is love...* (Galatians 5:22).

Love must have preeminence in the virtues of the Christian life because God is Love. John wrote, "Beloved, let us love one another: for love is of God; and every one that loveth is born of God, and knoweth God" (1 John 4:7). Throughout his epistle, John emphasizes that love is the evidence of true relationship

153

with God. Jesus taught His disciples: "By this shall all men know that ye are My disciples, if ye have love one to another" (Jn. 13:35). If the disciples thought it difficult to love one another, they must have cringed at the other command Jesus gave concerning love. He said, "...Love your enemies, bless them that curse you, do good to them that hate you, and pray for them which despitefully use you, and persecute you" (Mt. 5:44).

This command to love our enemies is impossible for the natural man to fulfill. This fruit cannot be produced by human effort; it is the result of the love of God Himself being shed abroad in our hearts. The love that the Holy Spirit produces is much more than ordinary human affection. It is God's very character, who He *is*. It is that love flowing through our spirits into our souls, and made manifest through our human flesh, that the Holy Spirit produces. It is only the love of God that will enable us to love our enemies.

Among all the words in the Bible, this simple word, *love*, stands alone as the supreme description of the very essence of the Christian life. Love binds all other virtues of the fruit of the Spirit together. It is the common denominator of Christian character. One cannot love completely and fail to cultivate the other virtues. To be filled with the Holy Spirit and display the fruit of the Spirit in our lives is to be filled with love. One might ask, "Why is love of supreme importance?" Many reasons could be given. Let's examine some of them.

## THE SIGNIFICANCE OF LOVE

### God Is Love

First, the Scriptures teach that love is not just one of God's attributes, but the very essence of His being. We must remember that God *is* love, He doesn't *have* love. There is a real difference between what one has and who one is. All true love finds its origin in God and flows forth from Him. God intended that love, the essence of who He is, would be the essence of His creation as well. All redemption is designed to restore this reality of God's intention for a loving creation.

### Motive for Creation

Second, love is so important because it was the motive for all creation. This God of love needed someone to respond to His love. Because of that need, God created mankind as an object of His love, to share His life, His wisdom, His holiness, His character, His eternal riches, and ultimately His glory. Even before the foundation of the world, God in His omniscience knew that man would fail. So God made a provision for the devil's interruption that tried to destroy His plan to have a human family He could love. God demonstrated His love to us in that He provided the remedy for that interruption even before He made man. The Scriptures teach that Jesus was "the Lamb slain from the foundation of the world" (Rev. 13:8).[1] After God made man, man's choice to disobey God resulted in a broken relationship with God. Yet God's love continued to reach out to him, so that "while we were yet sinners, Christ died for us" (Rom. 5:8b). What incredible love! God's love for us is unconditional and undeserved. He loves us in spite of ourselves.

## Fulfilling of the Law

Third, love is of supreme importance because it is the greatest commandment that fulfills all the law of God. When the scribe asked Jesus which of the commandments was the greatest, He replied:

> *Thou shalt love the Lord thy God with all thy heart, and with all thy soul, and with all thy mind. This is the first and great commandment. And the second is like unto it, Thou shalt love thy neighbor as thyself. On these two commandments hang all the law and the prophets* (Matthew 22:37-40).

You remember that the law was written on two tablets of stone. The first four commandments are regarding our love for God and God only, and the last six deal with our relationship to man, loving our neighbor. Therefore, Paul declared that "love is the fulfilling of the law" (Rom. 13:10).

## Our Sure Sign of Discipleship

Fourth, Jesus gave His disciples a new commandment to love one another. He declared, "By this shall

all men know that ye are My disciples, if ye have love one to another" (Jn. 13:35). Our doctrine should be sound and our faith should be strong. Still, those are not signs of our testimony to the world that we are disciples of Christ. According to the Scriptures, only God's *agape* love manifested in our lives is the sure sign that we are His disciples. For that reason, love must be foundational in our lives, motivating everything we do. Paul admonished believers to follow the way of love (1 Cor. 14:1), and to do everything with love (1 Cor. 16:14).

## THE PRINCIPLE OF LOVE

*Though I speak with the tongues of men and of angels, and have not charity [love], I am become as sounding brass, or a tinkling cymbal. And though I have the gift of prophecy, and understand all mysteries, and all knowledge; and though I have all faith, so that I could remove mountains, and have not charity [love], I am nothing. And though I bestow all my goods to feed the poor, and though I give my body to be burned, and have not charity [love], it profiteth me nothing* (1 Corinthians 13:1-3).

Since love is of supreme importance in our spiritual lives, we need to understand the principle of love as it is outlined in the Scriptures. The love Paul describes is selfless rather than selfish; it is a supernatural love operating through us, not the love of our self-efforts or natural affections. The Charismatic movement emphasized (a) tongues; (b) the gifts of the Spirit; (c) faith to move mountains; and (d) giving. In the "love chapter," Paul mentions all four of these areas of emphasis, contrasting them with the need for love. What is the Holy Spirit saying here? He is saying that even in the Charismatic movement, if we have all these supernatural endowments and do not have love, they are of no value to us.

The Bible teaches that our goal must be to put love first. The apostle John writes more about this: "And we have known and believed the love that God hath to us. God is love; and he that dwelleth in love dwelleth in God, and God in him" (1 John 4:16). We would do well to meditate on that powerful statement, "he that dwelleth in love dwelleth in God." Where do true anointing, power, and faith come from? Don't they come from dwelling in God? And dwelling in God means dwelling in love. Are we as Spirit-filled Christians aiming simply for gifts, power, anointing, and faith— or the love that produces these things? God will show up wherever love shows up. A person who dwells in love brings the presence of God to every life situation.

We have established that the fruit of the Spirit is the love of God developed in the believer. Now we are ready to study the other aspects or facets of this supernatural fruit that are descriptive of it. As we gain understanding of the characteristics of each virtue, we will be able to recognize them practically and make them operative in our life circumstances. The Scriptures offer us simple guidelines to show us how to allow each of these virtues to be manifested in our lives. As we yield to the Holy Spirit, He will cultivate His fruit in us and allow us to experience the love of God as He intended.

## JOY

*...these things I speak in the world, that they might have My joy fulfilled in themselves* (John 17:13).

The joy that comes from the Holy Spirit as He produces the character of our Lord in us can range in emotional response from a sense of well-being, tranquility, or quietness, to an exuberant gladness. That gladness can be expressed in singing, clapping, dancing, and even loud victory cheers. Whatever our response, we must remember that only the Holy Spirit can produce true joy in our lives. It will never be manufactured by our efforts.

I remember when I first came into the Spirit-filled walk, I would hear the church sing a lively chorus called, "The Joy of the Lord Is My Strength." One verse declared, "If you want joy you must clap for it, dance for it, shout for it." As we went through all those motions, I finally realized we were trying to work up joy by our own efforts: clapping, dancing, and shouting. Somehow we got the idea that if we did those things, we would have joy from God and then we would have strength.

I didn't understand then that God Himself is true joy. True joy is part of the character of Christ. So, since joy is part of God's nature and part of Christ's life, we become heirs to this joy as we allow His nature to be developed in us. "For the kingdom of God is not meat and drink; but righteousness, and peace, and joy in the Holy Ghost" (Rom. 14:17). True joy, then, is love's response to God's mercies, His blessings, and His benefits.

The joy of the Christian is not dependent on circumstances. It is not our environment, the people around us, or the events we are going through that determine our joy or lack of it. This divine joy lives in trust even in the most trying circumstances. Human happiness looks at things on the earth and is affected by its conditions, what is going on around it. But divine joy, as part of the fruit of love, looks Heaven-ward. It is unaffected by people, events, or surrounding conditions because Heaven's benefits are unchanging.

The genuine Christian will express the emotion of joy. David declared, "In Thy presence is fulness of joy" (Ps. 16:11b). Those who would suppress all expression of emotion in worship, condemning enthusiasm and rejoicing as emotionalism, do not rightly interpret the Word of God. Emotionalism, which is to be avoided, is the seeking of emotion as an end: emotion for emotion's sake. We carefully differentiate between emotional extravagance and the true operation of the Holy Spirit in our emotions. In keeping with the teaching of the Scriptures, we exercise self-control over our feelings so as not to grasp selfishly for attention in our emotional experiences.

On the other hand, we believe in singing joyfully, praying earnestly, preaching zealously, testifying forcefully, and giving cheerfully. Not one sentence of condemnation for enthusiasm and rejoicing can be found in God's Word. The Scriptures are full of commands to rejoice, to shout, to dance, and to sing unto God. Paul uses the words *joy* and *rejoice* 17 times in his short epistle to the Philippians. Emotionless worship is cold worship. Joy is an expression of godly emotion in the inner being that is inwardly moved by love for God. The joy of the Lord is our strength, and as the Spirit of the Lord fills a person, joy will be manifest in his or her life.

Two years ago we buried the last member of my immediate family, my only brother. His death left me without family: mother, daddy, grandfather, grandmother, aunt, uncle, or brother. When it dawned on me that I didn't have a birthplace or family to go back to, an emptiness and loneliness settled in my spirit that pierced me deeply. Just as I was experiencing that deep pain, I heard a song inside my spirit. A line from an old hymn that declared the Comforter had come was running through my mind. I looked up at my husband and said, "Honey, the Comforter I preach about is now comforting me." In the midst of my pain, despite my loss, I could still experience the comfort and joy of the presence of the Lord. You might ask, "Did you feel like singing and dancing?" No. I was grieving. But I realized that nothing in this world could steal what I had inside: the comforting presence of God that is so eternal. Even though I was walking through the valley, my God was with me, and in that fact I could rejoice. I didn't have to go through the seven steps some prescribe for resolving grief because the joy of His presence brought infinite peace.

It is true that life is sometimes painful and that we do not always have answers for the difficulties we encounter. In those times I have discovered that true joy doesn't depend on our outward circumstances, but on our inward responses to God and to those circumstances. When we learn to see our lives from God's perspective, we can draw on the strength that comes from His joy.

### Joy in Heaven

Jesus said, "I say unto you, that likewise joy shall be in heaven over one sinner that repenteth, more than over ninety and nine just persons, which need no repentance" (Lk. 15:7). Melody Green, a saintly woman and dear friend, made this observation concerning

Jesus' statement: "Think of it! The joyful angelic out-burst must be like celestial fireworks when people on earth become reconciled to God. All heaven has a display of heavenly fireworks because of the joy of the Lord they experience when a son has come home!"[2]

The Old Testament prophet declared, "The Lord thy God in the midst of thee is mighty; He will save, He will rejoice over thee with joy; He will rest in His love, He will joy over thee with singing" (Zeph. 3:17). The Hebrew word for *rejoice* literally means "to spin around exultantly." So God rejoices over His people with dancing, with singing, and with shouts of joy. The Lord on His heavenly throne is not blind or unfeeling toward the suffering, injustice, and sin on the earth. Yet overriding joy grips Him when one soul is delivered from the chains of sin and the grip of death.

On the Day of Pentecost, in Peter's first sermon, he quoted David, saying, "Thou hast made known to me the ways of life; Thou shalt make me full of joy with Thy countenance" (Acts 2:28). Just to see the countenance of the Lord fills us with joy. Joy was a characteristic of the disciples who were full of the Holy Spirit, even as they faced persecution (Acts 13:50-52). I have seen that when believers today are baptized in the Holy Spirit, they too experience a baptism of the joy of the Lord. I believe this great release of joy is a result of the dynamic overflowing of the Spirit of God when He takes up full residence within us, establishing

His purposes in our lives. What a wonder it is that God has made a way for us to become like Him! Surely this should be our highest priority in life, to allow the love of God to dwell in us so we become joyful ambassadors of His Kingdom of love here on earth.

## *PEACE*

*But now in Christ Jesus ye who sometimes were far off are made nigh by the blood of Christ. For He is our peace...* (Ephesians 2:13-14).

I had a beautiful experience that defined peace for me. I was taking a group of young people through Natural Bridge, Virginia, one of the seven wonders of the world. We were touring deep underground in the Endless Caverns. As we walked through those deep caves, we came to a ridge that was like a mountain underneath the ground. From that ridge we looked down into a deep ravine through which flowed the clearest stream of water I have ever seen. It looked as though it might be several feet deep, and it was running its own course—so tranquil, so undisturbed, so unaware of being walked over by the tourists above it.

As I stood there, the Holy Spirit whispered to my spirit and said, "This is peace like a river—the peace of God that passes understanding." I realized when I saw that natural example of peacefulness that there could be a river of peace inside me coming from the life of the Lord Jesus, a river that is fuller and deeper and in much greater harmony with God than anything this world could offer. No wonder the apostle Paul used the Greek word *symphoneos*, from which we derive our word *symphony*, to describe this peace that brings us into perfect harmony with God, without any discord.

Peace can be defined as a soul-harmony that comes from the Christ-rule living within us. This divine peace is an experience that is much deeper and more constant than happiness. This beautiful facet of love is an inner characteristic that manifests itself in peaceableness with God, with others, and with ourselves. It signifies freedom from an agitated, contentious, or quarrelsome spirit. Love seeks to live peaceably with all men. The Spirit-filled believer may enjoy this peace that is described in the Scriptures.

## Four Aspects of Peace

The Word of God teaches four different aspects of divine peace that we may experience in our relationship with our Lord. First, we can have peace *with* God (Rom. 5:1). This peace means the war is over in our spirits. We are not warring anymore with our conscience or with God. We have declared our armistice and have been reconciled to God through repenting of our sins and accepting the sacrifice of Jesus' blood to cover them. This born-again experience results in peace with God.

Second, there is peace *from* God. When Jesus was preparing His disciples for His death, He said, "Peace

I leave with you, My peace I give unto you: not as the world giveth, give I unto you. Let not your heart be troubled, neither let it be afraid" (Jn. 14:27). This aspect of peace focuses on the gift of God. Paul called peace a gift of God when he declared, "He is our peace" (Eph. 2:14). Jesus is the Prince of Peace. Therefore, if He is living in us, producing His life through us by the power of the Holy Spirit, then it is His peace that sustains us and keeps us from inward turmoil. We experience a divine peace that is not a result of any human effort.

Third, the Scriptures describe the peace *of* God. Paul told the Philippians, "And the peace of God, which passeth all understanding, shall keep your hearts and minds through Christ Jesus" (Phil. 4:7). In his salutation to the Thessalonians, he prayed, "Now the Lord of peace Himself give you peace always by all means..." (2 Thess. 3:16). This is a description essential to God's divine love: "peace always." He desires that we enjoy that peaceful state as we experience His love. The dynamic power of this peace is expressed in the phrase "peace that passes all understanding." No matter what kind of vexing situation or painful circumstance we have to face, we can go through it in the power of the Holy Spirit in the peace of God that is not dependent on our natural ability to cope.

Fourth, the prophet Isaiah referred to perfect peace *in* Him. He wrote, "Thou wilt keep him in perfect peace, whose mind is stayed on Thee: because he trusteth in Thee" (Is. 26:3). This aspect of peace describes that abiding relationship that comes as our minds are "stayed" on God. The Hebrew word for *stayed* carries the connotation of "nailing down securely." As our minds are nailed down on Christ, because of our trust in Him, He will keep us in perfect peace. That peace that is a fruit of divine love is real and genuine. The common greeting among the Jewish people was "Shalom," or "Peace." We will be at home in peace. May He who comes to look for fruit on our branches find peace growing profusely in the garden of our lives.

### LONGSUFFERING

*But the fruit of the Spirit is...longsuffering...* (Galatians 5:22).

*...giving all diligence, add to your faith virtue; and to virtue knowledge; and to knowledge temperance; and to temperance patience; and to patience godliness; and to godliness brotherly kindness; and to brotherly kindness charity* (2 Peter 1:5-7).

Although longsuffering, otherwise translated as patience, is a lost virtue among many Christians today, it is essential to the Christian walk. We have established the fact that the fruit of the Spirit is Christlike character, not the fruit of our own efforts. It is so with patience also; this godly aspect of character will be a "natural" result of a life that is controlled supernaturally by the Spirit of Christ.

Still, we must remember that the development of godly fruit is neither automatic nor instantaneous. Christlike character doesn't develop without diligence on the believer's part to yield continually to the Holy Spirit in each situation he confronts in life. The Greek word Peter used for patience can also be translated *perseverance*. This desirable fruit will only be brought forth by much prayer, study of God's Word, and perseverance in life's difficulties. Patience is the ability to endure graciously a less-than-desired state for an extended time.

James understood this when he wrote, "As an example, brethren, of suffering and patience, take the prophets who spoke in the name of the Lord. Behold, we count those blessed who endured..." (Jas. 5:10-11 NAS). James informs us that we develop patience through a process of endurance and determined struggle. Paul declared, "for I have learned, in whatsoever state I am, therewith to be content" (Phil. 4:11b). He *learned* contentment in life's less-than-desirable situations. In that statement he confirms that contentment is a learned virtue that must be developed.

Paul also prayed for the Colossians that they be "strengthened with all power, according to His glorious might, for the attaining of all steadfastness and patience; joyously giving thanks to the Father..." (Col. 1:11-12 NAS). Because patience is not an option for the Spirit-filled Christian, but a necessary virtue, we must cultivate it through prayer and surrender to the working of God's power within us.

The Scriptures give several reasons for the need to develop patience in our lives. For example, Paul told Timothy that patience should characterize the way we share the gospel. He wrote, "Preach the word; be ready in season and out of season; reprove, rebuke, exhort, with great patience and instruction" (2 Tim. 4:2 NAS). Second, patience is a key to receiving God's promises. The Scriptures teach, "That ye be not slothful, but followers of them who through faith and patience inherit the promises" (Heb. 6:12). Perhaps one of the greatest reasons we need to have patience is that through testings that produce patience, Christian character is perfected. James declared, "But let patience have her perfect work, that ye may be perfect and entire, wanting nothing" (Jas. 1:4). He also taught us that patience is the pathway to blessing: "Behold, we count those blessed who endured" (Jas. 5:11a NAS).

*Waiting Patiently*

A most difficult aspect of patience involves waiting. Waiting is something very few of us want to do, like to do, or can do. Most people consider waiting to be a negative experience. Yet true success is usually determined by how a person uses such waiting periods. What we may think is a time of adversity and "standstill" could be God's time element of preparation in our lives for a task for which we are not yet ready. The manifestation of patience, like the manifestation of other traits of godly character, may be seen in a single act, but the development of each is the result of many testings and trials. The character we develop as we respond properly in our trials may well be the preventative of failure in the future. Jesus declared, "In your patience possess ye your souls" (Lk. 21:19).

A distressed king by the name of Jehoram once asked the prophet Elisha, "Why should I wait for the Lord any longer?" (2 Kings 6:33 NAS) Many who are sick, economically deprived, tempted, abused, stressed, or otherwise unhappy, are asking the same question today: "How long, O Lord, how long? Why should I wait for the Lord to deliver me?" Elisha encouraged King Jehoram and charged the people to trust God and wait for their supernatural deliverance. That very night God drove the enemies away and gave His people all the food and treasure they needed from the enemy's camp. Even when the situation looks hopeless, patience does not surrender to despair. We need to persevere and be patient as we wait for the Lord, knowing that our deliverance will surely come. Though patience may be a lost virtue for many, it is part of the character of the fruit of the Spirit that should be predominant in our Christian lives.

## GENTLENESS

*But the wisdom that is from above is first pure, then peaceable, gentle, and easy to be entreated, full of mercy and good fruits, without partiality, and without hypocrisy* (James 3:17).

Even though the Scriptures use the word *gentleness* in other places, the only time this Greek word is found in the New Testament is when Paul describes the fruit of the Spirit (Gal. 5:22-23). It is the word we use for *kindness* and frequently depicts God's dealings with His people. Gentleness, or kindness, is Christ's tangible expression of His love in our lives. Jesus said of Himself, "I am gentle and humble in heart" (Mt. 11:29 NAS). Gentleness beautifully characterizes the love of our Savior for rebellious sinners.

Few words are so easily defined as kindness. For most people, this aspect of the fruit of the Spirit can be defined with words like caring, mercy, compassion, and concern, along with other words that express warmth of feeling toward another person. Only the meanest of "schoolyard bullies" would not aspire to possess and exhibit these qualities in his character. What this definition of gentleness fails to reveal, however, is the subtle transforming power that gentleness has on our own lives as well as on the lives of those to whom we give kindness.

## Demonstrating Gentleness

In order for kindness to be manifest in our lives, we must become involved in the lives of other people. Gentleness needs a neighbor. Like the other aspects of the fruit of the Spirit, it is not ornamental but practical. Fruit exists to be shared and enjoyed by others. For that reason, gentleness and kindness need a neighbor. In fact, I am convinced that gentleness cannot exist without a neighbor, for it can find no real expression without someone upon whom to lavish its caring. As we show kindness to others, its power is working quietly in us to free us from unhealthy preoccupation with ourselves. That involvement not only blesses the people we touch, but also acts as a wonderful door of freedom for us from unhealthy self-centered involvement.

## Gentleness in Confrontation

God's people bring glory to Him when they manifest gracious kindness to others. We all find some situations where it is easy to show kindness. Most of us are not so hard-hearted that we cannot be moved by a person's distress, and will try to find a way to minister love to them in their painful situation. Yet kindness is not only to be shown to people in distress; kindness is also love dealing with others in confronting their faults.

Perhaps nothing more frequently discredits one's testimony and ministry than showing unkindness in dealing with people. No conceivable circumstance can possibly justify a Christian's unkind treatment of others. No matter how firm we have to be in our correction and reproof, we never have an excuse to be unkind. There is no greater mark of nobility of character than the ability to reprove and correct in kindness. In Paul's "love chapter" he writes, "Charity suffereth long, and is kind" (1 Cor. 13:4a). This is a beautiful picture of the fruit of gentleness at its best, after it has "suffered" a person who has been difficult. It is a most important trait to be cultivated in preparation for working with other people.

## Jesus Is Gentleness Personified

*Now I Paul myself beseech you by the meekness and gentleness of Christ* (2 Corinthians 10:1a).

Gentleness not only helps us relate to others; it also interprets Jesus for us. Jesus is gentleness. We may not understand many things about Jesus, but we do understand His kindness because we experience it every day. Gentleness is a tangible manifestation of Jesus' love and is the avenue through which His love finds expression. Jesus is not a distant, benevolent deity. He is our Savior and our Friend who provides for our personal needs.

Paul also tells us that we are God's workmanship, created in Christ Jesus unto good works (Eph. 2:10). These good works become God's outlet for our kindness. Cultivating gentleness involves a conscious decision *to value the other person more highly than we value ourselves*. True kindness is not demonstrated on an occasional special event like a holiday fruit basket. It shouldn't be confused with "voluntarianism." Being a volunteer is a vehicle through which we can transmit kindness to others. But true kindness is an integral part of the Christian character that is to be demonstrated in all our daily activities.

Those "small" kindnesses of a smile, a caring word, a listening ear, a touch of the arm, a note of encouragement, an act of including someone who feels left out, or simply being there when we are needed, are of great value. Especially to those closest to us, our mates, the fruit of gentleness needs to be displayed. We need to remember that when we speak harshly to our Christian mates, we are speaking to Christ in that tone because He lives in them. So when we speak sharply, we are mistreating Christ with our lack of kindness. There are many opportunities in the home to demonstrate the gentleness of God that will make our homes tender places of caring, a refuge from the unlovingness of the world.

Gentleness protects and affirms the dignity of the other person. How important it is to cultivate the fruit of gentleness in our lives, not only to nurture our families, but to affirm everyone we meet. God expects us to be kind to those who are different from us, even those whom we may dislike. Sometimes disagreeable people are the ones who need our compassion more than anyone else, and often they may be the least able to return our kindness. Jesus taught us to love even our enemies (Lk. 6:35). We should pray daily that God will allow people to cross our paths and give us the opportunity to reveal Jesus through kindness. Without the continual practice of showing kindness to others, we will inevitably lapse back into our self-centered ways.

Gentleness doesn't require us to become heroes, though simple acts of kindness can have such a profound impact on others as to evoke their admiration. Believers who have developed the fruit of gentleness have learned to affirm and love one person at a time. They see love where others see hatred; forgiveness where others see offenses; reconciliation where others see separation; acceptance where others see rejection; hope where others see despair; and life where others see death.

A recent study suggests that people who regularly help others live longer and feel better than those who are concerned only about themselves. As we have mentioned, we will discover that showing kindness is good for us as well as for those to whom we are kind. As the people of God, we are instructed to put on "bowels of mercies, kindness, humbleness of mind, meekness, longsuffering" (Col. 3:12). May we be those people who evidence that they have been chosen of God to be clothed with compassion and with gentleness.

## Notes

1. Dr. Fuchsia Pickett, *God's Dream*, (Shippensburg, Pennsylvania: Destiny Image Pub., 1991). This 140-page book deals with this theme completely.

2. Melody Green is director of Last Day Ministries in Tyler, Texas.

# Chapter 8

# *The Fruit of the Spirit*

## *Part III: Divine Goodness, Faith, Meekness, and Temperance*

### *GOODNESS*

*(For the fruit of the Spirit is in all goodness and righteousness and truth)* (Ephesians 5:9).

Goodness can be defined as the state of being virtuous, benevolent, generous, upright, and righteous. The root word for *goodness* is *God*. So the fruit of goodness is Godlikeness demonstrated in works or acts shown to others. As it so closely relates to gentleness and kindness, it is a very practical expression or outworking of love. If man is truly good at heart, he does good to others. Those who show God's goodness will be motivated by a compassion that does not change even in the face of controversy. Goodness is the Christlike nature of Godlikeness that is manifest in our lives by the power of the Holy Spirit.

How do we become like God? The only way to show forth the character of God in our lives is first to partake of His divine nature. Peter understood this when he wrote to the saints:

*According as His divine power hath given unto us all things that pertain unto life and godliness, through the knowledge of Him that hath called us to glory and virtue: whereby are given unto us exceeding great and precious promises: that by these ye might be partakers of the divine nature, having escaped the corruption that is in the world through lust* (2 Peter 1:3-4).

God has given us everything we need through His divine power to live a godly life. When we are born again, the Holy Spirit "lifes" us with the life of Christ in order that through faith in God's promises, we can have His divine nature developed in us.

## A Mode of Conduct

Although true goodness is a quality of divine character in our hearts wrought by the Holy Spirit, it is more than that in its expression. The term *goodness* is not simply a symbol for God, but is a mode of conduct that becomes a way of life expressing itself in action. We might say that goodness is a habit of doing the "right" thing as defined by the Scriptures. As God's ambassadors on earth, we are to manifest God's goodness to this world (2 Cor. 5:20).

The Scriptures teach us that it is the goodness of God that leads people to repentance (Rom. 2:4b). It is wonderful to think that the goodness we show to people can be God's way of bringing them to repentance. When God's righteousness is manifested in our actions to people, men and women will come to God and become partakers of His divine nature themselves. That is why our Lord Jesus commands to "do good to them that hate you, and pray for them which despitefully use you, and persecute you; that ye may be the children of your Father which is in heaven..." (Mt. 5:44-45).

Doing good to someone who does not treat you well is the zenith of benevolence; it is not the "normal" behavior for the non-Christian. A non-Christian's mode of conduct would be more like this: "Don't have anything to do with them because of the way they treated you," or "Find a way to get even with that one who hurt you." Our returning goodness to those who are unkind to us catches the world's attention because it is totally contrary to their self-centered mentality. Jesus taught us to express God's goodness in our actions toward our enemies. That vertex of goodness becomes the power of God that will lead our persecutors to repentance. In that way the world will know the power of God's love as it is displayed through human vessels.

## Pharisaical Goodness

There is a pharisaical, self-righteous goodness that is more of a blight to Christianity than a recommendation. Selfish goodness can be a kind of "badness" that is heaping good acts upon someone out of selfish motives to gain favor or other personal benefits. True goodness is love in action, heaping benefits on others, not with gritted teeth or ulterior motives, but motivated by compassionate love and caring without desire for personal gain.

The Christian does good acts because he is yielding to the power of the Holy Spirit. When the Holy Spirit permeates our lives, there is a positive outflow of goodness to all men. We might work with someone who is a troublemaker, who tries to upset our every effort, and who gossips about us behind our backs. Although that person is not treating us right, Jesus taught us to do good to those who despitefully use us, so we must find a way to bless that person. The Holy Spirit will show us what to do to show His goodness and, as we yield to Him, He will enable us to perform it.

The church I founded in Texas was located in a neighborhood of people who were not sympathetic with our beliefs. We were the first Charismatic group in their city at that time, and we had great difficulty trying to witness to those neighbors. Then one autumn a violent storm damaged many beautiful homes in our neighborhood, flooding them and leaving a mess in its wake. As president of our Bible College, I suggested to our students that we take this opportunity to show goodness to our neighbors. So our college students volunteered to help them scrape up mud, wash walls and drapes, and help clean up the mess. Those simple acts of goodness made an impact on the entire community. They became an example to our neighbors of the goodness of God manifest through our students by the power of the Holy Spirit. We heard statements such as, "We have never seen anything like it before, the way those young people worked...."

We didn't yield to the temptation of being offended with our neighbors or developing a plan of retaliation because of their attitudes. Instead, we yielded to the Holy Spirit and found a way to bless those who had spoken against us. Some of our students baked pies and cakes for them, and offered to take care of sick babies. Many simple outworkings of the goodness of God through us became a way of "turning the other cheek." Our students made such an impression in that neighborhood that a news reporter covered the "story." The article printed in the newspaper reporting their acts of goodness erased the negative opinions in the community of our church and student body.

## Goodness in Sternness

In defining goodness, we stated that it is motivated by compassion and does not shrink from controversy. Sometimes doing good to others involves more than gentle acts, as when it requires opposing evil. Along with the gentle aspects of goodness, there are also stern qualities. Goodness will boldly represent what is right and true even when the truth hurts. Jesus demonstrated this stern aspect of goodness when He found the moneychangers in the temple and ran them out. He declared, "Is it not written, My house shall be called of all nations the house of prayer? but ye have made it a den of thieves" (Mk. 11:17). His manifestation of divine goodness declared to all who witnessed that His house would be a house of purity, power, and prayer. After Jesus cleansed the temple of the evildoers, the blind and lame came to Him there and He healed them.

It may be difficult for the natural mind to comprehend that Jesus' actions with the moneychangers was good. But when Jesus saw that what was going on in the temple was not right, He was moved with compassion to cleanse it so hurting people who came into the temple could have their needs met. After all, the purpose of the temple was not buying and selling. The temple was built to be a house of prayer for people who wanted to serve God. That godly purpose was made possible when Jesus threw out the moneychangers.

The priority of goodness is to identify the real needs of others and find a way to meet those needs, even when such actions meet with opposition. As we have seen, it was not until Jesus had shown the stern side of goodness by cleansing the temple of evil that He was able to show the kindlier side of goodness by healing the sick. Today as well, goodness needs to take a bold stance against what is wrong so what is right can prevail.

When we take our stand against the lottery and gambling that is introduced in our cities as a way of collecting taxes, we demonstrate the stern side of goodness. Although society tries to sell us a bill of goods, declaring that the lottery is a good idea, Christians know that gambling is disastrous to cities, so we must stand against it. Abortion, the murdering of innocent babies, is another issue that Christians must oppose. This national sin must be confronted and repented of so goodness can prevail. In many such ways the quality of sternness is manifest through the fruit of goodness.

How do we know when the gentle side or the stern side of goodness is needed? The key to that discernment must be found by walking in God's love and becoming sensitive to the Holy Spirit as He develops Godlikeness in us. As the character of God grows in us, it will indicate our mode of conduct for every life situation.

## FAITH

*Faithful is He that calleth you, who also will do it* (1 Thessalonians 5:24).

When Paul listed faith as part of the fruit of the Spirit, he used a Greek word for *faith* that can be translated *faithfulness* as well. Both translations are correct, though neither is complete in itself. The Greek word, *pistos*, involves the concepts of trustworthy, trustful, sure, and true in its meaning. To divide our thinking between faith and faithfulness would not do justice to the original meaning. Both faith and faithfulness involve utter reliance on God.

Faith, on one hand, involves learning to depend on God and to stand on His Word in every situation and circumstance. Faithfulness, on the other hand, is learning to yield to the Holy Spirit so we become dependable people. It is impossible to cultivate faithfulness without faith. And faith, which is complete reliance on God, is expressed through our faithfulness. We can think of both as a single coin with two sides. However, the key characteristic of each is *dependency and reliance* that leads to *trust*, which is developed through our personal relationship with God.

Perry Brewster describes faith and faithfulness this way: "While faith in God and His work is the basis of our relationship with Him, and the avenue through which His blessings flow into our lives, what is in view here is the faithfulness of character in conduct that such faith produces."[1] This fruit of faith is an aspect of character that must be carefully cultivated. It is a calm, constant, unchanging trust in God's goodness, His sovereignty, wisdom, power, and trustworthiness.

## Faith Is Stability

In its expression, faith is demonstrated through stability. The fruit of faith doesn't panic or get frustrated, it doesn't lose the victory, and it never thinks of turning back and giving up. It maintains a serene, tranquil, and persistent reliance on God based on relationship with Him. The apostle Paul expressed this attitude of trust when he wrote, "And we know that all things work together for good to them that love God, to them who are the called according to His purpose" (Rom. 8:28). Of course, that promise is conditional, as stated, to those who love God and are committed to *His purposes*. If we meet those conditions, then no matter what happens, we know that God will cause it to work together to fulfill the *plan of God* in our lives and thus perform the destiny for which we were *ordained*.

Paul powerfully illustrates this reality in his second epistle to Timothy, which he wrote near the end of his life in the most discouraging of circumstances. Forsaken by once faithful friends, he is now an elderly man in jail, undoubtedly suffering physical pain and lack of warm clothing, awaiting trial, and facing execution. Yet this is what Paul said in that dismal situation: "...I also suffer these things: nevertheless I am not ashamed: for I know whom I have believed, and am persuaded that He is able to keep that which I have committed unto Him against that day" (2 Tim. 1:12).

The key word here is *committed*, which means entrusted. To depend on God is to entrust ourselves to Him. If we know that we have put our lives without reservation into God's hands, we have committed our total selves to Him. Then we will know that whatever comes into our lives after that commitment is God working in us to will and to do of His good pleasure and eternal purpose (Phil. 2:13).

## Cultivating Faithfulness

To understand the other aspect of faith, that of faithfulness, we need to first lay hold of the reality that God is faithful. The fruit of faithfulness in our lives will be manifest as we let God work out His quality of faithfulness in us. We must realize that this process takes time. It doesn't just happen overnight, nor is it received by having someone lay hands on us. All fruit must be cultivated, and no fruit requires more cultivation than the fruit of faithfulness.

How do we cultivate a faithful heart? Jesus taught us that it starts with small things. He said, "He that is faithful in that which is least is faithful also in much: and he that is unjust in the least is unjust also in much" (Lk. 16:10). We reveal clearly what kind of person we are when we take charge of small and seemingly insignificant responsibilities. That's when our characters are being tested. In God's Kingdom, if we are not faithful in small things, how can we ever be promoted to be trusted with the "big" things?

Let's check ourselves to see how faithful we are in the small, apparently unimportant things of life. For example, do we make promises, perhaps to our children or our spouses, and then consistently break them? Sadly enough, some Christians are more faithful to keep their commitment to their employers than to their families. Do we continually arrive late for appointments? I believe that continual tardiness is an evidence of a weakness in one's character. God is never tardy. His sun never rises late or sets late. Everything for which He is responsible in this universe is punctual. We reveal His faithfulness in our punctuality.

Another area that reveals faithfulness is the way we handle our finances and how we pay our bills. Do we allow our bills to be overdue? Are we faithful in keeping up our accounts? According to Jesus, how we deal with money is the acid test of our faithfulness. He said if you have not been faithful in the use of unrighteous mammon, the biblical word for money, who will entrust the true riches to you (Lk. 16:11)? Finally, perhaps, for more examples of faithfulness in "small" things, what about the way we return things we borrow? What about the books or other items that we borrow and do not return? In such seemingly unimportant matters our faithfulness is tested each day, for faithfulness must begin to be manifest in small things.

## Trustfulness

We must always keep in mind that the purpose of bearing fruit is not for our own consumption, but for others' enjoyment. Oh, that we would realize this! The fruit of the Spirit is not for our personal benefit, though we do benefit by becoming Christlike. Our purpose as fruit-bearing vines is to produce His fruit for those who are hungry. So these beautiful characteristics of faith show the Christian attitudes we should reflect toward the people whose lives we touch. In His commentary on Galatians, Martin Luther made this wonderful statement:

> In listing faith among the fruit of the Spirit, Paul obviously does not mean faith in Christ, but faith in men. Such faith is not suspicious of people, but believes the best. Naturally the possessor of such faith will be deceived, but he lets it pass. He is ready to believe all men. Where this virtue is lacking, men are suspicious, forward, wayward, who believe nothing nor yield to anybody. No matter how well a person says or does anything, they will find fault with it. If you do not humor them, you can never please them. Such faith in people therefore, is quite necessary. What kind of life would this be if one person could not believe in another person.[2]

What a delicious fruit we have discovered in faith! May many who come to our tree find this fruit abundant in the life that Christ lives through us. As we learn to depend on God, His faithfulness will be revealed to us in fulfilling His promises to make us the kind of people who are trustworthy and dependable. We should want to be men and women who are faithful to God and faithful to one another.

## MEEKNESS

*Take My yoke upon you, and learn of Me; for I am meek and lowly in heart: and ye shall find rest unto your souls* (Matthew 11:29).

Perhaps we should begin by stating emphatically that meekness does not indicate weakness. On the contrary, a truly meek person is one who displays great strength of character. Meekness is the gentle humility exhibited by those at peace with God, with themselves, and with their fellow men. The meek are accepting and doing the will of God. They are slow to anger and willing to bear offense. They are not boisterous, noisy, or selfishly aggressive. They are not boastful or contentious, but teachable and lowly in spirit.

This description of meekness must not be construed, however, to reflect a shy, timid, or weak person. Neither must the fruit of meekness be considered synonymous with cowardice or lack of leadership ability. The Scriptures declare that Moses was the meekest man in Israel (Num. 12:3), and he was their greatest leader. He was humble and patient, but also capable of firmness and great courage. His life proves that meekness is an essential characteristic of a true leader.

Growing up as the son of Pharaoh's daughter in the palace, Moses had all the advantages of wealth and power. Before the Lord could use Moses as the deliverer for His people, however, He had to strip him of Egyptian vantages and benefits. Then He had to allow the Holy Spirit to give him favorable time and occasions (40 years in the wilderness) for the purpose of God to be fulfilled in developing meekness in him. It was precisely that gentle humility that would qualify him for the task of becoming a deliverer for God's people. This meekest of all men displayed great courage as he confronted the powerful Pharaoh, divided the Red Sea, led several million of God's covenant people for 40 years through the desert, transformed slaves into warriors, received and taught the law of God, administrated the first theocratic government, and stood alone before God to intercede for a rebellious nation.

Jesus declared in His sermon on the mount, "Blessed are the meek: for they shall inherit the earth" (Mt. 5:5). Even though Jesus described Himself as meek and lowly of heart (Mt. 11:29), no greater strength and power has ever been displayed on earth than that which He exercised in His ministry. He fearlessly proclaimed the truth in the face of religious leaders who plotted His death. He exercised authority over devils, disease, death, and the elements of nature by the power of His spoken word. He did not shrink from the agony of the cross. And He completed His mission on earth by totally defeating satan and securing complete redemption for mankind.

William Vine makes this comment about meekness: "It must be clearly understood therefore that the meekness manifest by the Lord and commended to the believer is the fruit of power. The Lord was meek because He had the infinite resources of God at His command."[3] As we have seen, both Moses and Jesus were characterized as meek men, and both were men of great authority and strength. Their lives, by demonstration, help us to define the fruit of meekness.

## Meekness Defined

We have established that meekness has no resemblance to weakness. We have also seen that meekness is not simply gentleness. I have seen people be very kind, tender, and gentle when they pet their dog or hold a little child. But that doesn't make them meek. When we see someone who is obedient and submissive to another's will, we often classify him as a meek person. However, obedience can be a result of wrong motives such as legalism, bondage, or fear. It does not proceed necessarily from a meek heart. Meekness is not simply submission either, for one can submit to external codes of behavior because of "cultural" pressure and have absolutely no meekness in his heart.

How, then, should we describe meekness? In the biblical sense, it is a combination of three characteristics—gentleness, obedience, and submission—expressed through a humble, unpretentious attitude. The meek person reflects a joyful *willingness* and a genuine *teachableness* in life situations, as well as an *acceptance* of the will of God, whatever it may be. Meekness, like the other fruit of the Spirit, is acquired by yielding to the working of the Holy Spirit in our lives. Though it may be manifest at times in a particular act in a specific situation, it won't appear fully grown in our lives overnight. First comes the blossom, and then the small fruit that needs time to grow, develop, and ripen. Like the other characteristics of love, meekness is only cultivated by our continual yielding to the Holy Spirit in all of life's circumstances. If we truly desire meekness in our lives, we must seek the things that cause it to grow.

*Cultivating Meekness*

Jesus gave us clear instructions about cultivating meekness. He said, "Take My yoke upon you, and learn of Me; for I am meek and lowly in heart..." (Mt. 11:29). Jesus simply calls to us and invites us to submit to His yoke. He does not force us to come, but extends an invitation to take up His yoke and learn of Him. The picture of a yoke that harnesses oxen to walk together gives us the understanding that walking with Jesus will give direction to our lives and, at the same time, limit our independence. Taking His yoke willingly into our lives and submitting to His will marks the beginning of the development of the fruit of meekness. Sadly, our natural flesh life does not want to stay in His yoke. It wants to rule. Staying in the yoke with Jesus is the secret of maturing that fruit.

## Impact of Meekness

Jesus was really teaching us how to have a true impact on our generation through developing meekness. I believe with all my heart that meekness will be one of the strongest weapons of the Church against the enemy. Jesus said that the meek would inherit the earth (Mt. 5:5). Unless we understand the true power of meekness, it will be difficult for us to see how this strategy can work. But Jesus portrayed that power of meekness in His own life. When the enemy came to Jesus and found nothing in Him, he fled screaming. Through His gentle submission to His Father's will, Jesus changed the destiny of mankind.

The Scriptures are filled with instructions for us to walk in meekness. When the apostle Paul wrote guidelines for restoring a believer who had fallen, he insisted that those who restore someone do so in the spirit of meekness (Gal. 6:1). Teaching us how to deal with unrepentant people, he wrote that in meekness we instruct those who oppose themselves (2 Tim. 2:25).

Regarding treatment of fellow Christians, he instructs us to put on meekness (Col. 3:12). He wrote to Titus to show meekness to all men (Tit. 3:2). Without the cultivation of this fruit, the true nature of Christ will not be seen through the Church.

## Promises to the Meek

The call to meekness also is accompanied by divine promises for our personal lives: "But the meek...shall delight themselves in the abundance of peace" (Ps. 37:11). Jesus said that those who learn meekness from Him would find rest for their souls (Mt. 11:29). Could the lack of peace in our families and our society be traced to the sad reality that so few Christians have found peace because the fruit of meekness has not been developed in their lives? If so, then our need for repentance is urgent. We must determine today to submit to Jesus' yoke and begin to cultivate the firstfruits of meekness in our lives. May we truly hear Him say, "Come unto Me, all ye that labour and are heavy laden, and I will give you rest. Take My yoke upon you, and learn of Me; for I am meek and lowly in heart: and ye shall find rest unto your souls" (Mt. 11:28-29). This rest that we find through cultivating meekness and learning of Him surpasses all human explanation.

## TEMPERANCE

*He that is slow to anger is better than the mighty; and he that ruleth his spirit than he that taketh a city* (Proverbs 16:32).

Temperance can be defined simply as self-control. Among the graces of the Spirit that are the fruit of abiding in Christ, none are more important than self-control. Temperance is the true kind of self-love. He who respects himself as the temple of the Holy Spirit will exercise control over his impulses and motivations. We usually think of temperance as moderation in the areas of eating and drinking. Temperance, however, is self-control over every phase of life. One who shows the fruit of temperance shows self-control over anger, carnal passion, appetites, desires for worldly pleasure, and our self-centered lives. Of course, this can only be accomplished by the power of the Holy Spirit who works in us His divine control that overrules the self-life, our carnal nature.

The Scriptures teach that he who rules his spirit is better than he who captures a city (Prov. 16:32). Many people have not brought their "desire to rule" to the cross and are creating ungodly situations by trying to control others according to their selfish desires. Until the fruit of self-control is working in a person's character, he is not qualified to govern or take a place of authority in even one other life. In every area of delegated authority, whether in the home, the church, or the workplace, the fruit of temperance needs to be manifested. What peace and harmony will result when leaders, counselors, pastors, and parents cultivate temperance. This understanding should cause godly parents to cultivate this fruit so they can rule their homes properly. It is important that every Christian allow the Holy Spirit to work self-control into his character.

To cultivate the fruit of temperance, our own appetites and desires must be submitted to the Lordship of Jesus and not allowed to rule us. Paul declared that all things were lawful for him, but not all things were expedient, or profitable, and that he would not be brought under the power of anything (1 Cor. 6:12). "Meats for the belly, and the belly for meats: but God shall destroy both it and them..." (1 Cor. 6:13). He went on to say in that verse that the body is for the Lord and the Lord for the body. With this perspective, we will respect ourselves and others too much to allow our carnal desire for power to rule our lives or the lives of others.

*Summary*

Samuel Chadwick makes the interesting observation that, in newspaper English, Paul's description of the fruit of the Spirit would read something like this:

The fruit of the Spirit is an affectionate, lovable disposition, a radiant spirit, a cheerful temper, a tranquil mind, and quiet manner, forebearing patience in provoking circumstances with trying people, a sympathetic insight and tactful helpfulness, generous judgment; being sold to charity, loyal and reliable under all circumstances, humility that forgets self in the joy of others, in all things self-mastered, self-controlled, which is the final mark of perfection. In summarizing the subject of the fruit of the Spirit it is emphasized that these characteristics are not imposed upon the Christian from without. They are the result of the life of Christ within. They describe the character of Jesus Christ in the life of the believer.[4]

The wonderful mystery of "Christ in you, the hope of glory" (Col. 1:27) is revealed through fruit-bearing. That is only possible as we yield to the work of the Holy Spirit to become a true branch, receiving the vital life-giving sap from Christ Himself. Then we must submit to the dealings of the divine Husbandman, the Father Himself, who will not be satisfied without finding fruit in His vineyard. When He finds it, He will prune away any unnecessary material to ensure the increase of that fruitfulness. It is wonderful to think that the character of Christ Himself can flow through our lives as we submit to this precious work of the Holy Spirit to produce the fruit of love in us.

Lest we despair in thinking we cannot produce such beautiful fruit as described here, we must understand that we need only come to Christ continually in submissive obedience to the Holy Spirit for this godly character to be cultivated in us. We need always remember that these beautiful facets of divine love have as their source, not our human efforts, but the life of God Himself. As we cultivate an intimate relationship with Christ, learning to abide in Him, we will become fruitful Christians.

## *Notes*

1. Perry Brewster, *Pentecostal Doctrine*, (Cheltham, England: Reed Hearst Publishers, 1976).

2. Martin Luther, *Commentary on Galatians*, Tr. by Theodore Graebner, (Grand Rapids, Michigan: Zondervan Pub. House, 1939).

3. William Edward Vine, *Expository Dictionary of the New Testament Words*, (Old Tappan, New Jersey: Fleming H. Revell Co., 1966).

4. Samuel Chadwick, *The Way to Pentecost* (New York: Fleming H. Revell Co., 1937).

# Chapter 9

# *Walking in the Spirit*

## *Part I: Divine Purpose Fulfilled*

*If we live in the Spirit, let us also walk in the Spirit* (Galatians 5:25).

The Scriptures teach that if we walk in the Spirit, we will not fulfill the lust of the flesh (Gal. 5:16). As Christians, many of us have heard this biblical admonition all our lives. It gives us a beautiful picture of life in Christ and sounds like a simple command: Walk in the Spirit. However, many Christians do not know what it means to walk in the Spirit. It remains a vague concept to many, even to ministers. Yet the Scriptures declare that we must live and walk in the Spirit, so we dare not settle for a vague understanding of what that involves. Instead, we need to search the Scriptures until we grasp the significance of what life is like when we walk in the Spirit. Only then can we expect to be victorious in our Christian lives.

A simple definition of what it means to walk in the Spirit is *to allow the Holy Spirit to do the work in us that God sent Him to do.* In order to cooperate fully with the work of the Holy Spirit in our lives, we need to understand why God sent Him to us. Just before our Lord left this earth, He said this to His disciples:

> *And I will pray the Father, and He shall give you another Comforter, that He may abide with you for ever; even the Spirit of truth; whom the world cannot receive, because it seeth Him not, neither knoweth Him: but ye know Him; for He dwelleth with you, and shall be in you* (John 14:16-17).

As we have said, the Father sent the Holy Spirit to dwell in us and to fulfill God's eternal purpose through our lives. Unless we can grasp the greatness of His mission and His work in the earth, we will try to satisfy ourselves with a small portion of that eternal work. We may receive a few of His gifts, mistakenly thinking that is all there is of the Holy Spirit and His work. In that way many miss the reality of the eternal purposes of our Father being worked out in our lives.

We saw in our study of the gifts of the Spirit that spiritual gifts are not a prerequisite for walking in the

Spirit. Paul taught the spiritually-gifted Corinthian church that there was a more excellent way. He declared that if they did not follow that way of love, they were nothing, regardless of the impressive spiritual gifts they had (1 Cor. 13). That means that if we are not following the way of love, we are not walking in the Spirit at all, but are following the carnal ways of our flesh-nature.

Although some have erred in overemphasizing the gifts of the Spirit, others have quenched the Holy Spirit dwelling inside them by not acknowledging His presence or consulting Him. Thus He is unable to do in them what God sent Him to do. They may acknowledge the work of Jesus on the cross and say He abides in them, yet the work of the Holy Spirit can still be foreign to them. As a result, they will never come to know Him intimately. For them He will remain some mysterious being whose Presence is something they must accept by faith without ever really understanding who He is or why He came. These people will never be able to allow the Holy Spirit to do what God sent Him to do because they do not know Him intimately.

Unfortunately, the Church today has erred, I believe, in both settling for a small part of the Holy Spirit's work and in quenching His moving among us. Sometimes we become satisfied with thinking that the Holy Spirit's work in us was merely to give us spiritual gifts. We think we are walking in the Spirit because the gifts of the Spirit are operating through us. Others ignore the Holy Spirit, choosing to follow man's program instead of the leading of the Holy Spirit.

Do we talk to the Holy Spirit as we do Jesus? Do we know Him intimately and personally? Do we acknowledge His presence daily? Every once in a while the Holy Spirit seems to nudge us and remind us that we haven't been very friendly to Him, that we haven't kept in very close touch with Him. It is as though He is crying out, "Don't keep Me locked up. Acknowledge that I am here. Recognize what I have come to do." The time must come that we get serious about who the Holy Spirit is and learn why He came to earth. Then we must choose to cooperate with Him and allow Him to do all that God has sent Him to do. We need to ask Him, "Why did You come?" and, "Why did My Father send You to me?" Then as He answers us and reveals to us His divine purposes, we must yield to His work in our lives and churches.

## PERSON OF PURPOSE

The Holy Spirit is a divine Person with a plan and purpose for our lives. He doesn't come to us haphazardly; He is a Person of purpose. God has an eternal plan and purpose for every individual who accepts Him as Lord and Savior. The Holy Spirit is God bringing that purpose to reality as we learn to yield to His will for our lives. Paul declared to the Corinthians, "What? know ye not that your body is the temple of the

Holy Ghost...?" (1 Cor. 6:19) The Holy Spirit does not reside in the church building; He lives in us. Though He resides in our spirits, His work is limited by what we allow Him to do through our souls and bodies.

That is why we need to die to our soulish nature; it is so we can cooperate with Him to accomplish His purposes. Our carnal minds need to be renewed by the Spirit of God within us to think His thoughts. Our wills need to be yielded to Him to obey His will. Our emotions need to be filled with the love of God. As we begin to discuss what it means to walk in the Spirit, we need to understand the specific purposes for which God comes to dwell in us.

## A Place of Spiritual Discernment

What is His purpose when He comes into our temples to live in them? One of the first things He does is to make our hearts a place of *spiritual discernment.* In our study of spiritual gifts, we saw that the Holy Spirit Himself living in us gives us ability to discern what spirit we are encountering in a certain situation: the Holy Spirit, an evil spirit, or the human spirit. Though all may not operate the gift of discerning of spirits, when the Holy Spirit comes into our hearts, He brings His divine ability to discern and makes our "temples" a place of spiritual discernment.

Why do I list spiritual discernment first in considering the purposes for the coming of the Holy Spirit?

Until the Holy Spirit comes to us, we are living under the influence of another spirit. Paul declared:

*And you were dead in your trespasses and sins, in which you formerly walked according to the course of this world, according to the prince of the power of the air, of the spirit that is now working in the sons of disobedience* (Ephesians 2:1-2 NAS).

Before our salvation, we were cooperating with the spirit of this world that is inspired by satan. So our inner man was under the influence of that spirit. If we are going to submit to the Holy Spirit, He has to be able to teach us to discern which spirit is to abide there. We have a mind of our own, and the devil has one, too. If we can't discern, we don't know who is influencing us. We need to have a place of spiritual discernment inside of us. We call it "walking softly," or "ascertaining the voice of the Spirit." He needs to set up discernment inside us so we can recognize what is good and evil, holy and profane. If we can't discern righteousness from unrighteousness, we won't be able to walk with Him. If we can't discern truth, we can't relate to the Spirit of truth. The Holy Spirit will put a caution in our minds when we hear something that is not quite right. Those checks become safeguards that keep us from error. We need to learn to listen to those impressions and then learn to test them, trying the spirits.

## A Place of Victory Over Sin

He came to make us *victorious over sin*. The Scriptures teach, "For sin shall not have dominion over you" (Rom. 6:14a). There is the power of sin, the pollution of sin, and the penalty for sin. God came to deliver us from all the dominion of sin. When people do not live victoriously, they are not walking in the Holy Spirit. Even if they speak in tongues as an evidence of having received the baptism of the Holy Spirit, that is not a criteria for walking in the Spirit. He came to make this temple a place of victory over sin, and having that victory means we are walking in the Spirit.

Does that mean I won't ever sin again? No. But sin does not have to control me. As I yield to the Holy Spirit, He delivers me from the sin and I don't have to live in it. He changes my desires so I don't want to live the way I did under sin. I don't have to have people watching me to make me keep the rules. I walk obediently because the victory is dwelling in me. I don't have to be restricted to turn off immoral programs on my TV. My own desires scream against them. The Holy Spirit is controlling my desires and enabling me to hate the things God hates. So He came to give us that victory until sin no longer has dominion over us.

## A Place of Refreshing Rain

The Holy Spirit makes our hearts ready to receive the *refreshing rain* that God promises. He knows that without rain, we can't produce fruit. He knows that unless we have showers, our hearts will get hard. Have you ever seen rain fall when the ground was so hard that the water didn't soak it? That is a picture of people who come to church when the Spirit is moving and the rain of His presence rolls off like water from a "duck's back" because their hearts are too hard to receive it. The rain of the Spirit brings repentance. Repentance will break the soil and the fallow ground. He comes in conviction to our temples and prepares them as places where the showers of the latter rain of refreshing can fall.

## A Place of Healing and Deliverance

The Holy Spirit has come to make our temples places of *healing*. Jesus is the Anointed One who brings healing and deliverance to captives. He acknowledged the fact that the Holy Spirit empowered Him for every good work when He stood up in church to read, "The Spirit of the Lord is upon Me, because He hath anointed Me to preach the gospel to the poor; He hath sent Me to heal the brokenhearted, to preach deliverance to the captives..." (Lk. 4:18).

The good news of the gospel is for the poor. The "poor" does not refer to people who do not have material possessions, but to those who recognize their need of God. What is the first declaration of the constitution of the heavenly government? "Blessed are the poor in spirit: for theirs is the kingdom of heaven"

(Mt. 5:3). The poor in spirit are those who know they have a need and who look to God for help. What is available to them? It is the Kingdom. Under this anointing, by the Spirit of the Lord, Jesus proclaims freedom to captives in bondage to sin and disease. So anytime the Holy Spirit begins to move in the Church, part of the message is freedom from bondage, recovery of sight to the blind, and deliverance of the oppressed.

As we can understand from the passage in Luke 4, the healing that the Holy Spirit came to set up inside us is not limited to physical distresses. He came to bring divine help to the mind, to the will, to the emotions, to any part of us that has been injured or bruised. In whatever way we are lame or crippled—physically, mentally, or emotionally—He has come to bring divine enablement. We do not need to wallow in self-pity over our emotional hurts, or use the past as an excuse for present failure. We hear the cry so often today, "I was abused." Though it is sadly true that many have suffered deeply from traumatic experiences, it is equally true that the Holy Spirit came to bring healing. If, as Christians, we haven't experienced His healing in certain areas of our lives, is it not that we haven't allowed Him to do that healing work in us? We need to find a place of forgiveness and yieldedness to His love and power that will free us from the effects of our past.

You may ask me, "Have you ever been hurt or rejected or abused?" Of course I have. "Have you ever had anybody do something to make you bitter?" Of course I have. But I did not have to succumb to bitterness and other negative strongholds, for I discovered Somebody living in me who can handle it. When I am thinking about that difficult person or circumstance, He says, "Would you like to see your healed condition inside?" And He shows me that it is as though He has dropped a glass bubble between me and the difficulty, and I can look through the glass shield without feeling any disturbance of anger, retaliation, or hurt emotions. I have been given grace to forgive and that becomes my key to the healing of my hurt. The healing of the Holy Spirit, then, is for even the deepest pain: bruisings, batterings, broken hearts. He came to make us whole, not only in our bodies, but in our psyches and emotions as well. Though we are powerless to heal ourselves, the Holy Spirit brings our healing by His divine power.

## A Place of Soul-Winning and Missionary Zeal

The Holy Spirit comes to set up a zeal in our hearts for winning the lost to Christ. Jesus promised the disciples, "But ye shall receive power, after that the Holy Ghost is come upon you: and ye shall be witnesses unto Me…" (Acts 1:8). One of the sure proofs that He has come to our hearts is "after that" we become witnesses. Where do we begin to be witnesses? Jesus said we begin in our Jerusalem, the place where we live—home base.

Your world is where you personally touch lives. As you experience this zeal and power to witness to your world, it is an evidence that the Holy Spirit has come. It is the Holy Spirit's business to win the world to Jesus. Jesus commissioned His disciples to go to all the world. A Spirit-led life will have that mandate. A Spirit-led church has the same mandate to go into all the world with the gospel. Where the Holy Spirit is working, He is working to bring souls of men to Jesus.

## A Place Where Strongholds of Satan Are Conquered

Is conquering strongholds different from gaining victory over sin? Yes. It is even greater than gaining victory over sin. I know that some say the Church is not to be militant, that we are to be lovers of the Lamb, cultivating relationship with our heavenly Bridegroom. I agree with them that we are to be in love with Jesus, but I disagree with the extreme of saying we are never to be involved in spiritual warfare. God gave the Church the power over satan. He deputized us, equipped us, and sent us out with authority over devils and diseases. The Church is learning both to worship the Lamb and to do warfare—not by our power, but by the power of the Spirit. It is God pulling down strongholds, but He has to do it through the Church. If we can stand against the enemy with vessels that are clean and release the Holy Ghost in us, He will pull down the strongholds of the enemy.

In the 1500's, the queen of England said she feared the prayers of John Knox more than the whole enemy's army. He was a man of God who knew God's power over the enemy. What does the enemy think of us? The Church is not a weak, passive, defeated group of people. The Church is the Body of Christ anointed by the power of the Holy Ghost to preach the gospel to the poor, to set the captives free, and to tear down strongholds. The Holy Spirit gives us authority to take back what the devil stole.

## A Place Where Backsliding Can Be Removed

The Holy Spirit comes into our lives to bring restoration to our souls. Everything the enemy has perpetrated against the human race, God has purposed to restore. Jesus came to undo, outdo, and overdo everything the devil ever did. The Holy Spirit is restoring us to relationship with God the Father and God the Son, teaching us to walk with Him in obedience and to enjoy the Kingdom of God in righteousness, peace, and joy in the Holy Ghost.

These are the wonderful purposes of the Holy Spirit in coming to redeem a life from the power of sin. How does He come to fulfill these purposes? What must we do to enjoy the benefits of His coming? The first requirement for having the purposes of God revealed in us is we must be born again of the Spirit of God. There is more involved in this experience than simply signing a paper to join a church. Understanding what actually takes place when we are born of the Spirit will prepare us to receive all the fullness of God's purposes for our lives. Though I had been saved many years when the Holy Spirit began to teach me about the new birth, I realized I had not understood very well what was involved in this experience.

## BORN OF THE SPIRIT

Sons of God are described in the Scriptures as those who are led by the Spirit (Rom. 8:14). The Bible has much to say about our three developmental stages of walking with God: babyhood, youth, and adulthood. There is a vast difference between being a baby born into a family and being a son who has come to maturity. Sonship in the Scriptures indicates a mature relationship with the Father, involving both privilege and responsibility. God wants not only sons, but sons with knowledge. Sons with knowledge are those who walk in revelation and who know what their Father is thinking. There are some grown children who can't "run the company." The spiritual son with knowledge is the one who has been trained in the ways of the Father so that he can reign with Him.

The first requirement for becoming a mature son of God is that we must be *born of the Spirit*. What does it mean to be born of the Spirit? Nicodemus asked Jesus, "How can a man be born when he is old? can he enter the second time into his mother's womb, and be born?" (Jn. 3:4) Jesus told Nicodemus that unless he was born again, he could not *see* the Kingdom of God. Do we really know what He meant? As evangelicals, we have taught people that they must be born again to get to Heaven. That was all we offered in our understanding of salvation. We knew that one day we would die, and that in order to go to Heaven we must be born again. That is true, but that is not all God intended in offering us eternal life through the new birth.

We live in a world where there are two kingdoms. One is the satanic kingdom of darkness and of lies. The other is the kingdom of light, love, and truth, the Kingdom of God. Those who live in sin are being controlled by a satanic power that rules that kingdom. Though they might be considered moral, pay their bills, and choose a decent life style, they are living in the kingdom of darkness that is opposed to the Kingdom of God. When Jesus walked this earth, He said, "The kingdom of heaven is at hand" (Mt. 4:17). His Kingdom has come for those who are willing to receive it through repentance. Asking Jesus to forgive our sins and to be Lord of our lives, and acknowledging His sacrifice on Calvary, brings the Kingdom of God to us and ushers us into that Kingdom here on earth.

Entering the Kingdom of God through the new birth means our inner man has entered into eternity now. When we are born of the Spirit, we are alive to the eternal realities of the Kingdom of God. I am not simply going into eternity when I die. My spirit is already living in the eternal Kingdom of God as a born-again child of God. I can't see the Kingdom of God unless I am born of the Spirit, taught by the Spirit, and led by the Spirit because it is a spiritual kingdom. Jesus said, "That which is born of the flesh is flesh; and that which is born of the Spirit is spirit" (Jn. 3:6). To be born of the Spirit means to be born from above, to receive a new spiritual life of divine origin.

I had preached the gospel for 17 years when I was miraculously healed from what was believed to be a terminal illness. I received the baptism of the Holy Spirit at the same time, and both experiences were against my theology at that time. A little while after that, my heavenly Father talked to me about what actually happened when I was born again. I was a little insulted because I thought I had come into revelation of much deeper things than the new birth. I thought I understood the new birth experience.

The Holy Spirit gave me a vision of a Jewish girl, a little maiden in a kneeling position. I knew it was Mary, the mother of Jesus. She was enveloped in the shekinah glory of God. I saw a beautiful cloud around her as He let me look in on that scene. Then He asked me, "What happened to her that brought your Savior to earth?" I answered simply, "She became pregnant." He responded, "What produced that child?" I said, "A seed." Then He asked, "Whose seed?" I answered, "God's." He continued His questions to me as a patient teacher: "Where did I put that seed?" I responded, "In Mary's uterus." Then He asked me what her response was. I replied, "She said, 'Be it unto me according to thy word.' " She was saying, in essence, "Let me become pregnant according to your Word." The Father explained, "From My mind, I produced from Myself a Seed, the Word." When He said that, I remembered how John began his gospel: "In the beginning was the Word, and the Word was with God, and the Word was God. ... And the Word was made flesh, and dwelt among us..." (Jn. 1:1,14a). Then He asked me, "Who took that seed from God to Mary?" I said, "The Holy Spirit." Then He made me understand that in that same supernatural way, when I was born again, the Holy Spirit planted the seed of God's eternal life in my spirit, through His Word. That is how Christ comes to live in my spirit.

Paul called this experience a mystery: "this mystery among the Gentiles; which is Christ in you, the hope of glory" (Col. 1:27). A number of times in the Christological epistles he talks about our being "in Christ," and Christ being "in us." After the Holy Spirit visited Mary and impregnated her with the seed of God, Mary extolled the greatness of God in her lovely "Magnificat": "My soul doth magnify the Lord" (Lk. 1:46). She was expressing the wonder of that divine life within her. In that same way, there is a new creation living inside of us, in our spirits. "Therefore if any man be in Christ, he is a new creature" (2 Cor. 5:17a). Who is this new creature inside us? It is Christ. We are new in that we are born from above, and our eternal spirits are now alive to God. He is eternal life. If we have Jesus, we have eternal life; if we do not have Christ, we do not have eternal life.

The Holy Spirit hovered over us, just as He did over the earth when it was without form and void, and created new life in us. He said, in effect, "Let there be light, life, love, liberty"—and He lifed us with eternal life. Without that supernatural spiritual birth, we cannot even see the Kingdom of God. These human eyes can never see the Kingdom of God. That is the reason we don't look for God in miracles. Miracles do not reveal Jesus; they show you where Jesus has been. Everywhere He went, He did good. Miracles help the natural man to see that there is a God, but we don't have to have them to see God.

Paul told the Corinthians, "…Eye hath not seen, nor ear heard, neither have entered into the heart of man, the things which God hath prepared for them that love Him. But God hath revealed them unto us by His Spirit…" (1 Cor. 2:9-10). He understood that only by the Spirit of God can we know the mind and purpose of God for us. Why are we disturbed when unsaved people can't understand what we Christians do about worship and praise, for example? It is not possible for the natural man to be able to comprehend and see what is in the Kingdom of God. Why? The Kingdom is a spirit world ruled by King Jesus and administrated by the Holy Spirit. He is the Executor, Divine Administrator, and the Teacher. He came to make the Kingdom real to us, and to put us into the Kingdom. We are citizens of another world. Without experiencing a supernatural new birth by the Spirit of God, a person cannot enjoy this wonderful Kingdom, a Kingdom of peace, joy, and righteousness in the Holy Ghost (Rom. 14:17).

I have a King in me now who has started to reign and rule in the eternal part of my inner man. One day He will be released to be King over all. Even as Christians, having experienced the new birth, we must be careful to focus our minds and hearts on the eternal Kingdom. Although we must live and work in this world, we dare not set our affections and pursuits on the values of this world system. The more we crave what is here, and the more the system of this world takes hold of us, the less we will know about the Kingdom of God. If we expect to grow from babyhood to youth and into sons with knowledge, we will have to concentrate our energies on the pursuit of God and His holiness and righteousness in every area of our lives.

## *OUR DILEMMA*

*Therefore if any man be in Christ, he is a new creature: old things are passed away; behold, all things are become new (2 Corinthians 5:17).*

If we do not understand what it means to be born again and become a new creature in Christ, we will be disappointed and discouraged in our walk when we discover that some of the old things of our lives still seem to be very present. The anger that ruled us before salvation may continue to plague us at times, though we do not want to give place to it. If we dogmatically declare that we are new creatures and that old things are passed away, but our behavior and attitudes do not show it, it is because we haven't understood what is really involved in this experience.

A translation of this verse that is closer to the original Greek would be, "Therefore if any man be *in Christ a new creature*, old things are continually passing away." This shows the progressive work of salvation in our souls. We must learn to allow the Christ-life in our spirits to permeate our soulish natures—our wills, minds, and emotions—by yielding to the Holy Spirit within us instead of to our sin nature. We still have our soulish nature to bring to the cross of Christ, surrendering its evil deeds to the Lordship of Christ. We are in Christ and He is in us, so all things are becoming new as the old are passing away. We have Someone new living in us as the pregnant mother has the new creature inside her. Christ's life was breathed into us when we asked Him to save us from our sins, and He took the Word and made it alive, planting His life inside us. As we yield to His wonderful divine life, we can be changed into His likeness.

We can be delivered from our dilemma as Paul so graphically describes it to the Romans:

> *For I joyfully concur with the law of God in the inner man, but I see a different law in the members of my body, waging war against the law of my mind.... Wretched man that I am! Who will set me free from the body of this death? Thanks be to God through Jesus Christ our Lord!...* (Romans 7:22-25 NAS).

As we yield to the life of Christ in our spirits, we can overcome our nature that is given to sin and grow into Christlikeness to become mature sons. We have to give up our lives in order to receive His. To the degree that we exchange our old nature at the cross, choosing to die to its sinful ways, we receive His life. John the Baptist understood this principle when he declared, "He must increase, but I must decrease" (Jn. 3:30).

Paul declared, "I am crucified with Christ: nevertheless I live; yet not I, but Christ liveth in me: and the life which I now live in the flesh I live by the faith of the Son of God, who loved me, and gave Himself for me" (Gal. 2:20). So as that new life comes forth, the life I now live, I live by the faith of the Son of God. Judicially I am crucified with Christ; the death of my sin nature has been legally accomplished. It was nailed to the cross on which Jesus died. My old Adamic, sinful, ungodly nature is reckoned dead, powerless to rule me any longer, as I bring it to the cross and refuse to

yield to its ways. We are powerless to change ourselves, but as we allow the Holy Spirit to birth the life
of Christ within us, we can continually yield to Him
and be changed into the image of Christ.

If I am in Christ, I am a new creature. I don't even
have to rely on my faith to experience that reality. For
a long time the devil told me I didn't have any faith,
until one day I was able to refute him with the Word.
Faith is a gift of God, not something we work up ourselves. Paul taught, "For by grace are ye saved through
faith; and that not of yourselves: it is the gift of God"
(Eph. 2:8). Now I say as Paul did, "...the life which I
now live in the flesh I live by *the faith of the Son of
God*, who loved me, and gave Himself for me" (Gal.
2:20, emphasis mine).

We are saved by grace through faith. It is not ours;
it is His. It is His grace, His faith, His wisdom, His
knowledge, and His holiness. The beautiful thing is,
when we go into business with Him, He furnishes all
the capital. We don't have much to invest. Whose
grace is working? Whose mercy? Whose wisdom?
Whose righteousness? We don't have much to "boast"
about except the new Person who is living inside us.
He does not take us over and possess us like a demon
spirit does. But to the degree that we give Him our
wills, He gives us His will in exchange. To the degree
we give up our carnal minds and opinions, He gives us
His mind. He uses our mind, He doesn't destroy it. As
we yield our carnal minds to Him, He gives us the

mind of Christ. And to the degree we yield our emotions to Him, He fills us with His joy and peace.

The development of the Christ-life within us is so beautiful! We have been breathed upon by the Holy Spirit as Mary was, and this holy thing within us is Jesus. We can call it "eternal life" or "Christ" or "glory." It is He! In our born-again experience, He has moved in to give us what we don't have and to furnish everything we will need to live our lives in Christ. The more we let the life of Christ grow, the more His divine nature becomes our nature. We begin to realize that we don't get angry like we used to, for Christ doesn't react like that. We begin to love people we could not love before. We are delivered from fear because "perfect love casteth out fear" (1 John 4:18). All of our sin nature loses its power over us as we allow the life of Christ to mature us into responsible sons and daughters of God.

As we begin to understand the work of the Holy Spirit in salvation, we can learn to yield to Him in such a way that we will fulfill the requirements for walking in the Spirit and receive the blessings that are a result of living a Spirit-filled life.

# Chapter 10

# *Walking in the Spirit*

## *Part II: Divine Requirements and Blessings*

As we explore the divine requirements and inevitable results of walking in the Spirit, we can evaluate whether or not we are living a life that is fulfilling the biblical mandate to walk in the Spirit and not fulfill the lust of the flesh. God's truths are not difficult to understand when the Holy Spirit gives revelation to our hearts. But He always waits for us to choose His way. He will never violate our wills in the matters of relationship, even though He knows we will suffer loss if we do not obey His commands. In the Scriptures,

God has given us many beautiful examples of people who followed Him in obedience and of the blessing that came to their lives as a result. We see this in a beautiful love story in the Book of Genesis, which typifies our relationship with the Holy Spirit.

## THE HOLY SPIRIT TYPIFIED IN GENESIS

In the story of Abraham sending his servant, Eliezer, to look for a bride for his son, Isaac (Gen. 24), we find a beautiful revelation of the Holy Spirit. This Old Testament type shows us the relationship between the believer and the Holy Spirit, as well as the relationship of the Godhead. Eliezer, a type of the Holy Spirit, is the faithful servant who leaves the father's house to go to a far country and seek a bride for the son. The drama begins with this journey of the servant from the father's house and ends in his triumphant return with a bride of Isaac, the son. Eliezer made a covenant with the father, Abraham, to bring back a bride for his son. As surely as this servant returned with Rebekah to present her as the bride for Isaac, so shall the Holy Spirit return to the heavenly Father with a bride for our Lord Jesus Christ. What actually happened in Rebekah's life should be of great interest to every believer who desires to be a part of that bride.

The name *Eliezer* means a "mighty divine helper." This faithful servant's entire mission and purpose focused on one thing: to fulfill the father's desire for a bride for his son. He realized he would have to get the girl to choose to leave behind her family, friends, home, and all she had. His commission was that she become enamored with Isaac, as well as espoused or engaged to him. As Christians, we have been chosen to be the Bride of Christ. The Holy Spirit has come to be our "mighty helper" to help us become that spotless Bride. We must understand, however, that bride-ship is not an *appointment*; it is a *relationship* of choice. To me that statement unlocks the entire mystery of who is going to be a part of the Bride.

We will become the Bride of Christ in eternity because of our love relationship with our Lord here on earth. If He is truly our Bridegroom by choice of relationship, and we have a passion for Him, He will one day be our Bridegroom. The heavenly Father sent the Holy Spirit to bring us into this love relationship with Jesus. As we learn to trust Him, He will woo us, win us, teach us, lead us, and bring us safely home as Christ's eternal Bride.

As Eliezer began his search for a bride for Isaac, he prayed for God to help him find the right girl. He asked that she would be at the well drawing water at evening time, and that she would offer to give him water and to water his camels as well. We can easily understand the application of this type as we are admonished in the Scriptures to draw water from the wells of salvation and to become servants of all. It was Rebekah who displayed this servant's heart, and Eliezer knew she was the answer to his prayer.

He then gave Rebekah many gifts: gold bracelets, earrings, jewels, and silver. Eliezer received those gifts from the father before he left home. The father sent them for the bride and wanted the servant to give them to her along the journey so they might give her a little understanding of the generous nature of her bride-groom. In that same way, the Holy Spirit gives us spiritual gifts to reveal our Bridegroom to us and show us the benevolent heart and kindness of the Father.

The purpose of the gifts, however, was not that Rebekah became satisfied with them alone. She could have stayed in her home with her new gifts, delighting in the fact that she had been chosen to become a bride. These gifts did not obligate her to choose to leave her home. But to become the bride of Isaac, she had to choose to be chosen. That choice would require her leaving all that was familiar and taking an arduous journey by camel across the desert to be united with her bridegroom. As we know, Rebekah made that choice and became the bride of Isaac.

The Holy Spirit is our divine Eliezer whom we must choose to follow as Rebekah did this earthly servant. Learning to walk in the Spirit will require following the Holy Spirit in obedience wherever He leads us. Just as Eliezer was successful in bringing home a bride for Isaac, the Holy Spirit will also be successful in finding those who will choose to follow Him to their heavenly Bridegroom.

In contrast to Rebekah's obedience, we can observe the disobedience of the children of Israel who were also chosen of God to be a special nation. A whole generation who had known the miraculous gifts of God never followed Him into the Promised Land. They were stubborn and rebellious, living in spiritual adultery. Yes, they were chosen by God, but they had never chosen to separate themselves unto their God and be cleansed of their unbelief so they could fulfill His purposes. So when it was time to go into Canaan, God could not take them into it. It was as though they had learned nothing of God during their 40 years in the wilderness. They were still self-centered, seeking only for the provision that God had given them without loving and trusting the person of God Himself.

This is a sad picture of so many Christians today who have received the gifts of the Holy Spirit, but who have not allowed the Holy Spirit to lead them into holiness of life, into the character of Christ. They have gloated over being chosen and called of God. However, they have not wanted the discipline of separation that Rebekah chose, or the rigorous "camel" journey that would prepare them for meeting the bridegroom. Instead, they want to rebuke the testings that have been sent to work in them the character of holiness. If we shoot our camels, how will we make the journey home to see our Bridegroom? Those lumbering beasts of trials and tests, as uncomfortable as they may be, are the only vehicle that we have been given to get us to our destination.

Do we see ourselves in the story of Rebekah as humble servants choosing to follow our divine Helper? Or do we fit easier into the story of the grumbling, unbelieving Israelites? If we see ourselves in the latter, we need to ask the questions, "Do I love the Lord Jesus with all my heart? Is He the lover of my soul? Is my passion for Him growing and consuming me more day by day?" Rebekah was asked the question, "Wilt thou go with this man?" What would our answer be to leaving all and following the Lord? Rebekah made her choice to follow the servant and become the bride of Isaac.

If we read the story of Eliezer carefully, we understand that this servant had focused on this one ultimate intention and purpose: to please his master by bringing home a bride for his son. The entire work of the Holy Spirit is related to His divine purpose of bringing home the Bride of Christ. He didn't come simply to help us cope with life or to bless us with spiritual gifts.

## Our Comforter

Although it is true that the Holy Spirit became our divine Comforter, that is not His ultimate purpose in our lives. Every manifestation of Himself, every divine touch we feel on our lives, is intended to reveal Christ to us and in us, preparing us to meet our

Bridegroom. Neither did He come simply to give spiritual gifts to the Church. Every gift has a purpose.

If He wants you to prophesy, your prophecy is to glorify Christ. If He lets you speak in divers tongues, it is so a person in that language may hear of the glorious works of our Lord. In everything He does He is saying, in effect, "Behold Jesus. Consider Jesus. Isn't He wonderful? He is the Alpha and the Omega, the Beginning and the End. He is the Healer. He is the Revelation of the Father." The Holy Spirit came to reveal Jesus to us so we can fall passionately in love with Him and be prepared to be His Bride.

Jesus said, "When the Counselor comes, whom I will send to you from the Father…He will testify about Me" (Jn. 15:26 NIV). The Holy Spirit's prime message is Jesus. He came to serve Jesus, to reveal Jesus, to quicken our lives with the life of Jesus in and through us. We need to remember that we are not our own; we have been bought with a price. We have been chosen to be espoused to Christ. The Holy Spirit came to guide us into all truth, and the truth will set us free from every bondage to sin and unbelief. We are not of this world. We are on a journey toward a glorious meeting with our Bridegroom. We are being prepared for the presentation of the Bride and the coronation of the Queen.

## Our Guide

We often hear believers say that the Holy Spirit "led them" into something they desire to do, and many cry out for Him to give direction when they are in trouble. Yet, many times when He is trying to lead us, we don't yield to His guidance. We spend time trying to decide what to do for ourselves and figuring out how we can do it. Somehow we cannot quite comprehend that the Third Person of the infinite Godhead lives inside us, whose eternal purpose is to fulfill the eternal plan of our Father in us. If we yield to Him and walk in His love, we will not fulfill the lust of the flesh. Why? The Holy Spirit is continually showing us Jesus in all His beauty, the beauty of holiness. He is enamoring our hearts with Christ and changing us from our selfish desires to an all-consuming desire to please Him alone.

It seems to me that in these days the Holy Spirit is opening the eyes of His chosen ones and answering the prayer Paul prayed for the Ephesians:

> *That the God of our Lord Jesus Christ, the Father of glory, may give unto you the spirit of wisdom and revelation in the knowledge of Him: the eyes of your understanding being enlightened; that ye may know what is the hope of His calling, and what the riches of the glory of His inheritance in the saints* (Ephesians 1:17-18).

When the Holy Spirit prayed this prayer through Paul, He was praying the will of God for the Church today as well as for the Ephesian church. Paul addressed his epistle not only to the church at Ephesus, but to the faithful in Christ Jesus. That includes everyone who loves Christ. The Holy Spirit will be faithful to open the eyes of every church that wants His presence and is praying this kind of prayer. This revelation comes to believers who have no concern other than to see the Body of Christ conformed to the image of our Lord Jesus Christ. We have had the era of a "word of wisdom" and a "word of knowledge," but the Holy Spirit is praying that we might have the *Spirit* of wisdom and the *Spirit* of knowledge and revelation.

## The Bride

The Holy Spirit's mission will be complete only when He does what He promised the Father He would do: bring back the Bride for the Son. What kind of bride do you think He is going to present to the Father on the day when our Lord is finally revealed in His ultimate glory? Will He choose her from among those who live with a Sunday morning mentality, who are filled with apathy and love for material things, and who worship as a religious duty once a week? Or will she be among those who are not devoted to Jesus and haven't cared about an intimate relationship with the Lord—those who are not truly in love with Him? I don't think that is the kind of bride He is going to present to Jesus.

The Bride of Christ will include those who are willing to "ride the camels" that represent those painful trials in our lives. Rebekah chose that long, tedious camel ride over the hot desert, following her guide, enduring the bumps and dust, and being willing to leave her personal comforts of home. She set her eyes on reaching her destiny. If we truly love Jesus, we will be found following the Holy Spirit wherever He leads us, despite our personal discomfort, because we have chosen to leave all to find our Bridegroom.

The Bride of Christ will have the yearning of the heart that says, as did David Wilkerson, "Jesus, You are the only happiness in this world. I have tasted and seen that You are good. And all I want is You." This is the deep inner cry of those who hunger for holiness. They suddenly begin to feel a deep remorse and anguish over their sins and iniquity that are revealed to them by the Holy Spirit. When they begin to pray, the Holy Spirit Himself comes to help their infirmities and to pray according to the will of God for them (Rom. 8:26-27). He is praying with such profound emotion that it becomes "groanings which cannot be uttered." He intercedes for the perfect will of the Father, the purpose over our lives that was ordained before the foundation of the world to be fulfilled in us. Our hearts long for Christ. This Holy Spirit-breathed "longing" is a powerful experience, and He groans in us because He knows the will of God is not yet accomplished. We begin to realize how far He has yet to take us before we are transformed into the image of Christ and evidence His character in our lives.

Where are those today who are experiencing this yearning and groaning to be more like Christ, with a thirst for righteousness and a passion for God? Many churches seem to be filled with people who never evaluate their love for Christ. They don't want to be disturbed. But the Holy Spirit is finding people who are allowing Him to take control of their lives. There is a "church within the Church" of believers who are learning to hear the voice of the Holy Spirit and are beginning to yield to Him.

The more they yield, the more His inner groaning comes forth. They are praying in agreement with the Holy Spirit. Their cry is, "Holy Spirit, do what the Father sent You to do. Whatever it takes, reveal Christ in my heart so I may be totally weaned from this world." They are allowing the Holy Spirit to convict them of sin and cleanse them so they can live holy lives. They are learning to walk in the Spirit so they will not fulfill the lust of the flesh.

If this is your testimony, you can rejoice. The Holy Spirit wants you to be cleansed from every spot and wrinkle to fulfill His ultimate purpose to bring home to the Father a spotless Bride for His Son. If you walk in the Spirit, you will be yielding in obedience to His leading. If you let Him do His cleansing work in you, allowing Him to fulfill the Father's eternal purpose, you will know what it means to walk in the Spirit.

## REQUIREMENTS FOR WALKING IN THE SPIRIT

### Dependence

As we observe Rebekah's choice to follow the servant, we can see that she was completely *dependent* on him for her future. In that same way, we are dependent on the Holy Spirit. Not only does He save us and give us spiritual gifts, but He is responsible for our entire well-being: spirit, soul, and body. We are completely dependent on Him, whether or not we consciously feel His presence. All believers know what it is at times to enjoy the conscious presence of the Holy Spirit. When I was first filled with the Spirit, I thought I was always going to feel His presence and be aware of Him.

Then one day when I was distressed because I did not feel His nearness, He gave me a beautiful object lesson. He said to me, "You loved your daddy dearly." That is true. He continued, "When you went to bed and said good-night to your daddy, did he have to stay in the room all night to prove to you he was there? Did he have to wake you up every few minutes and say, 'Daughter, I am here'? Or did you go to sleep trusting him, knowing that he was there, and if the slightest disturbance came, you would be conscious of his presence?" I understood then that I did not always have to have a consciousness of the presence of the Holy Spirit with me. I needed only to trust Him with my life as I had trusted my earthly daddy unreservedly as a child.

Our dependence upon the Holy Spirit becomes a life-force, like it did in Jesus' life (Jn. 5:30). Andrew Murray defines humility as "the place of entire dependence on God."[1] We must humble ourselves to recognize the Holy Spirit as the One who quickens our lives. We must depend on Him not only for our spiritual life, but also for the needs of our souls: our minds, wills, and emotions. To be totally dependent on Him doesn't make us puppets. It simply means that we have chosen to yield our wills to the Holy Spirit who furnishes the ability to do what we could not have done without Him. Instead of relying on our natural minds, we learn to consult our divine Guide and Teacher.

## How I Learned a New Dependence on the Holy Spirit

The Holy Spirit required total dependence of me at a critical time in my life. At the same time that I was healed from a terminal illness, I received the baptism of the Holy Spirit. I discovered that the Third Person of the Godhead had come to live in me. Though I had thought He had been in control of this body during 17 years I had been in the ministry, I was mistaken. I thought I had known Him in His fullness as a minister and college professor in the old-time Methodist faith, struggling to live a victorious life over my sin nature. When I would miss the mark, I would come under condemnation because of the legalism I had embraced. Then when I was gloriously healed and baptized in the Holy Spirit, I became very aware that a divine Person had come to take up His residence inside me whom I knew very little about. I had preached about Him in theory and had preached that He sanctified us because that was what I was taught. Now I felt the presence of a divine Person and heard Him speak inside me.

At that same time, to my dismay, the Scriptures seemed to become meaningless to me. I would read my Bible, but it was like a blank book. I couldn't even recall what I had preached all those years. For the next few months, the Holy Spirit gave me only four verses of Scripture to sustain me. They became life to me in a new dimension. The first one was from the Book of Proverbs: "Trust in the Lord with all thine heart; and lean not unto thine own understanding" (Prov. 3:5). The Holy Spirit was cleansing my mind of the way I had always understood the Scriptures. He was making me become dependent upon Him for revelation. I had to become dependent upon Him to teach me the Scriptures.

The second verse He gave me was this: "In all thy ways acknowledge Him, and He shall direct thy paths" (Prov. 3:6). I knew He was putting me on a new path and that I was going to start walking a different way as He directed me. Though I had quoted that verse hundreds of times before, He made it live to me during those months. A divine Person had moved into my spirit and He began to reveal the Word of God to me. He took this professor and preacher who had taught this Book for years and said to me, in essence, "I am here now, and I am your Teacher."

The Holy Spirit had to bring me to a place of willingness to admit I didn't know anything. I realized that I had not even understood that healing was a part of Jesus' atonement before I was healed. I had not believed that speaking in tongues was for us today until I received the baptism of the Holy Spirit at the time of my healing. So I had to admit I could be mistaken about other things I thought I knew. This was a place of dependence that I had not known before. The Holy Spirit would have to teach me how to walk this path.

The third verse He spoke to me was in Habakkuk: "For the vision is yet for an appointed time, but at the end it shall speak, and not lie: though it tarry, wait for it; because it will surely come, it will not tarry" (Hab 2:3). The verse preceding this one carries the instructions to write the vision and make it plain. In these many years following the direction the Holy Spirit gave me in seed form, it has grown to become a mandate over my life. I did not know then that I would be privileged to share with the Body of Christ the wonderful truths He revealed to me from His Word.

The fourth verse He quickened to my spirit during those months was this one: "If any of you lack wisdom, let him ask of God, that giveth to all men liberally, and upbraideth not; and it shall be given him"

(Jas. 1:5). When I would read the Word or pray, these were the only Scriptures that lived to me. With time, I came to a new place of surrender to the admonitions given in those four verses of Scripture.

Meanwhile, a "glory" cloud came to rest over my kitchen the day after I was healed. It was as if a literal cloud of His presence had moved in. It never left me. From the morning in April when I was healed until the night that divine revelation of the Word broke upon my mind, that cloud went everywhere I went. It got fuller and blacker, more "pregnant," like a cloudburst preparing to break. Although it was not visible to others, people who walked into my house could feel it. A Pentecostal pastor came to see me and asked, "Have you just been praying?" I replied, "No, I was just making biscuits." He said, "This place is full of God's presence." My husband responded, "It has been that way ever since my wife was healed."

When I went to the grocery store, that divine cloud of His presence hovered over my cart. It was over my automobile when I drove, and I could sense it over the foot of my bed at night. I was a Methodist professor who knew nothing about the spiritual world that I began experiencing after receiving the baptism of the Holy Spirit. Finally, the day came when that glory cloud burst, and I was lost in the presence of God that broke in upon my mind and heart for 22 hours.

I had been invited to preach for the first time in a Pentecostal church. So overwhelming was the presence of God when that cloud burst, that the lady in whose home I was staying had to assist me in dressing for the meeting. When I stood up to preach, I couldn't speak. I just stood there and cried, experiencing the wonder of God's presence. The people came forward spontaneously to pray at the altar, and revival came to that church. For three months I ministered daily, simply sharing the fresh revelation that God had given me each day. The Book began to open to my understanding in revelation because I had met my Teacher.

The greatest day of my life was the day I said, "I don't think I know anything." With that acknowledgment comes a brokenness of spirit that opens our minds to receive the wisdom He gives that is not of this world. Through my miraculous healing and baptism of the Holy Spirit, I was forced into a world where much of the theology I had taught for 17 years didn't work anymore. I had to find out where I was. To get acquainted with the Holy Spirit, this wonderful Third Person of the Godhead whom I had just met in a new dimension, I had to get into the Book.

So I got a lexicon, concordance, and notebook and categorized every verse in the Scriptures where I saw the Holy Spirit working (this was before today's computer software). I spent many hours a day for the next five years searching the Scriptures regarding this divine Teacher. It was during those hours of study that I found He came to do 66 different works inside me. I learned that He had seven different moods and seven offices that He fulfilled.[2] Because of the dependence God worked in my life during those years, I gained insight into some beautiful truths that changed my life.

Jesus Himself said, "I can of Mine own self do nothing..." (Jn. 5:30). He taught His disciples the principle of abiding in Him in order to become fruitful. Without learning to abide in Christ, in dependence upon the Holy Spirit, all we will have is theory, up-and-down emotions, and a seeking for spiritual gifts. That is not what God intended as the Spirit-filled life. If we don't cooperate with the Holy Spirit, He can't do what the Father sent Him to do. So our total dependence on the Holy Spirit makes available to us the help we need from God. He doesn't expect us to be perfect; He came because we weren't perfect. He didn't come because we already knew, but because we don't know. He came to bring us what we don't have and can't receive in any other way.

### Obedience

If our disposition must be one of dependence in order to walk in the Spirit, our response must be that of obedience to His Word. The first step of obedience is to hearken to what He says. We must be sure we are listening to His Word and set ourselves to hear Him. Often Jesus said, "He that hath an ear let him hear what the Spirit saith" (i.e., Rev. 2:7). He told His disciples, "But blessed are your...ears, for they hear" (Mt. 13:16). Then, after hearing Him, we must come to Him with a surrendered will so we can obey Him. The psalmist understood this when he declared, "The meek will He guide in judgment: and the meek will He teach His way" (Ps. 25:9). He has promised to guide the meek, those who are teachable. Those who are arrogant are not qualified to learn. No matter how much education we have, until we see our need of Him and cry out at the feet of Jesus, "I need the Teacher," He cannot reveal His will to us. If we don't obey the Word we have received, why should we expect to receive more revelation? Sometimes we pray for more light when we haven't walked in the light we have received.

Peter declared that God has given the Holy Spirit to those who obey Him (Acts 5:32). Those who obey God will receive the baptism of the Holy Spirit. Many people have received this experience without understanding, doctrinally, what happened to them. They do not really know who this One is. They simply obeyed God, and He filled them with His Spirit. In that same way, our continued obedience keeps our relationship growing and allows Him to continue to work in our lives.

Failure to continually walk in obedience will result in discontent and despondency. The cause of every despondent cloud that falls over the soul can be traced to the neglect of some particular instruction from our "divine monitor." Of course, this does not apply to places of testing where God may allow us to experience darkness for a season. It does explain, however, the difficult places we find ourselves in because we didn't listen to or obey the voice of the Spirit, but insisted that God let us go our own way.

## Keeping in Step

Not only must we learn obedience to walk in the Spirit, but we must learn to *keep in step with Him* in our obedience. Oftentimes we fall way behind in our obedience, not finding a willingness in our hearts to commit to Him completely or depend on Him fully. A halfhearted obedience will not allow us to keep in step with His purposes in our lives.

Jesus called Himself the Good Shepherd and said that the sheep hear His voice (Jn. 10:3,11). Did you know that a shepherd does not keep all the sheep close to Him? A professional shepherd from Cyprus told me that sheep that walk close to the shepherd are those that choose to be there. As the shepherd stands among the sheep in the morning, he doesn't line them up in a certain order. He simply calls to them and begins to walk. When he calls, some of the sheep begin to run toward him, pushing others out of the way, to get to him first. These are the sheep that want to be close to the shepherd, to feel his touch and hear his voice. Others that want to kick around and do their own thing stay aloof from him.

The shepherd knows all the names of his sheep, but he can't talk to those that are not walking close to him. The ones He talks to the most as they walk along are those that keep in step with him, rubbing his leg to get his attention. What a picture of our Good Shepherd! He has given us the Holy Spirit to be our gentle guide—kind, tender, merciful, understanding. He is patient with us and willing to walk with us all the way. We need to acknowledge that we want to be near Him. Then we will do what is necessary to keep in step with our Lord.

## Availability

As we learn to walk in step with our Lord, we will make ourselves available to Him to fulfill His purposes, not our own. Our continual *availability* is one of the greatest prerequisites for walking in the Spirit. The secret of abiding in Him is to continually make ourselves available as servants who are waiting for His instructions. This does not mean, however, that we have to try to "find" the will of God every day, begging Him for His presence and guidance.

It disturbs me to discover that some people are always trying to find the will of God. I don't believe I have to find what the will of God is for me every day. That doesn't mean I don't yield to the will of God continually, but I don't have to hear a word from God to tell me to do my ministry today. He gives guidance as it is needed, and is faithful to show us when He needs to change our path. Jesus promised He would be with us to the end. We must believe that He does not lie or leave us at every whim. Our responsibility is simply to rest in faith and to be available to His will.

## Friendship

In order to walk in the Spirit, we also need to acknowledge that the Holy Spirit is our indwelling Friend. Jesus called His disciples friends, and He told them it was expedient for Him to go away so He could send them the Comforter who would dwell in them. The Holy Spirit is our Friend. How great a value we place on friendship will help determine how we value our relationship with the Holy Spirit.

A real friend is one who cuts covenant with you, promising not to leave you when you are facing trouble. One of my favorite definitions of a friend is "one who sees you through and through and understands the things you do, and keeps on pulling just for you."[3] When we walk in the Spirit, we are never without a friend. Never! When we feel lonely, it may be because we are looking only to people for friendship without reckoning that the One who dwells in us comes to bring us divine fellowship with the Godhead.

The Holy Spirit is not here to pet our sins or condone ungodliness; He will convict us when necessary. But He will also be with us in every time of need. We can count on Him in the painful situations of life. He is all-sufficient in every crisis, and He is our constant companion. He is the One who has undertaken our cause, and He expects us to call on Him when we need to know what to do in any situation. He wants to be included in the details of our lives. We might be surprised at what this Friend would do for us if we asked for His help more often.

Fulfilling these prerequisites for walking in the Spirit will cause us to fulfill our destiny as believers and as the Church. He is redeeming us back to relationship with God as He originally intended it should be. The first Adam chose to be independent from God; the last Adam lived in complete dependence upon Him. As we choose to obey the Word of God and make ourselves available to be servants of God, walking closely to Him, we will find ourselves cultivating a divine friendship with Him. Cultivating this walk in the Spirit will result in eternal blessings for us and for His Church.

## RESULTS OF WALKING IN THE SPIRIT

God doesn't tell us to do something without a good reason. Everything He commands us to do is for our ultimate good. He doesn't make rules to be hard on us. They are to deliver us from destruction, to make life easier for us, and to allow us to live a life that is victorious over sin. He gave the Ten Commandments as an expression of His loving nature, to teach us how to relate to Him and to our fellow man.

When I was a young girl, I didn't understand that the reason my daddy made me come home at 10:30 p.m. was because he loved me and wanted to protect me; I thought he was being hard. Now I understand that his discipline and guidelines were proof that he cared for me. In that same way, God proves His love to us by giving us His instructions for life that will make it possible to live in such a way that we can receive His blessings.

## Deliverance From Sin

One of the first blessings that comes as a result of walking in the Spirit is a complete and delightful deliverance from sin. Paul wrote, "But now being made free from sin, and become servants to God, ye have your fruit unto holiness, and the end everlasting life" (Rom. 6:22). He taught that as we become servants of God, we will live holy lives and be freed from sin. He was declaring our freedom from the law of sin and death (Rom. 7:6). In this same epistle, Paul says clearly that if we live according to the flesh we will die, but if we yield to the Holy Spirit, we will know a life freed from the destructive power of sin. Daily walking in the Spirit is our only guarantee of having power over sin.

## Peace

The second blessing of walking in the Spirit is that we will experience a delightful serenity, tranquility, and steadfastness. God's wonderful intention for His people is that they walk in peace, free from the tyranny of fleshly drives and impulses. There is a rest promised for the people of God that we will not find until we learn to live in the Spirit. As the Scriptures declare, "There remaineth therefore a rest to the people of

God" (Heb. 4:9). Another simple way of describing that rest is to say that "we are at home in God."

In my home, there is serenity, contentment, and peace. For me there is no place as peaceful as home. When I am away from home I am a "visitor." No matter how gracious the treatment I receive, it does not give me the sense of serenity and haven that my home does. Similarly, the rest we find when we walk in the Spirit will be a haven to us. We will experience the peace of God and not be subject to ups and downs, becoming a victim of circumstances or of our own emotions. His rest gives us a stability in the face of every life situation.

## God's Providences

The third blessing that comes as a result of walking in the Spirit is the ability to meet the providences of God as they come to us with victory in our hearts. A "providence" is something that God chooses for us and promotes, although we may not always perceive it as something positive. We will be able to maintain perfect harmony between our inward disposition and His outward leadings or providences when we are walking in the Spirit.

Though we may be led through a difficult situation, our inside responses will be in harmony with it; we will not be disturbed. Of course, God doesn't bring to us the difficulties that are a result of sin. God doesn't promote divorce or other sinful behavior, for example (though we must remember that God loves the sinner and forgives). However, there are difficulties in our lives that God in His providence has permitted to cross our pathway for our ultimate good. Living in such a way that the providences of God can come into our lives always results in blessing.

For example, Simeon, the priest in the temple to whom Jesus was presented, probably didn't think his job was very significant—just keeping oil in the lamps. He could have become discouraged and said, "The glory is gone." By being faithful, however, he was in the right place at the right time to receive a blessing. When Mary brought her baby to the temple to be blessed, Simeon received the promise he had asked of God to see the salvation of the Lord. In the providence of God, he lived to see the Messiah, and he recognized Him because of his walk with God (Lk. 2:25-35).

It was no accident that Jesus met the woman at the well. He was obeying His Father when He said He must "needs go through Samaria" (Jn. 4:4). How many souls were saved that day because He obeyed the providence of God? We must learn to trust our unseen Guide, sometimes without understanding or seeing results, but knowing we are obeying Him. When Philip, the evangelist, obeyed the instructions of the Holy Spirit to go to a desert, he met the Ethiopian eunuch who needed to know how to get saved (Acts 8). Because of Philip's obedience, a whole nation received the gospel in the providence of God. The Scriptures give many other examples as well of people who walked in obedience and received the providences of God.

If we don't walk in the Spirit, we too will miss the providences of God for the important decisions of life. I don't agree with those who say that we can marry anyone we want to and that God doesn't care about that decision. I think God should give direction concerning something as important as marriage. How can we trust God to work it out the rest of our lives if we don't trust Him to arrange it from the beginning? God's divine providences are just as needed in many other areas of guidance as well.

There will be many who receive rewards for having walked faithfully in the providences of God who never received recognition while on the earth. When God hands out rewards, it won't be just great preachers who are in the front of the line to receive them. Some of those little grandmothers who were locked up in the closet praying for the nations will be there as well. We may be surprised to see a Sunday School teacher who taught a junior boys' class faithfully for 20 years every Sunday as if it were the greatest congregation on earth, in the front of that line. Unless we learn to walk in the Spirit, we will miss some rich experiences that the providence of God would bring to our lives.

Walking in the Spirit brings great blessings to every life that surrenders to Him. First, as we have seen, it secures us in complete and delightful deliverance from sin (Gal. 5:16). Second, it enables us to have a serenity, tranquility, and steadfastness in our lives. And third, it enables us to meet the providences of God that He has ordained for us. Surely the requirements for walking in the Spirit are well worth the life of blessing and happiness God has ordained for His people.

We must remember that what God requires of us is always for our ultimate good. Then we will surrender our lives without reservation, becoming available to Him, dependent on Him, and learning to be obedient to His instructions. The greatest blessing of our learning to walk in the Spirit will be our deepening friendship with God. In learning to know the Holy Spirit, that blessed Third Person of the Godhead, we will come into intimate relationship with God that will satisfy our hearts and fulfill the eternal purpose of God in us.

### Notes

1. Andrew Murray, *Humility*, (Springdale, Pennsylvania: Whitaker House, 1982), p. 10.

2. Dr. Fuchsia Pickett, *Presenting the Holy Spirit: Who Is He?* Vol. 1, (Shippensburg, Pennsylvania: Destiny Image Publishers, 1993).

3. Author unknown

# Appendix A

# *The Deity of the Holy Spirit as Affirmed by the Scriptures*

**1. He is spoken of as God.**

*...Why hath Satan filled thine heart to lie to the Holy Ghost...thou hast not lied unto men, but unto God* (Acts 5:3-4).

*Know ye not that ye are the temple of God, and that the Spirit of God dwelleth in you?* (1 Corinthians 3:16).

*If any man defile the temple of God, him shall God destroy; for the temple of God is holy, which temple ye are* (1 Corinthians 3:17).

249

*Now there are diversities of gifts, but the same Spirit. ...the same Lord. ...it is the same God which worketh all in all* (1 Corinthians 12:4-6).

## 2. Divine names and titles are ascribed to Him.

The following names and titles used of the Holy Spirit prove His deity and oneness with the Father and the Son, and each one also unfolds another aspect of His divine personality.

He is called Holy Ghost 89 times.
He is called Holy Spirit 111 times.

The Spirit of God (Gen. 1:2; 1 Sam. 19:20,23; Mt. 3:16; 1 Cor. 3:1,16, New English Bible).
The Spirit of the Living God (2 Cor. 3:3).
The Spirit of the Lord (Judg. 3:10; Is. 11:2; 61:1; Lk. 4:16-21).
The Spirit of Christ (Rom. 8:9; 1 Pet. 1:11).
The Spirit of His Son (Gal. 4:6).
The Spirit of Jesus Christ (Acts 16:7, New English Bible; Phil. 1:19).
The Spirit of Burning (Is. 4:4).
The Spirit of Holiness (Rom. 1:4).
The Spirit of Promise (Acts 2:33; Eph. 1:13).
The Spirit of Truth (Jn. 14:17; 15:26; 16:13; 1 John 4:6).
The Spirit of Life (Rom. 8:2; Rev. 11:11).
The Spirit of Wisdom (Is. 11:1-2; Eph. 1:17).
The Spirit of Understanding (Is. 11:1-2).

The Spirit of Counsel (Is. 11:1-2).

The Spirit of Might (Is. 11:1-2).

The Spirit of Knowledge (Is. 11:1-2).

The Spirit of the Fear of the Lord (Is. 11:1-2).

The Spirit of Grace (Zech. 12:10; Heb. 10:29).

The Spirit of Supplication (Zech. 12:10).

The Spirit of Glory and of God (1 Pet. 4:14).

The Spirit of Your Father (Mt. 10:20).

The Spirit of Prophecy (Rev. 19:10).

The Spirit of Adoption (Rom. 8:15).

The Spirit of Intercession (The Intercessor) (Rom. 8:26-29).

The Spirit of Judgment (Is. 4:4; 28:6).

The Eternal Spirit (Heb. 9:14).

The Comforter (Jn. 14:26, 15:26).

The Counselor (Jn. 16:7 NIV).

The Teacher (Is. 11:1-2; 61:1-2; Jn. 14:16-17,26; 15:25-26; 16:7-15; 1 Cor. 2:10-12).

My Spirit (Gen. 6:3).

Life (Greek, *neuma*, "breath") (Rev. 13:15).

The Spirituals (1 Cor. 14:12).

The Glory (2 Cor. 3:8-18; 1 Pet. 4:14).

The Seven Horns (Rev. 5:6).

The Seven Eyes "Before the Throne" (Rev. 1:4-6; 3:1; 4:5; 5:6).

## 3. Divine attributes are ascribed to the Holy Spirit.

Eternity and self-existence (Heb. 9:14)

Omnipresence (Ps. 139:7-10).
Omnipotence (Lk. 1:35; Acts 10:38).
Omniscience (Jn. 14:26; 16:12-13; 1 Cor. 2:10-11).
Creation (Ps. 104:30; Jn. 3:4-8)
Holiness (Rom. 1:4).
Love (Gal. 5:22-23).
Joy (Gal. 5:22 23).
Peace (Gal. 5:22-23).
Longsuffering (Gal. 5:22-23).
Gentleness (Gal. 5:22-23).
Goodness (Gal. 5:22-23).
Faith (Gal. 5:22-23).
Meekness (Gal. 5:22-23).
Self-Control (Gal. 5:22-23).
Fellowship (Phil. 2:1).
Glory (2 Cor. 3:8-18; 1 Pet. 4:14).
Life (Rom. 8:10-13).
Wisdom (Is. 11:2; 1 Cor. 12:8).
Knowledge (Is. 11:2; 1 Cor. 12:8).
Immutability (Heb. 6:17).
Invisibility (Jn. 3:8)

# Appendix B

# *Scriptural Purposes for the Gifts of Healing*

1. To destroy the works of the devil (1 John 3:8).

2. To establish Jesus' astonishing claims (Jn. 10:36-38).

3. To authorize the gospel message as preached by God's servants (Acts 4:29-30).

4. To establish the resurrection of Jesus (Acts 3:15-16).

5. To draw people to hear the good news of the gospel (Jn. 6:2).

6. To turn people to God (Acts 9:34-35).

7. To convince the unbeliever of the truth of God's Word, mysterious though it may be (Jn. 10:38).

8. To bring glory to God (Mk. 2:12; Lk. 13:17).

9. To inspire faith in God (Jn. 2:23).

If you have enjoyed
*Presenting the Holy Spirit,* we would
like to recommend the following books
and studies by Dr. Pickett:

*How to Search the Scriptures*

*SpiritLed Woman Bible Study: Ruth*

*SpiritLed Woman Bible Study: Esther*

*SpiritLed Woman Bible Study: Deborah*

*Stones of Remembrance*

*Receiving Divine Revelation*

*The Prophetic Romance*

*For Such a Time As This*

*The Next Move of God*

Available at your local Christian
bookstore or from
Creation House
600 Rinehart Road
Lake Mary, FL 32746